# SERMONS ON JEREMIAH
# BY
# JEAN CALVIN



Translated by

Blair Reynolds

Texts and Studies in Religion
Volume 46

The Edwin Mellen Press
Lewiston/Queenston/Lampeter

**Library of Congress Cataloging-in-Publication Data**

This book has been registered with the Library of Congress

This is volume 46 in the continuing series
Texts and Studies in Religion
Volume 46 ISBN 0-88946-835-4
TSR Series ISBN 0-88946-976-8

A CIP catalog record for this book
is available from the British Library.

 For information contact

The Edwin Mellen Press
Box 450
Lewiston, New York
USA 14092

The Edwin Mellen Press
Box 67
Queenston, Ontario
CANADA L0S 1L0

The Edwin Mellen Press, Ltd.
Lampeter, Dyfed, Wales
UNITED KINGDOM SA48 7DY

Printed in the United States of America

## TRANSLATOR'S PREFACE

In 1954, in Princeton, New Jersey, the Alliance of the Reformed Churches holding the Presbyterian Order resolved "that a Committee be appointed to explore the possibility of editing and publishing the unpublished manuscripts of Calvin's Sermons, now deposited in the library of the University of Geneva." This resolution took up a task begun by Dr. Hanns Ruckert of Tübingen in the 1930s. It succeeded in the publication of sermons by Calvin (*Suplementa Calviniana*) through the combined efforts of an international team of scholars.

However, English translations of Calvin's sermons on the Old Testament have yet to appear. This is a serious omission in Calvin scholarship in the English-speaking world; for Jean Calvin (1509-1564) was not only the author of voluminous theological and polemical writings, but also an outstanding preacher who, according to Beze, delivered about 286 sermons a year in French, which was his native tongue. His sermons are a major literary accomplishment, and, along with his other writings, may well represent the beginnings of French literature.

They also represent the very foundations of Calvin's thought, for his theology arose out of his exegetical method. It is true, however, that Calvin was not a systematic exegete in the modern sense of the term. Indeed, his biblical citations are generally very free; they are often non-referenced paraphrases, sometimes in error, and in some cases represent the combination of two tests into one. It is often, then, a matter of conjecture what specific biblical passages he had in mind.

Calvin's sermons, which lasted about an hour, were delivered from memory and were taken down word for word in shorthand by Denis Raguenier, who supervised their transcription into longhand. The sermons that I translated and others that I examined in *Supplementa Calviniana* are intact beginning to end and include even the specific date they were delivered.

Calvin preached approximately three hundred sermons on Jeremiah. We have, however, only twenty-five of them. These stem from a series of sermons that began in October 1548. Although sermons are missing in this series, the reader should have no difficulty picking up on Calvin's train of thought. Each of his sermons incorporates the major points of its predecessors. Indeed, he generally begins with a summary of his previous predication. Furthermore, his sermon style is straightforward and unostentatious. He speaks in the common language of the people and avoids technical, theological terms. He uses very picturesque imagery and often sets the scene as a dialogue between adversaries.

A definite affinity existed between Calvin's own situation in Geneva and that of Jeremiah. Just as Jerusalem was menaced by enemy empires, so Calvin's Geneva was menaced by Henri II of France and Charles V of Germany. Just as Jeremiah found himself in disfavor, so Calvin was incurring strong opposition from the public and from the Conseil and its anti-Calvin magistrate, Ami Perrin. Calvin, like Jeremiah before him, is struggling for the honor of God and the salvation of his people. That is the fundamental theme of his sermons.

For a more complete account of Calvin's situation in Geneva and as well of the transcription and preservation of Calvin's sermons, I refer the reader to the excellent commentaries by Bernard Gagnebin in *Volumen* II of the *Supplementa Calviniana* and Rodolphe Peter in *Volumen* VI.

My translation is taken from *Volumen* VI of the *Supplementa*. This gave me the advantage of having the original, handwritten French set in modern type with modern punctuation.

# CONTENTS

(1) Friday, June 14, 1549

Have you rejected Judah? Is Zion an abomination to you? Why do you smite us so there is no healing? Jeremiah 14. Get them out of my sight. Let them go. Jeremiah 15.

After the prophet proclaimed God's judgment, he prays for a way to render God merciful. Not only does he pray for himself, but he encourages the faithful to do the same. Because the people have offended God, it is just that He torments them. Nevertheless the prophet prays for mercy and encourages all the faithful to do so. That, in brief, is his plight.

God revealed to him that this prayer will not be answered as matters stand. It is not that God does not hear the prayers of His people, for He always accepts them, but most often He does not fulfill them in the way they have requested. Their prayers are answered, but not according to their desires, as we shall see. For our benefit, listen to what the prophet says: "Lord, have you rejected Judah? Is Zion an abomination to you?" as if he were saying, "True it is you may reject us for our demerits, but consider what is Jerusalem: It is the place where your temple is built. You have wished your name be invoked in this place and wished people to come from afar to invoke it, and you have said that you will fulfill those who pray in this place. What will happen now? People will say that you have defaulted on your promise."

Here the prophet speaks for the people. This is why he says, "Do not destroy the Throne of your glory," as if to say,

"When Jerusalem will be destroyed, you will no longer have dominion, and your name will no longer be invoked. Where will your Throne be? It will not be among the pagans, for it is necessary it be sacred. Now, you have consecrated it here. What will happen when it is thrown down?" This prayer is not founded on the merits of men but on the fact that God founded His Throne in Jerusalem. Because God has been so gracious to us, we ask, "Do you wish your grace to be lost?" For it is His office to pursue the good He can do us.

Furthermore, it is not only a question of God's grace, but also of His majesty. He has said that He wishes to be honored in this place. When it is razed, where then will God reign? That would detract not only from ourselves and our salvation, but also from God. It is true that God has given us no reason for complaint. Indeed, what wisdom have we to do so? Do we think that He lets things happen inadvertently? No! We must not presume to counsel God in any matters whatsoever. Our prayers are not made with this intention. There is no need for this audacious wish to make God wiser by our promptings. But God has given us the authority to proclaim the grace He has shared among us in order to console us through the hope of having even more. God has promised to dwell in the midst of us, who are the congregation in His name. Nevertheless, we encounter so many difficulties in the poor Church that it seems it must perish. What is to be done? It is necessary to resort to His promise; in doing so, He will make obvious that He does not default on His promises, but fulfills them to the hilt.

Thus we see that the remonstrances we make against God serve us and not Him. They serve us, for otherwise it would seem that we are blocked from attaining what we have in God's promises. When such reveries float through our heads, we must reject them; we must take all the deficiencies and afflictions that torment us and cast them upon Him, that they be remedied, as we will see. When we are afflicted in some way, we say, "Alas, Lord, we endure so much!" In saying this are we speaking to God as if He were ignorant of our condition? No! But this does serve ourselves, for God wishes that our prayers be efficacious and that we tell Him our needs. Now, this is not to inform Him, but is for our own good.

Suppose we speak to God of the difficulties in the Church, saying, "Alas, Lord, if you permit enemies to exercise their rage, all will be lost. We hold nothing in greater esteem that your glory, but it will be annihilated. Since you bear a very special love for your own, it is necessary that you remedy this situation." When we say that to God, we are all the more comforted and our heart is lightened, as we have cast the burden of our cares upon Him.

Will God permit His name to be annihilated? No! That is what consoles us, giving us confidence there is another way. That is why the prophet says, "Alas, Lord, is Zion an abomination to you?" Zion was the mountain where the Temple was built.

After the prophet speaks of Jerusalem, he mounts a step higher and says, "Zion." Always the prophet returns to God's promise. This is important to note, for we cannot turn ourselves from God's promise. Let not our prayers be frivolous, for it is necessary they be made in faith. Should we attempt to regulate God as it would seem fitting to us? No, never! It is necessary that we always follow His Word. Note carefully, as I have just said, that the prophet always clings to the God's promise. When he is stuck for words, he always throws himself upon God's promise.

We are certain, then, that having recourse to God's promise, it is impossible for us to be confused. When all the men are moved by rage against the Church, God will step in and put them down. The reason is that He has promised to protect the Church and not that men have moved Him to do so. He does this purely by His own bounty. His will is immutable, so there must always be a Church. But this does not mean that the Church is affixed to a certain place. Since His office is to protect it, He has totally miraculous means to do so. Let us not, then, imagine methods to preserve the Church; let us be certain that He will protect it.

When the prophet says, "Alas, Lord, is Zion an abomination to you?" it is as if he were saying, "This is impossible, not that this city is more worthy and holy than others, but that you have built your Temple there. You have said it is your resting place. This is not in vain and necessitates you be there forever." All this came to pass, but only after Zion had been pillaged by enemies, undergone great slaughter, vomited forth blood, after all sacrifices had ceased and it had been a captive in Babylon. Afterward, God reveals that He did not hate Zion, for the Temple was rebuilt, His name was again invoked there, and the sacrifices were restored to their rightful place. That is why men had to be purged. Just as God is merciful, He is also faithful. Whatever He has spoken must come to pass; whatever He has said is eternal and will be accomplished, no matter what obstacles there are. Regarding this Word and how we must apply it, it is a matter of resting assured that God will never reject His Church. Why? This is not a question for us, but rather is a matter of God's promise, of His honor, and of His glory.

Consequently, the prophet adds a term we have already seen, namely, "the Throne of the glory of God." Pay attention to this term, for here the prophet reveals the quality and condition of the Church. It is named the Throne of God. Why? Because God is not known in this world, save where He is invoked. That is why God calls the Church the Kingdom of the Heavens. This is not because we are inheritors of the eternal life, but because that God rules over us and because we know our sovereign King. Where, then, His word is thrown down, there the Kingdom of God is abolished. In this we see what a great blessing it is to have the Word of God. Is it not a great honor that God rules over us? It is always necessary that we have some master; if God did not rule us, how quickly Satan would take possession. If we had not the Word of God, there would be only great evil, since Satan would rule over us. Thus let us consider the great good that God did us by giving us His Word, since by this He reveals that we are His own. Now God cannot be King if we are kings, for He does not rule like an earthly king; rather, He wishes to appropriate His Kingdom for our benefit. We must come to know the good He does by ruling from the midst of us. That is why Zion is called the throne of God.

We are also admonished that God declares His Kingdom to us in order that we be obedient, as Saint Paul says. What good comes from this obedience? It glorifies God. Certainly this must inspire us, for is there anything more desirable than serving the glory of God? What are we? Can the glory of God be augmented by angels? No! However more than useless we may be, God wishes us to serve His glory. When we make room for His will, He reigns in us. We must strive to do this all our life. On the contrary, if God is dishonored by our vices, if we are unhappy to serve His glory, how can we boast of being Christians? Only as those who will say they are Christians simply because they are baptized! Therefore, let us be diligent in this sign; for we must obey God or we cannot boast of being His, and before all men He will reproach us that nothing of ourselves belongs to Him.

Let us turn to what I said earlier, namely, that the prophet prays in His name and encourages the faithful to do the same. When he says, "We recognize our faults," this must not be taken in general, that is, in the name of all; for if all were penitents, God would have pitied and have been merciful to everyone. Does, then, Jeremiah wish that one prays by hypocrisy? No! He prays in the name of the Church, which is only a small number. God never lets go of those who are regenerated in Him, save by their disobedience.

Thus God says to the prophet, "Well now, although these people are so malicious in rejecting My Word, still there is a small number who think you have secret books. Although you are the only one who can read them, they are too difficult for you to bear." Thus the prophet encourages those obedient to God to pray saying, "Alas, Lord, we are yours. Although the people have abandoned you, we are a small number who remain obedient. True our number is not as great as all those You have blessed. Many have rejected your Word. Nevertheless, we are a small number who know our faults. Take pity on us. Behold yourself, not us, for we can do nothing except inflame Your wrath more and more. Behold yourself, that you be merciful."

Although perversity reigns everywhere, those who fear God must join together and not lose courage to pray. Each must encourage the other, as we see in the example of the prophet. Sometimes things become so overwhelming that we lose courage, for it seems that all have conspired against God. We have no claim on God. True it is that He says, "Where two or three are gathered in my name, I will be in the midst of them." But how can we assemble ourselves? If I go outside, I see nothing but blasphemers among men. What access do we have to heaven above? For the ones wallow in one vice; the others, in another. None live by a clean conscience. This discourages us, as I have just said. Now the prophet shows us that we are a small number that must unite. We must encourage each other to pray; in doing so, we will become aware that God will answer us, even though we may think He has forgotten us. That is the crux of the matter.

When God afflicts us, let us learn to be humble, that we know that He is just in punishing us. Let us not place the blame on others, but know that we are all culpable, even the most just and innocent. In whose name did the prophet pray? In the name of those who were the most holy and were as angels among men, as were Daniel and his companions. Does the prophet speak here in fantasies? Do those who pray with him do likewise? Do they seem to be humble and yet think themselves worthy of God's mercy? No, certainly not! When we are afflicted for the iniquities in the world, the more righteous among us must not place the blame on others. So many think that if all the others resembled them that such-and-such an affliction would not have come to pass. Indeed, but because we live together, we constitute a body. Thus if the greater part of the members abandon themselves to all vices, we are all culpable, in as much as we are all members of one body.

True it is that we are not all equal. Those who abandon themselves to all evils are not equal to those who strive to live righteously. But because each is a member of a body, none can console themselves that they are not culpable. Are we able to resist each other as we should? No! Suppose some men rebel, do we attempt to put down this rebellion as we should? Far from it, for we would not even involve ourselves a tenth part in such a matter. Our nonchalance is condemnable. When vices are present in a great number, they are like a pestilence. True, some will try and escape the pestilence, but they will get sick. The air stinks. There is contagion everywhere.

We should not be astonished that the prophet holds himself culpable and encourages the most holy to do likewise. This teaches us that we must not point the finger and accuse others, though we are all quite adept at passing the blame onto others, saying, "We are punished because such-and-such evildoer did such-and-such." It takes no great intelligence to see that. Alas, we are all culpable; but the first person passes the blame on to the second; the second, to the third; the third, to the fourth. If they all recognized themselves as sinners, God would not have to punish them. When God afflicts us, let us voluntarily renounce condemnation and ask Him to pity us in His name.

This is not to deny that there is a great deal of difference between evildoers and ourselves. Let us not overlook the grace of God. When we are governed by the Holy Spirit, do we live according to the flesh? No! But in so far as we are not justified, it is a matter of knowing our culpability. By this, we can receive God's pardon. We cannot glorify God unless we recognize our culpability (Saint Paul in the third chapter of Romans) and account for our actions before God. Here God is exalted. But if we proclaim our innocence, what belongs to God will be cast away from Him.

Let us glorify God and confess that we merit punishment. Let us say, "Because of your name, lift your hand from us, that we be delivered from evil." God will do it because of His name, though we be the most unworthy. This is the consolation for poor sinners. When they are confused in themselves, what more can they do? Here God returns us to Himself, saying, "No, no, I have reason to be merciful because you say I do so for my name. I will shed my grace on you, provided that you do not think that I am indebted to you, but solely to draw you to me."

Let each meditate upon this consolation. It cannot be explained in words; it can be known only through experience. When our eyes are confused by our own sinfulness, it is God who comes, saying, "Although you only curse, my bounty spurs me to reveal to you that, though I be offended, I will not fail to be merciful when you ask me in my name." When God thus reveals His bounty, we have a way to God, notwithstanding the fact that our sinfulness overwhelms us so much that we know only to turn back.

Following this holy teaching, let us prostrate ourselves in the face of our good God. Let us pray that He never allow us to become so blind that we do not know our faults, that we never become so hypocritical as to think that He is obliged to pardon us. Let us pray that He shed His grace not only on us but on all, for Christianity is so alone. Let us also be moved to pray that His Kingdom be established in the midst of us, that He sustain true ministers in order that His assembly be maintained. Finally, let us pray that He give such zeal to the princes and magistrates that they serve nothing but His honor, and that He give them the grace to live for His glory, correcting all iniquities, so that all together we give God the honor that belongs to Him.

* * *

All-powerful God, we have been reconciled to you, as your Gospel witnesses. Yet, we do not cease to provoke your wrath daily. Give us the grace to gasp, bemoan, and condemn our vices without feigning or weakness, that we be truly displeased and sorry. May we learn in this way to cling to your mercy, not for one instant in our lives, but throughout each minute of time, until finally we understand that you are appeased by us and treat us not as we merit. Because you were pleased to reveal your paternal love through your Son, may you continue in such goodness and grace towards us, until we are finally purged of all stains and soil and are made participants in your celestial glory through Jesus Christ, our Lord, Amen.

(2) Saturday, June 15, 1549

Have you rejected Judah? Is Zion an abomination to you? Why do you smite us so there is no healing? Jeremiah 14.

And the Lord said to me, "Were Moses and Samuel standing before me, it would not turn my affection to these people. Get them out of My sight. Let them go." Jeremiah 15.

Following up what we claimed yesterday, namely, that the prophet finds his refuge in God's promise, let us examine what he now says. He speaks of an alliance God made with the Jewish people. "Lord," he says, "whatever happens, you remember the alliance you made with these people." But he does confess the sins of himself and of his people, even the most holy, to reveal that none are justified, that God will find enough on them to convict them all, even the most righteous.

Now, we learn here that God's alliance will not be broken by the multitude of our faults; it will always remain. If we return to God, we become aware of it; for, as I said, we cannot share in God's promise unless we adhere to Him. God's alliance extends through the line of Abraham. Nevertheless, the majority have rejected it, and this promise is of no benefit to them. Why? They have turned from God. It is necessary, then, that if we wish God to receive us in mercy by virtue of this alliance, we must adhere to Him. Thus the prophet says, "Lord, You know our maliciousness and the iniquities of our fathers, for we have sinned against you. We have provoked you. Yet, you will not dissolve your alliance." Here the prophet puts two ideas together, namely God's promise and his prayer for mercy.

God continues to be our God and holds to His alliance, provided that we wish it. Now this is a doctrine worth noting. Who can pray that does not experience remorse for his sins which block him from coming to God as confidently as he should? It is certain that as soon as we place our hope in God, scruples arise which block the way. As long as we fixate upon ourselves, we can find no way to God. This doctrine, that notwithstanding our faults His alliance is eternal, is then, very necessary. It is true that on our part we have wished to break his alliance; it is also true that we wish to receive God's mercy and wish His promises be everywhere fulfilled. To have the courage to pray for this latter, it is important that our knowledge of our own sinfulness does not overwhelm us to such an extent that we can no longer place our hope in His promises. When the prophet speaks of the glorious Throne of God, which is the Church, and when he speaks of Zion, we know that he does not ground himself upon the merits of men, but solely upon God's promise.

Not only should the most holy confess their own sins before God, but also the sins of their fathers. This is not to place the blame on them, but to more clearly delineate their faults. We sometimes mention the faults of our neighbors, but that is solely to place the blame on them, which is contrary to the prophet's intention. He says, "We know our iniquities" and he adds, "We are not the first evildoers, but certainly we persist in evil. Our fathers were the first to do evil, and we have done even worse things than they did." That is his point. Let us learn not to make frivolous excuses for our faults and those of others; let us learn to confess our faults and those of others with whom we converse. Our punishment is aggravated when we place all the blame on others as if to say it is all their fault. Here we see the folly of those who use the sins of their fathers as a shield against God. It seems to them that because they merely followed their fathers, they should be granted absolution for whatever they do. They claim they have done only as their fathers instructed them and so God must excuse them. What presumptuous foolishness. Let us learn to condemn ourselves before God, who alone is righteous. If it is a question of a particular rule to live by, let us submit ourselves to the ordinances of God, so that He alone is the sage. Let the Word of God alone have authority over us.

Let us turn now to the prophet saying, "Lord, are there any among the vain gods of the gentiles that can make it rain? Are not you alone our God? Do we not wait upon you because you are all-powerful? Do not reject us." Here the prophet is instructing the faithful that once they lose faith, they will find no power in heaven or earth that can comfort them. He is saying, "What else do we need, save our God? Do we have any power? There is none who can aid us other than He. We must pray to Him alone." When he refers to God's power, he says, "Who will aid us other than you?" When he refers to the power of God, he speaks of rain, which means that God is all-powerful. He means that everything we see comes from God, that it is God alone who gives the power to the earth to produce what we have. It is God who gives heat to the sun to warm and pollinate the earth. Because everything is in His hand, where will be find remedies if we turn from Him? We would be totally excluded from goodness. As we are predisposed to attribute the power of God to creatures, so much the more must we attend to this teaching.

Why does each wish to have his own patron and to have recourse to the saints? Because we imagine God to be decapitated and cut in pieces, as if God said, "My power to whoever can have it!" One saint heals fevers; another, catarrahs; another, inflammations: another, persons plagued by gravel; another, tooth problems; and others heal all sorts of other ailments. It is as if they carved up God and shared the pieces of His power among themselves. True it is they say that God gave them their power; but however this may be, the fact remains that God becomes an idol left in the lurch, as if He resigned His office to others because He was no longer pleased to carry it out. This is why we go after the saints and superstitions. The power of God is not known as it should be, as the prophet says. We must pay close attention to this teaching. We fall not only by superstition but also by pride. We leave God behind when we think we have a way to curtail evil.

Because we are possessed by this diabolical pride, by which we usurp that which belongs to God, we are well advised to note carefully what the prophet says: "Are there any among the vain gods of the gentiles that can make it rain?" He does not speak solely of idols, but also of the sky, meaning that we must not attribute to them the glory that belongs to God alone, for He alone governs all. True it is, when we are oppressed, we well recognize that God alone is our aid and refuge; but this is when we have no other recourse. If we had no rain, would we go higher than the clouds? If we had no heat, would we go further than the sun? No! Because our souls are brutish, we fixate upon creatures and do not go to God unless we are forcibly compelled. The prophet teaches that no celestial or terrestrial creature can aid us, so we must go higher. When he speaks of the rain, he is saying, "When we eat the goods of the earth, we must not think they come from the power of the earth itself; we must not fixate upon the earth; rather, we must come to know that God disposes the earth to produce its fruit, that He sends the rain to make seeds grow, that He gives the heat to warm the earth, and that by His commandment all creatures are subordinate to our needs. Therefore, it is necessary for us to fixate upon God and not down here; men abuse themselves by fixating upon themselves and so are blocked from having the things which God promised.

That is why the prophet says consequently, "We have waited upon you, for you have made all things." He means that we can have no refuge in God, save we recognize that it is by His providence that all creatures are sustained. If we did not know this, we could not put our hope in God. True it is that we can feign a kind of hope, but this is mere hypocrisy. Who are those who do not wish to be respected because they trust in God? Even the infidel knows himself preferable to the most faithful, when it is a question of hope in God. It is true that God does not abandon His works because of our infidelity. We cannot strip God of His power so that He is unable to carry out what He has planned. The prophet teaches us to recognize that it is to Him alone that all things are subject. When we have this knowledge, we can put our hope in Him. But we must know yet even more about God, for devils know that God is all-powerful and yet do not put their hope in Him. Why? Because His bounty is not appropriate for them. We cannot have sure and certain hope in God unless we also know that He has us in His care and shares His bounty with us. In addition to His power, we must come to know His promises and bounty. When we have joined these together, hope follows. The faith of Papists is nothing more than a fleeting opinion that we must receive the Word of God; they think it unnecessary to know the will of God as contained in Holy Scripture. They do not have the faith they should, for true faith presupposes that we know God's will in order to accommodate ourselves to it. Any other faith for us would be mere imagination. If we wish to profit in faith, what remains to be done? We must remember all our days the power of God in all things. Whether we look to the sky or to the earth, whether we look high or low, we know that all we see comes from the power of God and is governed by His providence. That is what we must know in order that our faith not be just so much hot air, but a faith which engenders hope, so that when evil presses in on us, we go immediately to God without running around whilly-nilly for aid.

Let us turn now to the beginning of the fifteenth chapter. The prophet tells us the response God made to his prayer: "Do not pray to me; were Moses and Samuel standing before me, it would not turn my affection to these people. It is necessary they be taken into captivity, as I have ordained." It seems that God will not fulfill the prophet's request, and it is contradictory to Scripture that God will not answer the prayers of the righteous. This seems to overturn our faith, for its foundation is that we will receive what we ask in faith. What does it mean, then, to say that the faithful pray and yet God does not answer them? God always answers the prayers of His own, but not according to their desire, as we can take example in ourselves. We request something of God and assume it must be granted as we request it. God does not do that; He goes us one better. I am sick and pray to God to pity me, resting assured He will answer my prayer. Healing is what I want. But this does not come to pass; God keeps me ill in order to achieve a more complete healing afterwards. I am deprived of my wish and am ill for a longer time; but this does not mean that God did not answer my prayer; He chose another way. Because we know not how God has decided to aid us, we must leave the entire matter to His will, as we say in the prayer He gave us: "Your will be done." Thus we can say in brief that God always answers the prayers of the faithful, but not according to their desires; most often, they do not obtain what they pray for. When we see the Church tormented by tyrants, we wish that God would immediately strike down all His enemies. He does not do so, for He has a solution in hand of which we know not. Our biblical passage for today says as much; for when the faithful say, "Lord, have you abandoned Jerusalem?" they rest on the promises made to them. When the Jews are led into captivity, it seems that all is lost, that God's promises are not fulfilled. God has excluded them in regard to the specific way in which He fulfills His promise; but He still maintains the invocation of His name and preserves the seed of His Church, although they are all captive. When He says, "My heart is not to these people," He still sustains the faithful and does not reject their prayers. All who stand on the promises of God will not be rejected by Him and can proclaim the promises made to their fathers. God never abandons His people; He will even deliver them from the grave. Babylon was like a grave, and the people of Israel were buried in it, rotting away. Nevertheless, God delivered them through desperate means. Far from God refusing to answer their prayers, He fulfilled them through a greater display of His power than if He had done what they requested.

Why does God proclaim to Moses and Samuel that this sentence must be executed? Because they were the great zealots for the salvation of their people. Moses desired to be erased from the Book of Life, not that he could in fact be erased, but that he forgot himself, hearing the curse of God upon his people and that He wished all to be exterminated. Hearing this, he said, "Lord, I would rather be damned than that come to pass." He has no self-interest; he wishes only that the people be sustained. Because Moses had such zeal, it is not without good reason that God mentions him. For the same reason, He mentions Samuel. However great was the opposition and however much he had to endure, he persisted in his office. Thus Moses and Samuel are mentioned as if God were saying, "All men together would profit in nothing by praying to me for these people, for my sentence must be executed without opposition. I must be avenged."

Now the Papists take today's passage to mean that the dead saints can pray for us. Their reasoning is that God says, "If Moses and Samuel were before me and prayed to me, I would do nothing for them." Now, Moses and Samuel being dead, it follows that dead people can pray for us. They are so brutish--I do not say the most stupid but the most conniving--that they do not see this passage directly contradicts themselves. If the dead could pray for us, it is certain that Moses and Samuel would have been the first. God mentions them for this reason. Now let us hear well the words of the prophet. He does not say, "I do not wish to answer them;" he says, "If they were before me and if they were to intercede, I would not fulfill them." If I say to a man who is in fact standing before me, "If you were before me," is that not mockery? When God says, "Were they before me," He obviously means that they were not. If a friend asked me a favor and I said, "If my father asked me, I would not grant it," this is not to say that my father asked me. Let us conclude, then, that the dead cannot intercede for us. Here the brutishness of the Papists becomes so much greater in the face of Scripture because they do not harken to the prophet's intention. If they would examine minutely the books of the Bible, they would find a similar passage in the fourteenth chapter of Ezekiel, where it says that if Daniel and others prayed, that would not save the women and children. Does the prophet speak of them as though they were dead? No, he speaks of them as if they are living. This means that we must not think ourselves aided by intercession, as is the case among the Papists, who abuse themselves by each choosing a patron. One will have the virgin Mary, "Oh, she will be my advocate, she will pray for me." It seems that the saints oppose God and block Him from doing His will. So much do they give themselves free reign to offend God by their patronages! The same is true for those who live among righteous persons. They abandon themselves to all sorts of vices; they believe that for the sake of these righteous ones, God will pardon and protect them in the time of persecution. Such are the foolish expectancies of the people of Israel. On the contrary, the prophet says, "No, no! Do not trust in them, for their company is of no benefit to you." God can well distinguish among people, for the righteous will be saved and the evildoers will perish, as Ezekiel says. Here we see the iniquity of the Baptists. They did not found the intercession of the saints upon biblical proofs, for there are none. They simply plunder Scripture for whatever they want. They wish to have patrons, they cannot find this in Scripture, so they twist and pull at Scripture, turning it into a nose of wax, as they say. We cannot tell what passages they are using. Why? In the whole of Scripture, there is not one passage on patronage. Now the Papists wish to base their patronage on this one passage where it says, "Were Moses and Samuel before me, I would not answer," but it will not serve their goal; for their actual goal is to show that we must have recourse to the saints and must pray to them. Their claim does not accord with this passage; for even if one were to agree that the saints were intercessors, it does not follow that we must pray to them. A man lives one-hundred leagues from here and wishes to do all he can for me. Each morning, when I wake, I beseech him to do better, namely, that he have ears long enough to hear me! The Papists have no claim, save that the Saints see everything in God. The Papists, then, jump to conclusions, jump from the rooster to the ass, as they say. As I have said, there is not one single passage in Scripture which says that the saints pray for us. If we wish mercy, it is necessary we ourselves pray; it is necessary we be humble, and wish God to pardon our sins. That is when God will lift hand from us. But if we remain obstinate, there is not an angel or saint who could excuse us. Let us cling to what the prophet says.

Because the people are so hardened, the prophet says, "When you pray, God will be gracious, but it is necessary the people perish." Because that is said to the children of Israel, it is fitting for us. If, having offended God, we do not humble ourselves and ask for pardon, it is certain all creatures will perish and we will profit in nothing. Each must make a penitence for himself and must not doubt that the angels rejoice in it, for it is there office to serve our salvation. Let us not doubt that God receives us; let us know that all else fails us, as I have said.

Following this holy teaching, let us prostrate ourselves before our good God, in full recognition of our sins. Let us pray that He permit us not to become hardened, as were the Jews who were condemned, but that our hearts be softened and that it please God to abolish our sins. Knowing our faults may we learn to come to Him in the name of Jesus Christ, in whose name our sins are pardoned. May God be gentle and loving towards us, as if we never offended Him. May He shed His bounty upon us, though we be unworthy. May He shed grace not only on ourselves but upon all peoples of the earth.

* * *

All-powerful God, you condescended to allure us so sweetly and humanely to repentance. Your rod holds us in suspense. You gave us the leisure to reform. Grant us the grace that we no longer provoke your great vengeance by our obstinacy, but that we relinquish all governance to you, so that not only those who pray for us be fulfilled, but that we ourselves be pardoned at our request, having Jesus Christ for our intercessor and advocate, through whom we have been reconciled to you. May this intercession forever appease your anger towards us, until finally we appear before your face, purged and cleansed of all stains and soil, sharing the glory Christ won for us. Amen.

(3) Monday, June 24, 1549

Were Moses and Samuel before me, it would not turn my affection to these people. Get them out of my sight. Let them go! If they ask, "Where should we go?" you will say to them, "Those destined for death go to the dead; those for the sword, to the sword; those for famine, to the famine; those for captivity, to captivity. Jeremiah 15.

After our Lord proclaimed that there was no remedy for the Jews in captivity and that it was necessary His sentence be executed, namely, that these people be in captivity, he added that the prophet sets this in motion by pronouncing the sentence. Here God wished to reveal the power of His Word, as if He were saying, "When you have spoken the Word, this will not be as a game; it will assure that things be accomplished as you have spoken them."

Let us be advised that whenever God speaks or the prophet speaks in His name, be it of menaces or chastisements we must endure, these must not be taken as a fable, but believed as if we saw them before our very eyes. God does not speak in vain. We must respond as if we saw them before our very eyes. God does not speak in vain. Here is how we must respond to all preaching in the name of God: Either it speaks of His mercy, in which case we must not become idle in our task, or it speaks of His scourges, which must not make us desperate. Let us not abuse His patience. If He is punishing us, let us not think He has forgotten His Word. If we have all this engraved in our memory, it is certain we will profit so much the more from teaching. But, whenever one speaks of the deeds of God, we pass this off as a fable. Let us, then, be taught such that, stupid as we are, whenever He threatens us, we come to actually feel the blows of His rod upon our heads, even though we merely foresee this. When God says to the prophet that He "chases the people," He does not mean by an army, but solely by the prophet's word. God led the Babylonians who executed the prophet's word.

Now the prophet adds that in punishing, God will use horrible force and will lay a heavy hand on people. Sometimes God chastises simply by holding His hand in the air so we feel no blows. Having chastised us, He appeases us, giving us something pleasurable to make us forget our past misfortune. But now, to show what will be expected, He says: "Those for death, to death; those for the sword, to the sword; those for captivity, to captivity; for I wish to reveal to you that I am no longer your protector, as I was." This means God will discipline us more severely than He is accustomed to.

Some will say that God always punishes us in a way we can bear. We all need to be corrected by the hand of God; otherwise, we become too tardy. A student with good will needs only the lesson, but the stupid ones need to be taught by the rod. So it is said of us that we are all asses who need God's rod to goad us. Seeing we all need chastisement, we must pray it be done in all gentleness. It would be a horrible thing if He were to act as a judge and condemn us. That is what the prophet means when he says God took extreme measures to correct the Jews. This should not surprise us, for we are all equally unworthy and our life is so evil that it is an abysm of iniquities. Seeing that we resemble them in every iniquity, and seeing that God was as gracious to them as He is to us, we expect the same punishment. What will happen to us? Will we be poor, dispersed men ignored by a God to whom we are strangers? Would this not be a horrible punishment? That is what we must expect if we continue to offend God as we have done. We must understand His word as a warning, so that we humble ourselves and no longer fear God will vigorously lay His mighty hand upon us.

The prophet adds that He "appoints the sword to slay, the dogs to tear, the birds of the sky and the beasts of the earth to devour and destroy" and that "He puts them in a commotion throughout all the kingdoms of the earth because of what Mannasseh, son of Hezekiah, King of Judah, did in Jerusalem." God says, "It will seem to you purely by chance that you will be eaten by the birds, beasts, and the dogs. You will attribute it to luck, but know that it comes from my hand." Here the prophet proclaims what so often we find in Scripture, namely, that all the creatures that harm us are the instruments of God. When God created the human species, He did so in order that a union exists between ourselves and all creatures, even in goodness. When creatures raise up against us, let us know that God gives them license to do so and also that He subjugates them to obey us. When the order of nature is not disturbed, they obey us. Let us cherish this teaching so much the more so because it is found so often in Scripture. At first blow, God cannot chisel this truth into our imaginations, where we attribute to luck what happens to us and know not that it is by His hand. Neither the birds nor the other creatures rise up against us, save that God incites them. This is also true of the sword. No man can raise his sword against us, save that God sharpened his sword in the first place. Here, then, is how all things come from the wrath of God. Whatever may happen, we must cling to this knowledge. If men rise up against us, be aware that it is God who makes this happen and not without reason, for we have offended Him. That is the heart of the matter.

Let us note that God has various ways of punishing us. If we escape the sword, that is not all; we fall into all sorts of other difficulties, for it is said that His coffers are full of wrath. Men so unbridle themselves and do even worse deeds after some punishment is over: "Why? Ah! Evil will not return soon," they say. They forget that when God has used up one-hundred methods of punishment, He has yet another hundred in store. Therefore, the prophet says that God will send not only the sword, but also the birds and the domestic beasts and the wild beasts to devour us, as God has said, "When you are resting in your home, I will send a serpent to kill you, and if you are in the fields, the beasts will devour you." Note well, then, that just as God has all sorts of ways to deliver us from adversity, when He is angry He also has many ways in which to punish us, the likes of which we cannot imagine.

Because our punishment may seem strange and even vulgar, the prophet says that God always punishes righteously. If God had merely mentioned His scourges, such as birds, dogs, and other beasts that can devour us, that alone would be sufficient to horrify us. But why does God do this? We ask how it is possible that God can punish in such a way those who are created in His image. He does not do so without cause, saying, "O Jerusalem, who will pity you? Who will bemoan you? Who will pray for your peace? You have forsaken me and you persist in your rebellion. I am tired of so much repenting." First, the prophet jogs their memory, saying this is "because of Manasseh, son of Hezekiah, King of Judah." After declaring God's punishment upon the Jews, he adds that they are deserving of such chastisement. What sense would it make for God to terrify us by His wrath if we were all innocent in His eyes? What is the benefit from all this suffering and gnashing of teeth? God's threats serve two purposes: First, they shock us. Second, they make us aware of our sins; we become displeased with ourselves and desire to repent; this repentance makes us desire to invoke His name. That is how God's threats serve us.

Let us explore why he speaks of Manasseh. In sacred history, in the fourth chapter of Kings and in Chronicles, it is said that Manasseh rebuilt the altars that had been destroyed, that he polluted the Temple of God, where He wished His name be invoked, that he prayed to the stars, and that he had sorcerers with him. He was given to all sorts of superstitions and idolatry. He murdered so many prophets that Jerusalem swam in blood. As the drunkard vomits wine, so Jerusalem vomited the blood of martyrs. Nevertheless, he recognized his faults, which is an admirable demonstration of God's bounty. Here is an evildoer who shed the blood of his people everywhere. He destroyed his people, yet he received mercy, having recognized his faults. He made the necessary repentance and remained on his throne. But the people remained stubborn and idolatrous, although he wished to keep them in line. The prophet, then, says they were punished for the sins of Manasseh. If we ask whether or not it is just for the people to be punished for the sins of one man, it should be noted that these sins were not unique to just one man alone, for the people surrendered to evil along with their prince. True it is that Manasseh corrupted them all, but this was not without their consent to be polluted by idolatry. Thus it was not without divine providence that Manasseh ruled such a long time. When God lets an evil one reign, this is a sign that we are unworthy to be governed by the righteous. When God grants us a good magistrate, this is a sign that He wishes to demonstrate His mercy. On the contrary, when God abandons us to Satan, that is a sign of His strictness. That is what happened in the time of Hezekiah. Now, he strived to serve God faithfully; he was a good prince; but were the people subdued? No, for they worshipped idols in secret. When God saw that, He felt the need to raise up an evil king. If people lead orderly lives and recognize the grace of God, it is certain that He will send them a good king; but if they go on a rampage, as they did, an evil king is necessary.

Furthermore, the prophet mentions Manasseh, to warn us that an evil king or magistrate is like a poison that infects all lands. We know this by our experience. No matter how much sovereign authority a king may have, he always needs much more to govern his people. Why? Because he must force us to be good. But if it is a question of evil, if there is an evil prince, all he has to do is raise his finger and he is instantly obeyed, so committed to evil are we. The same is true of the magistrates. Well may they be mere idols. But if they, waving their hands up and down, say to evil ones, "Come, come, we will support you!" instantly evil bursts forth everywhere. It is not without reason, then, that the prophet speaks of Manasseh's works. Although all lands were overrun by idolatry, the seeds came from him. We must beseech God, then, that He permit no men to be in authority who would drive the people to perdition. When the magistrates make an instant debauchery of it all, this is a revelation of God's wrath against us for our sins. We are without excuse, for all are culpable. Those in authority should pay close attention to this point. They do not tolerate evil, but neither do they punish it, so they give free reign to evildoers, as even the Pagans know. Those who hold the baton of justice in their hands are accountable to God for all the faults incurred through their negligence, for God does not stammer in speaking. Is that what the passage means when it says that it was because of Manasseh? Yes, for as we have seen, "the children gather wool, and the mothers bake cakes for the idols." None are exempt. Why is every fault blamed on the king? He did not squelch evil, but aided it, omitting service to God. He is therefore responsible, especially in light of his repentance, as we said earlier. The fact of his repentance shows us that he had done little to abolish idolatry. Although he had the power to do so, the people had abandoned themselves to superstition. When the king ordained evil, he easily won over the people; when he tried to return them to goodness, he could not.

We are admonished, then, to refrain from giving free reign to scandalous living. For soon afterwards, in our attempts to set a good example, we will find that we send a hundred to perdition, from which we cannot extract three. Be aware that when God gives us the grace to repent and return to His mercy, we will deeply regret that we cannot redress those whom we led astray. Indeed, will we not feel terrible remorse over this? That is what the prophet means. Although King Manasseh attempted to restore order among his people, he is the one who bore their disgrace. Wherever and whenever God speaks of the rampage of His people, he will be named first. Be aware, then, that when God gives the opportunity to repent and we refuse, we will be reproached. God says that He repents so much to save us. This means that God had continued so long that nothing more could be done to warn the people, that God had sent prophet after prophet. It is written in the tenth chapter of Deuteronomy that "I will raise up a prophet," which means that the people will be abandoned, so that they have no prophet. Were the Jews able to complain that the Pagans have gods with whom they can speak? Must the Jews be ignorant of the will of their God? "No," God says, "you will have prophets," and then He adds, "I raise early and go to bed late to court you; nevertheless, you become hardened." Note that this threat was not made recently; for a long time they had been warned: "Will it not be necessary to have a day of reckoning? Watch yourselves." Now, the people mocked all this. The prophets were despised for their vigorous reprimands. The prophets shook them by their arms, saying, "What is your condition? Are you not all corrupt? Where is justice? Where is the loyalty that should be among you? Are you not full of all evil?" There was gnashing of teeth and vexation: "Ah! Are we not the people of God? It seems they speak to us as if we were dogs! Are we going to stand for these insults? No, never!" When the prophets spoke to them about the burden of the lord--"You will know that it is God with whom you must deal"--they responded, "What, what? The burden of the Lord? Alas! Is it necessary to burden us so?"

That is how matters go today, I do not say in Papist territories, but in Geneva. How is preaching received among the evil ones? When God does not press upon them, they mock. When they are called to account, there is much vexation and gnashing of teeth: "How? Will the ministers always scream at us? We do not know what we must do? Alas, this is too much to endure! Is it necessary to have so much screaming in the name of the Gospel? Hah! If we do not like this gospel, we will find another!" We see their debauchery, so let us be wary; for God has said, "I am tired of pardoning you." Can we say that God walks on egg shells among us? Has not God threatened us almost every day last year? True it is we could feign some excuse, but even a small child could see through it. Seeing all this, one might think that God has bandaged eyes and does not see a wink. Oh! Such abuse!

Therefore, after speaking of Manasseh, God says, "Jerusalem, who will pity you?" Specifically, God addresses this holy city, even though all the lands of Judah are consecrated to God; for His name is invoked in Jerusalem. The people say, "We are the people of God; He will sustain us." Yes, but only if they profit by the grace of God. We are all the more culpable before God, all the more we turn good into evil and transform what God gave us for our life and salvation into our damnation. When God says, "Who will pity you?" this means we have feigned excuses. When God adds, "You have abandoned me," this means that we must humble ourselves, that God does not see fit to punish us. We are familiar with such ways of speaking, for the prophet uses them so often. Why? Because it is necessary that the cause of our evil be revealed to ourselves. We are all given to evil, and the root of this is that we have abandoned God. If we are united to God, if we have lived well today, tomorrow we will profit; but, on the contrary, if we abandon God, tomorrow we will walk in confusion. This is what the prophet says, though men strive always to justify themselves. It is necessary we behold our iniquities before our very eyes. Instead of trembling in the face of their iniquities, men rebel against God. It is not merely a question of all the grumbling yesterday, but of those who were drunk. The minute they find out these matters were brought up in the pulpit, they will start up again. It is necessary that God reveal His majesty in opposition to them to render them confused. Regarding ourselves, we must come to know that we have no way to receive God's grace, save by humiliating ourselves and asking for it in the name of Jesus Christ. We must not look elsewhere, for our sole refuge is in Him alone. We will come to know that all creatures serve our profit and salvation, provided that we strive to live in accord with God. This can be done only by confessing our sins and praying that He receive us in the name of His beloved Son.

Following this holy teaching, let us prostrate ourselves before the face of our good God. in full knowledge of our faults, by which we offend Him daily. Let us pray that it please God to touch us with true knowledge and life, so that, struck down by the knowledge of our sinfulness, we may be redressed by God through living hope. Let us return to Him. Let us attend to no end, save that His name be honored everywhere. May He shed this grace not only on us, but on all peoples and nations of the earth.

* * *

All-powerful God, give us the grace that we do not provoke your judgment and force you to goad and persecute us with the point of the sword. Grant us that we may govern and conduct ourselves in such a gentle and agreeable way that all your threats easily melt away. Let us overcome your wrath and vengeance, by which we know all the stubborn ones and reprobate have been consumed and destroyed. Grant us that we win your grace and favor by true repentance. Grant us that we may receive the good things you so abundantly make every day, until finally we come to all the wonderful things you have prepared in your heavenly kingdom through Jesus Christ, our Lord, Amen.

(4) Tuesday, June 25, 1549

I will fan them with a fan in the gates of the earth. I have deprived and destroyed my people, since they will not turn from their ways...Yet they all curse me. Jeremiah 15.

The prophet often repeats that when God torments us, we come to know His love. It is a sign that God thinks of our salvation, insofar as He does not wish that we perish. The torments He sends upon us are medicines. A physician shows he loves a sick person by treating him. So it is with God. We all wish to be comfortable, but God cannot allow this. He must correct our faults because such corrections are necessary to keep us in His grace and to lead us to salvation in the end. It is out of His special love for us that God torments us. This love is even more obvious when He complains that we do not amend our ways. Here He well reveals to what end He chastises us. He complains to Isaiah that there is no holiness in His people from head to foot, from the largest to the smallest. Our Lord, nevertheless, did everything to correct His people as a father would his child. Seeing that He could not succeed in converting people to the path of righteousness, He laments, "Alas, am I not very unhappy? I have done all I can to make men righteous. Yet, I have not succeeded." It was not that our Lord was subject to emotions, but that He wished to speak to us in a way fitting to our nature. So much the more was He angered when He saw that we did not profit by His corrections. In another passage, He says, "Alas, must I avenge myself of my enemies?" as if He were speaking of the Jews. When He says, "Alas, I must avenge myself," that signifies He will rely solely on the use of force to afflict us.

This is the matter the prophet treats. God attempted all sorts of means to correct the Jews, yet they would not amend their ways. The prophet says that the punishments had been multiplied seven times, yet they did not amend themselves. The number of widows has multiplied; those who have had seven children are now barren. Their land is full of chaos and confusion: "I turned upside down all the world and nature to bring them to penitence. Has the brought them to obey me? No! They will not turn from their ways. They continue to do even worse. What must be done? They must be dispersed throughout the world." God had collected together these people in the holy land so that they would not be mixed in with the infidels. Yet it became necessary to disperse them throughout the world. Now we understand what the prophet means.

Furthermore, we see how this situation is relevant to us today. Look at all the slings and arrows people complain they must bear. Can you find any place on earth where people do not complain? The ones complain of the brutality that has been heaped upon them. The others complain of afflictions. When pests are rampant, we must endure famine. So much is imposed upon us that we are eaten up. There is not a corner in all the earth where we do not see the scourges of God. Where do we see people returning to God? God does not torment His people for a time; His scourges are continuous. Yet the evil and obstinate ones grow in number. Thus God does not speak of momentary torments, for our condition has not improved.

What does it mean to say that "the sun went to bed when it was yet day," save that God has so weakened us by this natural clarity that we cannot see a wink? We allow adversity to unfold around us without learning how to turn it to our profit. God continues to flail our backs, but we pay no attention to the hand that strikes us. We make false prophets out of the Rolands and the rebels; we do not heed that God sees us. Nevertheless, God's scourges are not in vain: "I can well enumerate your faults to you. If I have warned you by famine, I will warn you by war; if I have awakened you by war, I will send plagues. Each of you in particular will be tormented after you all have been afflicted. Each of you will be awakened." What is there for us to say? Here is a teaching to meditate on day and night. If God could complain of His lack of success at the time of Jeremiah, He can do as much today. There is not a corner of the world without God's scourges, as I have just said. Yet this all seems in vain. There is a conspiracy of men with the Devil to vex God more and more.

Let us note well that God reveals His love when He complains that His scourges have been to no benefit. He shows how precious our salvation is to Him, when He complains that He cannot convert us. Does not sensing His love melt away our hard hearts? What a great shame it is to us that God is frustrated by our wickedness. To what end does God strive? To turn us to repentance. What does it mean, that our wickedness frustrates Him? Who are we? We are the scum of the earth, yet He cares for us. Must we not, then, strive so much the harder to return to Him? Pay attention: God, in tormenting us individually and as a whole, wishes only to convert us. Let us act so that we be not reproached His warnings were in vain. If the patient does not take the prescribed medicine, it is unreasonable that he dies? Would that be grounds to indite the physician? No!

It is of great consolation to the faithful that God, even in tormenting them, wishes them to taste His love. What can we say when He treats us so gently, sharing so much goodness with us? Does that not reveal His unfathomable love? Does that no reveal His bounty and paternal love, despite the afflictions He has sent upon us. Was not His eternal beatitude revealed to us when we were strangers and yet He shed His grace on us? On the contrary, when God afflicts us, it is to teach us not to go astray in the world. He knows our weaknesses and inspires us to conquer them. That is why we must always place our hope in God, whether He afflicts us or delights us.

Be aware, then, that God is reproaching us when He says He did all He could and yet the people would not turn from their ways. God can well enumerate His gracious acts; yet we let them slip in one ear and out the other, and fail to profit from them. "When I see that I have not succeeded the first time," God says, "I will return several other times." When a father smacks his child excessively and then regrets having been so cruel, that serves nothing. But when he chastises his child little by little, has the child any excuse not to be disciplined? When we do not pay attention to God's scourges, we turn His paternal love into our condemnation. Will we be excusable? Certainly not! We will be indited. God's scourges are not without His kindness. God gives us the leisure to examine ourselves. What does this mean? After He has chastised us, He lets us rest for a while. That is how He disciplines with kindness. After He has warned us once, twice, and thrice, He says, "I regret my efforts to save you." Now when this word "regret" is attributed to God, it means that He abandons us, not that He is mutable. Scripture uses this word solely to accommodate God to our understanding. When our Lord afflicts one day and relaxes the next, that is a change. But what are we looking at? At the act lone, not at Him. Therefore He says, "I know your weakness, I mold myself according to your comprehension. I pardon you once, that you have the leisure to examine yourself and say, 'God has revealed to me that I was asleep.' I grow weary of having to save you after you have been chastised and mistaken my love." By this abuse of His patience, we no longer merit His mercy towards us. Therefore, He says, "I regret my efforts." True it is that God does not experience regret. But this statement makes it clear that His mercy no longer has any place in our lives.

Now let us turn to how God saves us after we have offended Him. Certainly we do not call to mind even the least of our offenses. There are a hundred thousand offenses that we cannot call to memory. We are not, however, so insensible that we cannot find another hundred thousand that we do remember. Any of us can say, "In my youth God treated me in such-and-such a way, but I went astray; yet He did not abandon me. I became more and more evil. What opportunity is there left for change in my life? Nevertheless, I find signs of His wrath. Yet does He strive to transform me in all mercy and gentleness, although I abuse Him." Would it not be fitting, then, for God to say finally that he is "weary" from having to endure so much? Let us underline this word "weary", for He will hit us over the head with it when we abuse His grace. So much for the basic gist of God's complaint; let us go into more detail.

When God says, "I have admonished you in such-and-such a way," this means that He afflicted us with evil to make us return to Him, that we be not like the cattle who see the ox but not the hand the wields it or like the dog who chases after the rock but sees not who threw it. But so it is with us. We are well aware of our afflictions, but we pay no attention to the hand that laid them upon us. We know not it is God who wishes to return us to Him. So much the more must we pay attention to this teaching.

After the prophet sees that all his warnings serve only to inflame the obstinacy of the people, he says, "Woe is me, mother. Why have you borne me a man of discord and discontent throughout the world? Everywhere I go, the world quarrels with me. They say that I wish to torment the whole world. Must I be the mortal enemy of all? I have not practiced usury, so I am not the cause of quarrels." What brings about quarrels among men, save their transactions? When one borrows money from another, he will say, "It's clear the terms of his deal were deliberately set up so I cannot fulfill them." The lender will say, "Is it necessary my good will ruin me? I have lent money out in my hour of direst need. Now, to collect it back, I have to take drastic steps. Everyone speaks ill of me." Here we see how quarrels and enmities arise from the transactions among men. When the prophet says that he is not the cause of quarreling, that means that he is the enemy of all those who war against God: "It is necessary I be an obstacle to them. I bear the Word which uncovers the venom in their hearts." This statement shows us that it is not just today that people become vexed when confronted with their sins. Not only are men sick in their souls, but their sickness is incurable. There is no healing. But why? The Word of God and His remonstrances are certainly not the reason. Rather, the reason is that men transform into poison what God gave them for their salvation. That is what was happening at the time of Jeremiah. What was the purpose of God's scourges, except to turn the people to God? Does not one taste of God's bounty make our hearts cleave for God's great love? Instead of finding goodness, we find rebellion everywhere. Mankind has been a hardened lot since the very beginning of the world. But note carefully that this will not serve to justify us. Were those who cried out against Jeremiah, saying, "This man brings nothing but quarrels," excusable? We know well to pronounce sentence on them.

Let us turn to our affairs, for God will judge us solely by our actions. At the time of the prophet, the grumblers made war on God. If we do likewise now, we will also be condemned. Let us not think to be exempt, for none can escape His condemnation. Why is it that people grumble against ministers? Is it because of the dealings they have had with men? No, it is because of doctrine. Now is doctrine forged by us? Have we invented it to cause quarrelling? Certainly not. In fact, the prophet says that it is a gift of God. What, then, have we to say to these grumblers? We, like Moses and Aaron, can say that we have given them no cause. We have born the message of God, whereas the strive to rule us. But it is God who wishes to have dominion over us! So it is that the prophet, having proclaimed that God, not his own tongue, spoke, reveals that his opponents know well that God is his guarantor against the Jews. Odious as the Word may be to them, they will be brought to account by God despite themselves.

To better understand matters, let us examine the worthy doctrine of the prophet: Since all disputes are engendered by the trafficking among men, it is necessary to prevent all such furors. But how? Must each live separate and apart from the rest? No, that will not do. It is necessary to live harmoniously with one another. Those who have wealth must not use it as a sword to cut their neighbor's throat. They must aid the neighbor. If a man has a robe so large that it can cover his neighbor and he suffocates in it, what good did it do him? Let those who have great wealth know that it was not given them to hurt the neighbor, but to help the neighbor. That is how we must make use of the good things God has given us. We must attend to the way God makes prosper the goods He has given us. Those who are poor should be careful that their ingratitude does not cause disputes. Those who are ungrateful should recognize the good done them. That is why the prophet admonishes us to avoid quarrels. If we took him seriously, we would not have all the friction among ourselves that we now have. I believe that now that we have the Gospel in this city, there will be as much, if not more, quarreling among you as there was when you went around with your eyes shut. Yet God wants us to live in a harmonious union. How else did we get in this sad shape, save that there is stubbornness and misunderstanding towards some and ingratitude towards others. Let us bear this in mind as we move along.

Now there is a special doctrine for ministers, namely, that they must be careful not to start quarrels because of their membership, possessions, or persons. Why? Such quarreling deserves reproach. Thus the doctrine we profess would be stained, calumniated. It is necessary to avoid this. Let us not quarrel in the name of God. When one complains to us, let us console ourselves with the knowledge that we are like the prophet. No one is so perfect that they are without impatience, for it is not in vain that the prophet says, "Woe is me!" He has not been so steadfast that he had not been ready to quit both his office and his life. However that may be, he did not desist from his task. He does not grow faint, but says, "The Lord will assist me." So we see how those who wish to bear the Word of God must be patient.

It is true that not all those called ministers are in disfavor. Why? Some engage in all sorts of debauchery. When they come to Geneva, they are as easily recognizable as if they had a big sign on their forehead. It is certain they will not fall into disfavor. Why? They associate with the lechers. It will be said that they preach well. Why? They do not preach against vices; otherwise they would lose their credulity. They will be loved, as were the false prophets at the time of Jeremiah. Whenever the people were tormented by God's punishment, these false prophets said, "We can remedy that; it is necessary to put a salve on it." Oh, how they will rail against us! They support evildoers. Why? "Because it is necessary to consider the good they do us!" Ah! But what good can they do by making war on God?

What I say now is relevant only to those ministers God is pleased to convert in office. Here is what men charged with the Word must do. They must fortify themselves and say, "Whatever obstacles we face, we are completely committed to God." As I have said, all those who wish to faithfully bear the Word of God must prepare for war. God ordained Jeremiah a prophet by saying, "Go!" Then God said, "Prepare yourself, for they will battle against you." The third thing God said was that "they will not be the stronger." Here, then, are the three things that constitute our office. The first is that God calls us: "Let's go, let's go." The enemy is hidden. The ones are rebels, the others are rogues. So it is necessary to get on the march. Why? God sends us. There is a cry of "They attack!" That means if we wish to serve God faithfully, men will make war against us, as Saint Paul protested when he said, "If I am pleasing to men, then I am not serving God." But here is our one consolation: All they can do is to bump their heads. Why? God said that they will not be the stronger. We need not search for any other shield, for all the evil will count for nothing against us. They will fight one another and they will be in such disorder that they will well serve as an example to discourage others. Nevertheless, this battle recommences eternally. When those who attack us have been struck down by God, He will raise up others. But God is always striving to knock them down. That is our consolation. Nothing more can be said here.

Following this holy teaching, let us prostrate ourselves before the fact of our good God, in recognition of our faults. Let us pray that He not permit us to be so persistent in our opposition against Him that we remain the same despite all His efforts to transform us. Let us beg for pardon and pray He reform us, that we strive to be reconciled to God in total obedience. May we have access to the Word, that through it, we return to Him. Let us pray that God shed His grace not only on us, etc.

* * *

(5) Wednesday, June 26, 1549

Woe is me, mother. Why have you borne me a man of discord and discontent throughout the world? I have never lent on usury, nor have I borrowed on usury. Yet all curse me. Jeremiah 15.

We have begun to examine the prophet's complaint: He does not interact with men to cause disputes, he does not loan money on usury to heap litigations upon his adversaries and he does not borrow on usury. Yet he is assailed from every corner; each takes him for his adversary. He is odious to all the world. That does not come from a private quarrel, but from the fact that he is a servant of God and that evildoers cannot endure what he has to serve up to them.

This tragedy has been difficult for the prophet to bear. He is so tormented that he wishes he had not been born; he deems himself a most unfortunate man, as he would seem even in carnal matters. Nothing is more honorable than to bear the Word of God. But as soon as the flames leap up against us, we think it best to abstain from such a task. That is why God warns that those who bear His Word face war. Let up prepare, then, for war; let us recognize we will have many enemies. This does not happen to Jeremiah alone, for the Word of God does not change and will always enrage evildoers. Nevertheless, it does seem quite odd that we have war when we bear the peace teaching by which God wishes to reconcile us to Himself. What other purpose has the Gospel, except that God desires to receive us in mercy rather than punishing us for our sins? In essence, the Gospel is the reconciliation God wishes to carry out between Himself and men. He does not wish to punish us for our sins, but to swallow them up. So when we bear the banner of peace, why does it lead to war? Saint Paul says that "we are sent to exhort men in the name of God to be reconciled to Him." Will not God's grace soften hearts, however hard they may be? When we bear this message in His name, how can men be so moved against us? We should not be surprised that men are so perverse that God's gift of peace enrages them against ministers. Why not? God gave us His word in order that we come to recognize our sinfulness, know that all our nature is contemptible and that we give free reign to all our vices. Now it is upsetting for men to speak of renouncing their passions, so they change the subject. There is a contradiction in us so great that none can resolve it. That is the reason for the war. Although God softens our hearts, we find it most difficult to renounce ourselves. That is why we refuse God's grace and why men rise up against the Word. As long as God condemns our vices, men, at first hearing of the Gospel, will rise up in hate against those who bear the Word. As soon as God speaks to us, He makes it apparent that we will find only evil in ourselves and that we must change completely. That is why few accept God's teachings.

Now let us see if what I just said in not true. How many are there among men who obey God as they should? On the contrary, some mock God in one way, others in another.

The majority of men are possessed by the Devil. If we pay close attention, we find relevance in what Jeremiah says, namely, that ministers of God's Word are not exempt from quarrels. It is not that they are the cause, but that they possess His teaching, which is the cause. But perhaps you have little doubts, for He says "throughout the earth." It would be a terrible shame that none received Him. However that may be, the number of true receivers is quite small. Why? As I have just said, God commands that we come to hate all our passions, that we condemn all of our nature, and that we have no other desire than to accommodate ourselves to Him. Let us pursue matters further. Among those who have heard the Gospel, how many would find it disgusting to follow it? Why? It says, "Those who are lewd will no longer engage in lewdness, those who are robbers will no longer rob." After men have returned to God, there is no reason for them to return to their customary vices. Now, the first day, you preach against avarice. The wealthy ones will feel tormented, as happened to the young child who was as perfect as an angel. God said to him, "Go, give all you have to the poor and follow me." Now when he heard that he had to give up all that he had, so much the more angrily did he go. When you point out vices to people, they do not wish to listen, but to simply get out of a scrape. The second day, you preach against lewdness; the third day, you preach against hate and grudges; the fourth day, you preach against greed and mundane pleasures. But people cannot allow that. After they have been admonished that all such licentiousness must be abolished, they no longer listen. Here, then, is a new band of enemies given to blasphemy and cursing. We will see the vengeance of God upon these incarnate devils. Thus we will have a new war. God does not spare anyone; He treats each in his turn. The world, then, is full of enmities. Each of us is so discontented by our own iniquities that we quarrel: "Why? He said such-and-such. My crony is accused of this and my neighbor is accused of that. We will not stand for that!" Everywhere you will see what I am saying. We should not be surprised, then, that the prophet says "throughout the earth." We already know well how irritated we become when stung to the quick! Because our own iniquities upset us so, we quarrel among ourselves, as I have just said. If we find no hate in us, we have not searched far enough. Nevertheless, this is not to say that the friends of God must not receive the Word in all gentleness. Saint James says that we must be of a sweet spirit, whereas the unbelieving have a bitter spirit. The spirit of Satan is a combative spirit; God's children must have a spirit of peace. These will always be those who will not permit the Word of God to be in vain, but they are in a minority. The majority of people pay it no heed. Furthermore, those who obey God are not included in the expression "of this earth," for they are reformed and celestial creatures. They are not men who fear God, for they are no longer terrestrial or carnal, but new creatures. Here, then, is a consolation for the servants of God: Seeing that they cannot carry out their task without earning the ill will of men, they must realize that they are not more privileged than the prophet.

There is yet one other admonition for them. The prophet says with good reason that he is a "man of strife," for the evildoers who fight against God do not accuse us of evil. True, they are so impudent that each knows his own malice, but they do not wish to jeopardize their case by accusing ministers of God. They will not say who is right or wrong. They do not say, "I do not wish to be preached at." Instead, they say, "Is it necessary the Word of God be thus preached? Is it not necessary to do so in all kindness? Yet it seems those who preach wield the whip. What kind of preaching is that? It is good to see that they preach by love!" Praise be God that they say we walk by love; for if we have not love, what have we? But what about this kindness they demand? They wish God to hide their faults! The lechers wish that the minister would not speak of lechery. The greedy ones wish that he would not speak of their greed. The avarice ones wish God would conform to them. But that cannot be. To be united with God, we must change our perverse nature. Otherwise, we will be smashed and broken in the end, as the prophet says. This is why God chastises us. It is not without reason that the Gospel is said to be the sword to sacrifice us to God. We cannot change our nature unless we return to God. Then, the contradiction in our flesh will be abated. It will always be there, but God will restrain it. It is necessary we put up with contradictions. The evil ones will find out in the end with whom they have to deal.

Granted, we may protest that all this strife comes from the fact we bear the Word of God, not from our private affairs, and well ask what the point is in all this. Here we are given a double consolation. The first, as we have seen, is that the prophets preceded us. The second is that God assures the prophet that the outcome will be good. God says, "Those whom you battle against will come to repent themselves." They will not be converted to the truth, but they at least will put on a facade of goodness and say, "It is true that I have been irritated by preachers. I did evil." Having said this, however, they go back to their old ways the next day. When he is before the judge or the hangman, the evildoer may well put on a facade of contrition; but if he were released, he would go right back to his old ways the next day. That is why God says to the prophet, "They will cease opposing you and say, 'Alas, I have strayed, pardon me.'" It is no small consolation to know that we will always be victorious, however it may be, as we have seen. They will fight against us, but we are the stronger. So let us battle fiercely under the banner of Jesus Christ, while the evil ones battle under the Devil's banner. Saint Paul exhorts Timothy to do as much when he says, "I have fought and achieved my objective. Fight by my example and fear nothing, for God has given you the upper hand." Is this not a great consolation when we see the enemy fight in confusion? Will Satan lead them to victory? Not only are the gallows waiting for them, but the wrath of God is upon them. Yet they still fight. Will we not be happy to fight when we see our triumph is written in the heavens above? We may go into battle, with many reservations, but the evil ones will surrender and admit defeat. Those who scorn God will witness this great occasion, but they will soon forget it. Let them know now that God is admonishing them, that they not face this day of judgment when God will raise His hand to crush their skulls. May they return to God, that this judgment be no inflicted upon them.

This is not only true for the Papists. They are not the greatest enemies of the Gospel. True, they rage against us. But among those who say, "We wish to have the Gospel," how many contradictions to Scripture are there? Indeed, the prophet does not complain of Assyria, but of those who live in the holy city of Jerusalem, where God wished His name to be invoked. Nevertheless, it became a robber's den. Let us look to ourselves, for God has said that those who fight against the Word will come to terms with us. Note that the passage says, "The prophet will be as a fenced wall," so they will succeed only in banging their heads. Just as a horse who throws himself against the spur will have his belly ripped open, so the evil ones will know in the end that it is not man, but God with whom they must reckon. After God revealed through the prophet that the outcome would be favorable, He adds that those who resisted Him will be dispersed here and there, even to unknown lands where all sorts of calamities will befall them. Why? "Because my wrath is inflamed." Evildoers will be even more astonished, as we have already seen that God also says, "I will send you to the school of the Assyrians." "You do not wish to hear me, but I will send you to a school whose masters you know to serve well," as Saint Paul said of the reign of the Anti-Christ. Our passage for today makes the same point. When men do not wish to be subjugated to God, they will soon learn that god can well send them to other masters. So it is for those today who say, "Oh! We will have to be monks! How awful!" This is how it goes today. We have the remedy of the Gospel; but instead of using it as a remedy against Satan, we vomit up all this grumbling. No wonder the ministers weep; for if they are true servants of God, they will be struck dead by all this. Try and get someone to acknowledge his faults. He will deny all culpability and next esteem himself to be among the most righteous in the world. How, evildoers, do you expect Jesus Christ to demand your pardon before God, when you will not even wiggle your tongue to confess one fault to the glory of God? More and more do they become enraged against us, but we will keep fighting. What will the outcome be? These evildoers will come to know that God sends them to other masters to correct them. As it says in Ezekiel, "You have not wished to obey my laws, but you will have others which you must obey despite yourselves." That is to say, "You have not wished to obey me; you will be led into Babylon and there you will be tormented. You will profit in nothing, for no one owes you anything." Such was the fate of the people of Israel. Those who want a disguised Gospel, those who want a Gospel of quick and easy success, where are they today? Here, sirs, are the evildoers who feign to have the Gospel of God, but we see through their evil ways. They wish to have a Gospel according to their fantasies, but now they have the Spanish, who can well teach them another lesson. And ourselves, where are we today? Will God not be the master of Geneva as well as of Augsburg and Nuremburg? We go from bad to worse. All our balling and belly-aching around is to no avail. Do not think that God has failed to wait upon us, for He has said, "I am tired of saving you." We have seen that God punishes us ever so gently, this while the evil ones become wilder than ever. God has revealed to us that his measuring stick does not resemble ours, that He will not confine Himself to our standard of measure. Let us think on ourselves. Some ask whether what happened at the time of Jeremiah was written down for us. Hah! How insensitive we are to the blows on our heads!

The prophet continues, "Lord, you know me, remember me, and avenge me of my persecutors." This means that whatever course the evil ones take, he will always have God as his guarantor. How is this possible? Men do not make such a claim. Behind our backs, some will spread it around that the Word of God cannot be received because we are so stupid. Man's judgment cannot be trusted. Jeremiah says, "Lord, you remember me." This means that we cannot trust our judgment, as Saint Paul said to the Corinthians. Some will say of the minister, "Who does he think he is? Do we not know him well? Yet when he preaches, he flails us all? Does he think we will tolerate this?" That is how the ministers of God are always rebuked. If anything more is said against them, it is that they are all hypocrites. "No, no!" says Saint Paul, "I appeal to the judgment of God." Because the world is so insane, we must call upon God as our guarantor, provided our conscience testifies we do so for His glory. Let us be at ease, for the prophet brings us home when he calls God his guarantor. Whatever men may say about us, they judge in darkness, as if blind.

This passage, then, is of singular consolation to the ministers of God. On the contrary, those who wish to sentence all severely will sense that God will overrule their sentence. Like a judge who will overrule a too heavy sentence, those who have knowledge from above know well to rescind their sentence. God will chastise us if we usurp His office and condemn those who return to their vices. What gives us such authority? Do we not realize that God, having overruled their sentence, will have to chastise us again? God must reveal Himself to be the sovereign judge. Therefore, we are admonished, we, I say, who bear the Word of God, that we do not sustain any quarrels unless driven to do so by His zeal. Let us not only preach good doctrine, but walk in amity among men. If then we are accused of being men of discord and discontent, we can well say, "It is for you, Lord, that I have suffered rebuke." Do we think that the prophet can bear this without being avenged? No, certainly not! Furthermore, we are hated not only in regard to our persons, but because we bear the Word of God. Each and every one of us is admonished that whenever anyone calls ministers "men of discord," this remark is directed against God. Also we are admonished that we do not rise up against men, but against God. Make no mistake about it. Let us take to heart God's teaching that He will humble us to serve His glory.

Following this holy teaching, let us prostrate ourselves before the face of our good God, in full acknowledgement of our faults, by which we incessantly provoke His wrath. Let us pray that He not permit us to remain so obstinate, that we return in total obedience to Him. May we profit, that He have no occasion to send us to other masters. May He reveal Himself as always our prince. Let us pray that He give us the freedom of the spirit promised His children. We say with humble heart: Celestial Father, etc.

* * *

(6) Thursday, June 27, 1549

O Lord, you know: remember me, visit me, and revenge me of my persecutors. Do not rid yourself of me in your long-standing wrath. Know that I have suffered rebuke for you. Jeremiah 15.

Yesterday we saw the prophet complaining about those who rise up against God, those who fuss and fume against the Word. We also saw the menacing fate that awaits them: They will come to know with whom they have business.

Now the prophet proclaims even more acutely their ruin when he says, "Will iron break northern iron and steel?" It is easy for us to be proud and stubborn; but when God hurls iron and steel against us, how strong will we truly be? The prophet says "northern" to signify the Assyrians. God can well eradicate our hardness. If we were as hard as iron, He would send steel. Let us bend immediately to God. Those who do not wish to do so will be smashed and broken, not by His hand, but by ours. We have venomous-enough tongues and strong-enough backs to throw off His yoke, but He will send enemies strong enough to crush us all. Do not expect to be destroyed by His arm. As soon as we are menaced, let us come forth and pray for mercy.

When the prophet says that God will give over all their treasures to pillage, that is according to a prophecy by Moses. (All the prophets refer their statements back to what was said by him.) When we scorn God, it is very reasonable that He puts us up as booty, as if we were of no value. Sometimes it seems that God pays no attention to His people. When they are pillaged and plundered, it seems that God should have taken better care of them. Indeed! What care have we taken of his honor? Who is God? When all the world raises up against God, what will we do? We will trample Him under foot. Is that not a sufficient reason to destroy us all? That is why the prophet says that their treasures will be given over to pillage.

The prophet does not speak of God's vengeance out of envy. Let us note this point carefully, so that we do not use him as an excuse for ourselves. We must not be bitter; we must strive always to break our bad habits. If we have a cloak to put over us, that is enough. No, we must not imagine the prophet to be spiteful. When he speaks of vengeance, it is after having known the reprobate. We have seen how zealous he was for their salvation, how he begged and pleaded with them, notwithstanding the fact that there no longer seemed to be any remedy. When he now demands vengeance, this has absolutely nothing in common with the turbulence in our flesh. May we learn to be led by such a spirit. If we demand vengeance, let it not be out of self-interest and unbridled passion. Then we can say that our zeal is like that of the prophet. If there is the least bitterness in us, we have nothing in common with the prophet. So it is well for us to note that he says, "Punish these people," as if he were saying, "Amen." God had revealed that there was no way to convert the people, so it was necessary to punish them. The prophet acquiesces to God; he puts aside all thoughts of men; he desires nothing except that God carries out His sentence. He says, "Do not rid yourself of me in your long-standing wrath." Here he is emphasizing the patience of God. When God refrains from punishing His people for a time, it does not mean He has forgotten their faults; rather, it means that He has granted them a limited reprieve from the sentence He pronounced on them. "Because you ordained that these people be punished," says the prophet, "I consecrate this confirmation of your Word, that I be reconciled to the judgment of God and its execution."

He adds that the Word of God has been found and that he has eaten it. Why? Because God's name is reclaimed for him. When he says that the Word has been found, he means that he invented nothing of it by himself, for it is God who gave him the Word he proclaims. He says in effect, "I do not preach by adventure, I know the Word of God and therefore I preach." He says, "I have eaten it," that is, he has it in his heart. If we are to preach faithfully, it is necessary that we have the substance of the Word of God in our hearts, as if we had eaten some good meat of which the substance remained in us.

He adds that "the Word was a joy and rejoicing in my heart," that it had been a delicious meat for him. Why? He takes pleasure in having the sign of God. Now, above all, we must note that the prophet wishes to assure the faithful that his teaching is the pure Word of God. He also says that the evil ones will not escape the hand of God. Let us see how we might apply all this to our situation, if we have any doubts, which we generally do. It is necessary to be sure that the prophets did not dream up what ever seemed good to them. But how? They were certain that their teachings were infallible. That is how they answer us in order that our faith be founded in God and not in men. What will happen is we think our teachings come from men and not God? True, we would be able to hold with some sentence here or there, but there would be no certainty. It is necessary our faith be certain, so that all the devils cannot shake us from it. That is why God did not wish Jeremiah alone to speak but added His seal: "The word of God has been found," says the prophet, as if he were also saying, "I do not preach by adventure. What I proclaim to you I have taken from God. May your faith be confirmed in it." True, the Papists claim they have the Word of God. But what evidence do they have of this? When one compares what the Pope professes with what the prophets taught, there is a blatant contradiction. Now those who despise the teachings of God will have a fine time saying, "We do not know if it is God who speaks." Of course, in the end they will come to know with whom they have business. Here is how we must surmount the mockers who convert into mere fables all the exhortations and threats of God: We say to them, "The Word of God is found, and God will reveal in the end that there is no other judge but the Word," for it has the authority to condemn all.

Furthermore, those whose task is to proclaim the Word should not merely taste a drop of it on the tip of their tongue, but should be replenished by taking in its substance. What will happen if we are not certain our teachings are of God? In what assurance could we proclaim them? True, anyone can get up and babble, but will he have the majesty that comes from knowing that it is God who speaks through His Spirit? When God gives us His teachings, we must share them among ourselves, give all our hearts to them, and take pleasure in all receiving them. The prophet says that the word is so sweet to him, whereas the evildoers find it bitter, indeed a living hell. Whenever justice is mentioned to an evildoer, he thinks himself already on the gallows. Likewise, mention the Word to an evildoer and he thinks himself in prison. The prophet says that although the Word holds the evildoers in Hell, it does not fail to bring pleasure. Why? We must not find it strange that God avenges Himself on evildoers. We will never find the Word of God distasteful, even though it reveals His wrath against evildoers; once we have tasted its mercy, we cannot be diverted from it. Our difficulties stem from the fact we have not yet tasted the Word; as soon as we hear it speak, we know the promise of eternal salvation and adoption through Jesus Christ. Once we have heard and understood the Word, nothing can pull us away from it. When we learn of the grace God has shed upon us, we will ask only to be replenished by it. When we have been replenished today, we will want it again tomorrow.

Furthermore, we should not find it distasteful that the Word brings damnation to the evil ones. If the wine is poison to the drunkard, is it distasteful to us? No, certainly not! We do not loose our taste for it, oh, no, for it agrees with us. Thus, if the evildoers turn the Word of God into poison, it does not become distasteful to us. Let us know to what end God has ordained such. When we see that the Word is the smell of death to evildoers, let us sanction it and let us thank God that He preserves us in the Word. How are we different from the others? In no way, save that the pure bounty of the Word separates us from those who perish. We must realize that it is all to the glory of God that He is so harsh upon evil ones. That is how we should find the Word of God sweet, although it threatens these rebels with eternal damnation.

The prophet says, "Your name is reclaimed for me," which means that God has marked him as one of His own. Why is it that we take pleasure in the Word of God? Because God has chosen us, that His name be reclaimed for us. Are there not many who find only unhappiness in the Word when it is preached to them? What does the Word of God have to offer them? Only damnation. There will always be hypocrites and those dead as fence posts, who cannot take in one single item of the Word, whereas we draw our sustenance from it. Now the prophet proclaims that we would not know what is of God, save that God took us up again to be His own. That is why we must attribute all that we have to His gracious bounty.

Now the prophet adds a little later, "I did not sit in the assembly of mockers, I was not a mocker, and I sat alone because of your hand." When he says that he did not sit among mockers, he speaks according to the first Psalm; for it reveals the folly of man, saying, "Blessed is he who does not sit in the assembly of mockers." David, from the start, speaks of evil ones and sinners, meaning in general those who abandon themselves to evil and are alienated from God. No doubt, however, the word "mockers" is more important than these two; by this, David means men given to all iniquities. Now, this vice comes from the fact that men think themselves too clever. Consequently they mock God, as we see in Isaiah.

In Proverbs Twenty-Eight, Solomon reveals the brutality of men when they think themselves so wise and are so content with themselves. This gives them an excuse to completely unbridle themselves. That is why the prophet says, "I did not sit in the assembly of mockers." The word "sit" signifies not merely that he avoided their company for a time, but that he never associates with them.

He continues, "I was not a mocker, and I sat alone because of your hand." When he says he sat with the Word, that means there is no other remedy for us than to return to it. If we are blocked from doing so, we will be immediately seduced by the Devil and become mockers who give free reign to all forms of impiety. Let us note above that all men are by nature inclined to mock God, save that they bridle themselves. We all have the tendency to mock God unless His miraculous power works within us. Here, then, is our misfortune. The creatures to whom God gave reason do not obey their Creator. If God is not obeyed by asses, nobody finds that strange; but the fact that men are naturally inclined to mock God is extremely odd. It is unbelievable, just unbelievable, that we are rebels unmoved by the majestic glory of God, before which the mountains melt like snow in sunlight. We are extremely iniquitous until God remedies this fault. Now, since it is a matter here of such a loathsome vice, we should attempt to eradicate it. We must go to its source, which is our pride, to be rid of it. Here is the cause of our blindness. We do not know ourselves; we made idols, so that we are not subject to God; for it seems our own wisdom is sufficient to guide us. But why? Is our imagination but a dream? When he dreams, a poor man will make himself a king, yet he will wake to find himself as poor as always. Let us know ourselves, to be humble; for in knowing ourselves, we will see the abysm of evil within us. Let us then go before our judge. Now, let us compare our rottenness against the majesty of God, for our bodies and souls are nothing but an abomination. When we know this and present ourselves before the majesty of God, we will mock Him; we will see that His wrath is inflamed against us. Let us learn well this lesson if we wish to abolish all mockery of God. At a glance, men do not appear to banter about this mockery of God; but if you examine them more closely, you will find this evil habit in their hearts.

The majority of the Papists make a gesture of devotion to God, simply because it costs them nothing. Or, if it does cost them something, in as much as they wish to be acquitted of their sins, it merely amounts to going from one statue of a saint to another, trotting from chapel to chapel, running from church to church. "My iniquity is taken care of!" they say. Take a Papist aside after mass and ask him, "What do you think you accomplished? Have you appeased God by that?" "No, certainly not" is the answer. He cannot pay in such money, for it is necessary his heart be purged of all iniquity; otherwise, he does all this for nothing. Then he will spit out his venom and say, "If God is not pleased with that, let Him go elsewhere and bid me good day!" That is how it is among Papists, if we look at them closely enough. We will see this even more clearly among ourselves, for there are more trees to hide under in Papism.

When you preach the Gospel, it is easy to see the iniquities hidden in hearts. If you preach only stories from the pulpit, listeners will say, "Ah, how sweet is the Word of God." But if you land upon their faults, if you really put the pressure on, as if God were squeezing them in a vice, then this hidden impiety comes out and they who before had found the Word so sweet will say, "Hey! What Gospel is this? Best we chuck it!" That is how they show their evil. So it is true what I said before, namely, that men all have a hidden seed in them to mock God. It does not come out all at once, but little by little. It is certain that we will all become impious, unless God leads us! Solomon said that when man sinned, all was destroyed, for "he has abandoned himself to all evil." Because we are so accustomed to evil, we make fun of God. Here we come to the depths of our iniquity. The majesty of God means nothing to us, as we have seen in these examples. We have many mirrors before our eyes, if only we knew how to use them. We see this impiety in those who received the Gospel, so that we cannot even think without them insulting us. When they speak of Scripture in the taverns, it is all derision. Everyone jeers at God. They find the Word and the Gospel so distasteful that they wish never to hear them again. What impiety there is those who have received the Gospel! They are more out of hand than are devils. If you reprimand them, they mock even more, saying, "He yells alot. Will he send us all to Hell?" Oh, has the Word we preach the authority to send you evil ones to Hell! Seeing that the majesty of God means nothing to us and that we are so prone to evil, out of fear that He gives the Devil the power to blind us, let us return to Him; let us pray that He permit us neither to be seated among the mockers nor to be captivated by their impious rebellion against him.

The prophet, as I have said, reveals the only path to salvation: it is "to be seated" in the Word of God. If we pull away from the Word, we surrender to evil. It is our sole protection against Satan's power to turn us from God. When we stand on God's side we are well protected. Without the Word, we have no remedy and will be destroyed. The prophet says, "I am all alone," which means that we must not allow the fact that we are scandalized to block our path to God. Let us not be shocked when we see that the mockers of God cannot tolerate the Word. Let us, instead, pause and say, "Lord I give myself to you." We must bear this carefully in mind; for today so many are led astray, which is the sign of our times. The prophet does not say that there are two groups, the one given to evil, the other following God. He says, "I am alone." Now this does not mean that he is without others; rather, it means that however we have been led astray and that whatever stumbling blocks we may encounter, nothing can turn us from God.

Following this holy teaching, let us pray that God give us the grace to hate our faults and to follow Him, that we come to renounce the iniquities of the evildoers blocking our path. May we not only renounce their iniquities but ours as well. May God give us the grace to follow Him, that we share in His celestial glory. May He shed His grace not only, etc.

* * *

All-powerful God, because our sins provoke your wrath daily and because we are so ungrateful and disobedient to your teaching, give us the grace to know what end we deserve. Let this so displease us with our vices that we turn to you in truth with all our heart. Let us have no cure nor consolation other than to know the way you reconcile us to yourself, that we know your favor and grace. May it please you to govern us by the Holy Spirit. May you strengthen and fortify us to be obedient servants, until we finally come to our celestial beatitude, which is preserved in the heavens above by Jesus Christ, our Lord. Amen.

(7) Friday, June 28, 1549

Why is my pain eternal and my wound incurable? It refuses to heal. Will you be a liar to me, like waters that fail? They will return to you, but you will not return to them. Jeremiah 15.

Yesterday we explored how the prophet sits alone with the Word and not among the mockers. He avoids their company because that might give him occasion to sin; for we are all attracted to evil rather than good. He remains with God, although he could well be diverted from Him. This is what we must do. When all the world is given to evil, let us know that God does not change. We must hold to the Word, which we can do only if we return to God.

He says that he "has been filled with wrath." Now his wrath is holy. How have we abandoned God? We have seduced ourselves with our pleasures and we do not think we will perish, as we saw before. When we come to know that God is a just judge who punishes sinners, we will return to Him in full obedience. Note this will; for the prophet says that if the Day of Judgment had occurred before his very eyes, he would have been a debaucher along with all the rest and would not have been in horror of his sins. But when he realized that God is the judge of all who condemn His word, he was struck with fright. Time after time, he was inflamed with the zeal of God to punish sinners. Whenever God threatens us, let us, then, take these misfortunes to be present among us and not sluff them off. God can threaten us even when we sleep. Let us be content with the Word; let us not dare God to show what evil fate awaits us. Consider the example of Sodom. When God descended to see its abomination, He had already passed sentence. When Noah announced the Flood, people did not cease their merry-making and their total abandonment to all pleasures. The hand of God certainly surprised them. I can show many other examples that we must not wait upon His hand but that as soon as He speaks we must take seriously the evil with which He menaces us, for He acts as His Word dictates. It is good, then, that we become enraged. Indeed, Saint Paul admonishes us to be enraged. Likewise David said, "Be angry, but do not sin." Here he is again referring to those who war out of envy; he is admonishing them to reflect upon the evil plans they concoct in their beds. Next he adds, "Be angry and do not sin;" for if we become angry with our vices, it is sure that this anger is holy and that we will no longer sin. However, we often try to excuse ourselves by saying that we are irritated with our vices and enraged over having offended God. Yes, but if we truly hate sin, should we not begin with our own? If someone else sins, we are instantly angered; but if we sin, "Ah," we say, "it's no big deal." Another example of our hypocrisy: When one sins against a neighbor, "it is no big deal." But if one sins against us, we are enraged. We are not moved by true zeal, but only because sin has attacked us. May we be moved because God is offended, whenever we make a mistake. If we can come to react that way, God can save us from all deluges and we will have a good bridle to reign us in from sinning. This is why we must live in fear of God. When God calls us to ashes and sackcloth (as Isaiah says), there is no doubt we will go from bad to worse if we do not renounce our vanities and if we continue to love worldly delights more than we deplore our sins. This is why it is said that "the heart of the sage lives in the house of sadness; and the heart of the fool, in the house of joy." Why? We do not wish to be sad, but it is better to have this sadness that returns us to God than it is to rejoice in such a way that we go from bad to worse. Seeing how the iniquitous mock all God's warnings, let us be enraged against all vices; but let us start with our own.

The prophet asks, "Why is my pain eternal and my wound incurable?" He goes on to say, "Lord, you have been a deceptive fountain to me. I waited on you and everyone cries after me. Where is the aid I hoped to have? Lord, are you a little stream of water that has dried up? An incurable wound saddens me. Only living waters could have helped me. I know well the need for me to battle, but where is the aid you promised me?" The prophet has had as much as he can bear, for God permitted him to endure as much as he transgressed. There is no doubt that he is impatient and that this stems from his faith not being what it should. If we have full faith, we have hope; and hope brings patience. This is the order to observe when battling against the world. Saint John says that we must have faith and that this faith will be confirmed by hope. And when we have hope, we will not lose patience, no matter how we are afflicted. The absence of patience, then, is a sign our faith is weak. The prophet gives ample testimony that his faith is faltering when he complains that the fountain is tardy. This admonishes us not to allow our impatience to become a stumbling block and to pray that God does not abandon us. When we are far from blows, we seem to be ever so bold; but when they fall on us, we fold instantly. Seeing that the prophet falters, let us pray that God strengthen us; for if the prophet could be tempted to fear, certainly we could, too. Indeed, we have not profited in the teachings of God as he. Let us recognize well that if we were as oppressed as he, we would not only be as terrified, but we would lose all wisdom; we would no longer know what is God or whether or not He is in the heavens above. Let us return to Him, that He provide for our imperfections. However the prophet grieved, his faith did not fail; those who lose faith despise God; but the prophet says, "Alas Lord, I wait on you," which shows he still had faith in some aid from God. So let us go straight to God and pray that He makes us aware of His presence in us and that His promises are not fraudulent. That is what we must do.

When the prophet says, "Why is my pain eternal?" he shows that it is not for a mere day that he has been so afflicted. Let us learn to be that patient. I say this, because anyone can sustain one assault, only to fall with the second. We must continue on, we must not give up because at the end of a month or even a year it seems that God wishes all to perish. Let us note that the prophet speaks of such a long-standing pain that it seemed eternal. This means God was not testing his patience on a short-term basis. If God afflicts us for a year or even a whole lifetime without aid, let us expect it after death; for our hope must transcend this world.

When the prophet says that God has been a "flowing stream" to him, he expresses the hope we must have in God, as he says in the seventeenth chapter, where we read, "Blessed is he who puts his hope in me; he will be like a tree planted in living waters." God has said of evildoers, "They have abandoned me, the fountain of living waters, and have dug out cisterns for themselves." This means that we must hope in God as a fountain of living waters that cannot dry up. If our hope in Him is merely temporary, we honor Him no more than is due a mere mortal. It is necessary, then, that our hope in Him be eternal. Let us be resolved to eternal hope and it will aid us to the end of our life and even after we depart this world. That is the main point of my analogy. However, we do not always perceive of God as this fountain of living waters. It is not that we are void of His grace, but that we are not always aware of it. Yet we are very aware of our indigence. God permits that we be hungry and wish to eat, and this while we have no food. But we must not fear that the living waters have dried up. What is the source of the flowing waters that we never lack? Is it not God? When we come to Him, let us not fear our needs, provided that we look upon Him as the fountain of living waters. If we are upset over our needs, let us know that God wishes either to test or to punish us. If a man says, "Alas, I am dying of thirst," and if he must humble himself in order to drink, who is to blame if he dies of thirst? If we are well aware our needs and yet are such slow pokes that, knowing well God is the fountain of living waters, we do not wish to humble ourselves before Him and be replenished by His grace, then the blame is upon our shoulders; for God looks to no one other than ourselves. Let us see what follows.

God says, "If you return to me, I will return to you, that you be seated before me. And if you separate the precious thing from that which is not precious, you will be as my mouth. Be careful that they return to you and not you to them." This passage signifies that God wished to chastise him for his distrust. Here the prophet confesses his fault; indeed he even had it written down to make known he was tempted, in order that we have recourse to God and that He aid our needs. The prophet, then, wished his fault to instruct us; for it is a great human folly that men wish to conceal their faults, when confession of them is to the honor of God. He says, "When I was shaken up, God provided for me." God grants us a great favor: If God gives us His grace when we are almost conquered by temptation, this is a sign that He wishes us to be His. When we err, we must not be upset by reprimands, for all correction is from God. If a person reprimands us, it is really God who does so, even if that person bears enmity towards us. Seeing that God is our physician, are we not ingrates if we do not receive the grace He sheds on us? The prophet says, "I cried out and God aided me." That means if

God truly abandoned us in our time of need, we would be in great danger.

Let us turn now to the matter of correction. God says, "Where are you?" as if to say, "If I abandon you, would you not deserve it? But should you return, if you order yourself by reason, if you know I do not wish to abandon my own, and if you forget all your carnal thoughts, I will receive you to sit before me." When He says "before me," this means He will take back His own. This metaphor is frequently found in Scripture, so that God is likened to a man whose servants stand before him in order to provide the best service. When we quit the service of God, we will no longer be before His face. It is not that God does not see everything, but that we will be alienated from Him. We must note, then, that God is not like men who discharge servants without any reason. God could well give us leave because we have failed in His service; He could throw us out of His house. But why? If He were to do so, who would remain His own? Certainly a good servant makes a hundred-thousand mistakes. What would we do if God threw us all out and we were no longer His own? God supports us, so that, spoiled and as unwilling to serve our calling as we may be, God says, "Come, come!" God is like a master who runs after his servant, saying, "Hey, poor wretch, where are you going? You will die of hunger. Come back, come back!" That is what our Lord does. Our passage gives us a good example of the infinite bounty of God. When God says, "If you return to me, I will return to you, that you be seated before me," this signifies that the prophet deserves to be thrown out, but that he was not recalled only to be pushed out. When we see that the prophet quit the service of God, we know our fragility. In this manner of speaking, it is desirable we serve God in order that we are not reproached by Him. For it is said that if we no longer serve Him, He will no longer pay attention to us. Let us know, then, that there is no more desirable vocation than striving only to obey Him.

We see, then, that the office of those charged with the Word of God is to discern good from evil, approving what is good and condemning what is evil. When men rally to the teachings we bear, we can regard them as those in whom God works. On the contrary, we condemn those who retreat from the Word. Though they be among the most honorable in the world, we must condemn them. Here, then, is the office of ministers, and it is without exception of persons that they approve of goodness and condemn evil. They must allow nothing to dissuade them from executing God's sentence upon us. If they see a man who does his duty, they must honor him. On the contrary, if they see an evildoer, whatever position he may hold, they must condemn him. The Lord says, "If you separate the precious things from the vile, you will be as my mouth." This means that when we approve of goodness or condemn evil, we please God that we rally around Him. He adds, "Whatever the case, they return to you, not you to them." He means that if evildoers turn from God, we must not accommodate ourselves to them; we must break with our custom of compromising in order to have peace. "No, no," He says, "they must accommodate themselves to you. You must not be like a rose which bends with every breeze. If you want to have peace, they must return to you and not you to them." This instructs us that the Word of God brings the power to distinguish between good and evil. If God had not enlightened us by His Word, we would condemn goodness and approve of evil; although we have some discretionary powers, we understand nothing. Furthermore, men become so brutish that goodness is despised. But the Word of God illuminates us so clearly that we can see what was heretofore hidden. Know, then, that the Word of God is given, that we be not deceived but always have a clear path.

Not only does He speak of good and evil, but of that which is vile and that which is precious. If the prophet spoke only of good and evil, that would not have been as obvious as when he says vile and precious. When we see vices, we do not diminish them enough to be in true proportion to ourselves and we magnify what is really nothing at all. Thus the prophet reveals that we must have such powers of discretion that not only do we know to approve of goodness and reproach evil, but also that we know how to distinguish the vile from the precious when compared in all fairness. On the contrary, if we have no sound basis for our judgments, if we lack a pure, clean conscience and do not serve the honor of God, everything we do will go up in smoke. Now, it is certain that we must ask God for advice when we make discretions; it is His office to be judge and we must not usurp it. To say that God is judge means that it belongs to Him and Him alone to judge. We must avoid saying, "It seems to me such-and-such in the case." Our attempts to judge reek of our audacity. We must hear what God has to say about good and evil, and acquiesce to His decisions. Now, those charged with the office of ministry have recourse to the power of the Word to discern good from evil and therefore can condemn without any difficulty. When this condemnation is given, we must not complain, but follow it to the letter. Those charged with the Word have the Law of God to guide them. It is necessary to conclude, then, that the world will always war against us; how can it be otherwise? When preachers discern by the Word of God, it is certain that they will offend not only one or two but all and that each will have his turn at enlisting in the ranks of the disgruntled.

When God says "as my mouth," He reveals that we must speak only His word if we are to exercise the office He has given us. When a man speaks by his own will, he speaks not as a prophet, apostle or doctor of the church; he speaks for himself alone, as we will see in the seventeenth chapter. Do we wish to be known as prophets of God? His Word must be our discretion and we must not do things as we deem them appropriate.

He adds that "they return to you." This is important because those who are charged with the Word must be in harmony with those to whom they preach. Let preachers follow the Word of God, for they will be minded. Hatred is not necessary; we must reconcile ourselves. But what will this reconciliation be like? Will it be a mere drinking club? Will the minister say, "Because I see you cannot bear to be reproached, I will spare you any further criticism"? No, certainly not! A curse on such a reconciliation. The Word of God must always be in their hearts to condemn all vice. Those who wish to live in accord with the prophets of God must learn to correct their own faults. When God says, "They convert to you," this signifies that Jeremiah had carried out his office. When He says, "They return to you," He is not speaking of the person of Jeremiah but of the characteristics of a true prophet: "They must first be reconciled to me. Take care you make no compromises with them." Those who wish to be at peace with the ministers of God must take care to transform themselves and overcome their stubborn pride by which they say, "We will do as we have been accustomed to." Otherwise, let them make peace with the Devil, for they would have a sorry peace that brings only confusion.

Following this holy teaching, let us prostrate ourselves before the face of our good God, praying that we be forever vanquished of all temptation. Let us pray that if He tests us, this strengthen us so that we cannot be distracted from Him. Let us pray that more and more His image will be revealed in us. Let us pray that we be not spoiled, whatever spoilage we see in others. May He shed His grace not only upon us, but upon all the peoples and nations of the world, etc.

* * *

All-powerful God, because today it pleased you to so intimately reveal your will to us through the Gospel of your Son, grant us the grace to receive the certitude of faith contained in it, that we be content with you alone and rest in your truth. Let us be rid of and reject all the world. Let us not be disturbed by threats or fears. Let us not totter when we see the evil ones striving to turn the world from you. Let us render honor where honor is due, that we not only obey you but accomplish the task to which you committed us. Guide us, that in accomplishing our task, we do not create difficulties that enrage the world against us. Grant us that we constantly persevere in our vocation, until we reach the end of this war to which you have called us. Grant us that we enjoy the victory which has been won through your only Son, Jesus Christ. Amen.

(8) Saturday, June 29, 1549

The Lord said to me, "If you return to me, I will return to you, that you be seated before me. If you separate the precious things from the vile, you will be as my mouth." Jeremiah 15.

Yesterday we showed how the Word of God brings the power to discern between good and evil. Unless we are enlightened by the truth of God, we are confused. Although it seems that we are well advised, it is nevertheless the case that vice seems virtue to us. We do not perceive hypocrisy; but when God comes with the Word, that was heretofore hidden is revealed. This is why Saint Paul says that "if one preaches the Word as one must, men will be convinced of it." It is necessary for God to examine us by His Word, and those who think they are justified will find themselves culpable before God. If we are to discern good from evil, we must realize that we would be poor blind men except that God illuminates us through His Word. Ministers must put this teaching into practice, so that men whose lives had heretofore been inclined to vice now know the path to righteousness and can discern good from evil where heretofore they had no powers of discretion. If we are not to be more ignorant than we have been, we must hold to the rules of God reveals. In doing so, we will know how to discern the precious from what is of no value and we will realize that what we heretofore treasured was of no value.

Here is the fruit of this teaching: God picks fruit out of us, for it is not in vain that He is called "the seed of life." Now a field is barren and grows only bushes before it is seeded.

Likewise, we are all sterile until God cultivates us. What happens before God seeds us? Hah! Men think themselves to be saints, for there is only vanity in them. As Saint Luke says, "What is precious before men is an abomination to God." But after God seeds our field, we produce good fruit. It is a great consolation when we see God call precious the fruit he picks out of us after we have been instructed in the Word, for heretofore we were only scum. Is it not a great honor that he calls precious what he harvests from us? We will not profit in the Word of God until this separation takes place, as Jeremiah says. Until we are differentiated from the evil ones, we cannot say that we have profited in anything. There is of necessity a great difference between us and them: Whereas they are regarded as beasts, we are able to order our life. This is why Saint Paul says, "Do not be as you have been and as those who live by their brutishness. It should not shock you that they are all blind. But you, God did not give you His word for you to wander idly about but for you to teach others. Take care that this enlightenment was not given you in vain."

Here is how one can distinguish the precious from the worthless: Instead of finding only infection in us, He picks precious fruit worthy to be His honorable vessels, as He has elected us to this end. Now, the minister must always stick to the Word of God and never accommodate himself to those given to vice; he must stay pure; he must remain loyal to his task of returning to God those who were alienated from Him. Now this task requires a strength not found in men. Therefore, we must ask God to give us the strength and magnanimity of His Spirit, that we be not blocked from fulfilling our task. That is why ministers are exhorted to pray that God strengthen them so that they do not bend with every little breeze. Also we must not attempt to flatter ourselves in our vices; that causes all sorts of bickering simply because nobody is going to favor us as we would wish. True, we wish to be obedient to God. But why? To be courteous to Him as we would be courteous to any mortal man. We expect the same of others, even evildoers. We are ever so respectful to God because we wish Him to remain in the midst of us when we sin. This is why some have been turned from the Word. We must not imagine God or His Word, which resembles Him, to be mutable. God will not accommodate Himself to our changes; for "in Him there is no mutation," as Saint James says. We must not think that God will accommodate Himself to our concupiscence.

God consoles the prophet and says he will be a "well-fortified wall of steel," for war is inevitable. "But they will not conquer you," says our Lord, "for I will be with you to save you." The prophet has a special consolation, namely that God is his protector. He has deep need of God: What would happen if we went into this war where all the world fights against us, with only our two arms and armor? Alas, it would be all over for us soon enough, for where is our ammunition? If we are not sustained by God, how can we carry out our mission? But because God has foreknowledge of all our doubts, He said we will be a "wall of steel." Is not this sufficient to put us at ease? If we have an impenetrable fortress, we have nothing to fear. God fears not the armed forces of the world. He tells us He will share His power with us, so what have we to fear? We have an invincible force on our side, not that it comes from ourselves, but from God, so nothing can block us from carrying out our mission. Here is how we are consoled in carrying out our mission; for this was not said solely for Jeremiah, but for those who bear the Word of God. Let those who assail, torment and make war on ministers be advised that we can well counter-attack. When God says we will be a "wall of steel," He is referring not to the metal, but to the Assyrians; for He says that they are so hard that none can break them. What, then, will those who war against the ministers of God gain? We teach all not to make war against those God has sent: No matter how well these rebels fight, God will show that mortal men profit in nothing by raising up against Him.

Now, as I have said, if we must go to war, what do we need aside from fortification? What good will arms be when peace is everywhere? What use will swords be then? When God says that He will give us an invincible force, this is a sign we need Him. Now, we must not let our guard down when the enemy is near. This is a necessary precaution: Although we have the promise of God that He will deliver us, this does not mean we can go to sleep or be negligent. Our Lord foresaw all this and ordained that just as each of us must be sustained by His power, so each of us must go into battle; for we cannot carry out our mission without combat, not that this war comes from God or from ourselves, but from the rebels against the Word of God. What is the cause? Their malice. It is true that the Word has been called iron and sword; but this does not mean that it leads to war; war is not the nature of the Word, for it is the Word of reconciliation. But, then, why do men war against God? We resist the Word because we cannot bear what it says to us, namely, that all our passions must be reformed. That is a very hand and difficult affair for us. As soon as we begin to rebuke ourselves, the first shot is fired; for we cannot receive the Word in gentleness and in the spirit of kindness. The Word does not bring war, for it is we who rise up against it. The Word of God is not the cause of combat. But whether it is addressed to angels or to men, there will always be war; for what else is there in us, save total contradiction? The Word, then, will always be the stronger. The evil ones will know that they, not we, are the cause of war. As Elijah said to King Ahab, "I am not the cause of trouble, but it is you, King, who are the cause." Others will rail against us out of their righteous indignation, as Jeremiah reveals when he says, "I am a man of discord." But when they come before God, it is certain that they will know well to maintain the Word and condemn all evildoers. They will know who the malcontents are that make all the trouble. If they try to place the blame on us, we will well see their impudence. They know well that if they wished to subjugate themselves to God, there would be no war. Now it is said that "they will fight." Who is they? The people! We must combat not one or two, but a whole multitude. That is not surprising, for this rebellion is in all men in all nations. If you go from country to country, you find that each has its own unique way of life. But if you go all around the world, you will find that each has this perverse desire to rebel against the will of God. That is why war is common to all peoples, although there is a great diversity of mores and languages and so on.

If we look within man, we find two things that cause this rebellion. There is this pride such that we cannot help but rebel against God. Now this human wisdom, what exactly is this wisdom? It is the cause of all idolatry, for men think that they alone know what must be done. This wisdom is the mother of all superstition. From where does the idolatry of Papism come? From the wisdom of men. They presume to discern better good from evil without the Law of God. Men may express this presumption in a variety of different ways, but they are all in accord with this superstition. That is how the wisdom of men confuses all. Let us leave aside the example of the Paganism and take up one closer to home, namely, Papism. Why do Papists war against us? We say that there is only one God and that we must serve Him in spirit and not according to our whims, for He is spiritual. We say that He is the only one in whom we can hope. We say that all our goods are in Jesus Christ. We say that to serve Him we must hold to His teaching. Must these things be found so strange? No, but the Papists rise up against us immediately; for they have forged gods out of their own carnal ways. When it is a question of serving God, they throw up the matter of free will. Merits matter above all else. Jesus Christ is there, but totally shrouded. If it is a question of invoking God, they will say that not one of the Apostles knew Jesus Christ. How is God to be served? One will have one rule; the other, another. Yet we have only one rule which God has given us. Such is the pride of men. We have not invented new sacraments, for we wish only to maintain what God has ordained and add nothing of our own. Why are Papists, who claim to be Christians, not in accord with us? Why do they combat us? Because they think themselves wiser than God and call marriage a sacrament. They baptize with oil; otherwise it would be only a half baptism, as it says in their decretals. They also require spittle, salt, and a burning candle for baptism. That is where their wisdom led them. They pervert the Supper by saying that Jesus Christ is the sacrifice, as if the one He made were to no avail or else that He wanted to give us an example of being our own redemptors! Let us hope we do not fail to follow God's Rule; let us learn not to ground wisdom in ourselves and to find good all that God ordained. Then, there will be no war.

The second reason why we have war and why we do not find good what God has ordained is our evil passions. Even in Evil we wish to be free. But we cannot, for God has led us into His captivity to be subjugated to Him. This is why, in reproving our vices, we become so combative; for our vices are so common and must all be reproved. We cannot quell ourselves and cease bickering against God. However, we are not the cause of war. How much and for whatever reason we have spoken, all are moved as if someone sounded the tambourine. We demand only that each put his confidence in God and that, to have peace, each come to Jesus Christ, who is our reconciliation. That is what our doctrine claims. If the world does not wish to accept it, what can we do about it? Is it necessary to blame us? Let the papists who are so puffed up against the ministers of the Word know that in the end they will realize it is God Himself that they reproach. And among ourselves, if there is anyone who cannot bear the yoke of God, we can say that he has not held with us; for we have worked to be the sheep of God's flock. If men were sheep, there would be no war; but when men wish to be heard and to bicker with one another, then they are the source of war, not we.

Here is our one consolation: They will not be stronger. If we are faced by a great war, we would not be shaken, but follow always our vocation. There is no doubt that if we look to the mutabilities of the world, we will be shaken; for we see cruelty, on one hand, and the strength of our enemies, on the other. What prevents them from exercising their rage against us? God holds them down. That is a great consolation to us. Although we are not the most cunning, let us not doubt that we are the strongest, provided that we strive to draw to God those who pull back from Him. Let men be rebels to their heart's content; all they will succeed in doing is banging their heads against our wall of iron.

The Lord said, "I am with you to save you and deliver you." All our comfort rests in the Lord taking us as His own. When God reveals Himself to men, He does so through the truth of His Word. It is the true image of God that we must reflect upon, especially as it is revealed through Jesus Christ. Since we are certain of having the Word of God, let us not doubt that He will accomplish what He said through the prophet, namely, that we will be delivered from the hand of the iniquitous.

Here God warns those who battle against His Word. He calls them first evil, then hideous, and finally rebels. Scripture speaks of the children of God in two ways. It says that they receive the Word of God and next that they are meek, for the evildoers are always evil and iniquitous. Do we wish true justice to dwell among us? It is necessary, then, that God steps in and leads us by His Word, which tames us and directs us, not that we would wish anything else but to please Him. Justice consists of our humility before God. Once the Word has reformed us and we strive to live obediently, God will sanction our justice. This is why Scripture speaks so often of merit, for God receives from us the graces He shed, however imperfect they may be. If we wish to be children of God, we must obey Him. On the contrary, until God changes us, we will always be evil and rebellious; for if the will of God is just, what else could rebels be but evil? Why is it they are said to be rebels? Because the children of God are humble. Now, there is only one way to render us humble and that is to know God and to know ourselves. Those enlightened in the knowledge of God and of themselves will be dumfounded. Why are we so arrogant towards our neighbors? Because each of us prizes himself and thinks the other to be nothing. But when God reveals to us that we are all worthless, we are moved to kindness. On the contrary, those who have not received the Word of God are savage beasts with their horns aimed against God and their hoofs aimed against us. Therefore we must learn what is the office of the Word. Let us pray that God give us the grace to know the fruit of the Word. Let us pray that, so inclined to rebellion as we may be, He give us the grace to follow Him in total obedience. Let us pray God reign in us, that we bear fruit. Let us pray that nothing block Him from having dominion over us and that we may live charitably with our neighbors. Let us pray that He remove the bandage of human wisdom from our eyes. May He give us the grace to subdue our affections so that His kingdom be accomplished in us when we strip away all our passions.

Following this holy teaching, let us prostrate ourselves before His face. Let us pray that in this continual conflict between our passions and ourselves, we take His side and fight against ourselves, that we be glorified and victorious through His strength. May God shed His grace not only on us but upon all the peoples and nations of the earth, etc.

* * *

(9) Monday, July 8, 1549

The Word of God said to me, "You will not take a wife and you will have no son or daughter in this place." For the Lord says, concerning the sons and daughters born here and their mothers and fathers: "They will die grievous deaths. They will not be lamented or buried. They will be like shit on the face of the earth, they will be consumed by the sword and by famine, and their carcasses will be meat for the birds and beasts of the earth. Jeremiah 16.

We see here how such small things can block us from coming to God. Jesus Christ said that when God calls us by His Gospel to be His Church, we always find some excuse. One will say, "I have gotten married," so he no longer has the time to follow the Lord. Another will say, "I bought a farm. I must go look after it." Still another will say, "I bought some cattle." They use the least thing to excuse themselves from the path of righteousness. Nevertheless, as long as we are in this world, it is necessary for us to have cattle and to marry; for these are necessities to which God has subjugated us. What remedy is there? Saint Paul instructs in the seventh chapter of First Corinthians that he who is married should be as a widower and those who have possessions should be as they had none. This is in order that things of this world do not block us from coming to God.

There is another reason why the prophet is told not to marry in this land. God told him that "the fathers, mothers, and infants would be consumed by the sword and by famine." Now it is certain that when we marry, we do so in the hope of aid and in the hope of having descendants in which we can delight. That is what we all hope for in a marriage. But the Lord says that they will be afflicted from all sides. Who would want to marry under this shadow, where one sees only confusion? For each is preparing to depart this world and so does not search whilly-nilly for remedies, for it is certain all must perish. God forbids the prophet from marrying, to serve as an example to the rest of the people. Likewise, God commanded Isaiah to walk about in a wooden yoke like a poor captive slave, to warn the people their captivity was near. God wished the prophet to instruct the people. This is why we can do nothing but despise ourselves when called to repentance. Because the people are too hardened by sin to sense their purgation is at hand, the prophet must warn by example. True, marriage is not forbidden in itself; it is to be honored and prized, for it is a thing ordained by God for the salvation of man. But at the time of the prophet, men, as at the time of Noah, were totally abandoned to their pleasures and cared only to marry and have children. Our Lord, Jesus Christ, says that when the Day of Judgment is at hand, men will no longer care to marry even if they had to live forever. Jeremiah's celibacy, then, was intended as a warning that this Day was at hand. But the people believed nothing the prophet said. They mocked him, saying, "Indeed, you have sung your song for a long time. Yet we see nothing of that which you threaten us. We will have a good time and let the future take care of itself." Such is the mockery of men. True, the heads of households are not to relinquish their responsibility to marry off their children. The threats of the prophet are not directed against that; rather, they are directed against the vices of the people. When God threatens us, it is so that each can say, "It is God who remonstrates me for my sins." But insofar as we consider how totally abandoned to evil we are, we see that marriages can be made only in trembling. If we consider well the state of the world at the present time, we well have reason to cry over our lives. Because the people were so hardened by their sins, our Lord forbid the prophet to marry or to bear children, in order that he be a sign to the people of their captivity in exile. The prophet is not only a preacher, but is the sign to confirm his preaching. By not marrying, he shows that he is prepared to flee and does not wish to have followers. In this, we see our hardness, for we see no improvement in our life, despite God's warnings.

Seeing the people did not amend their ways, let us look to ourselves and see if we are not as equally, if not more, stubborn; for it is certain that our lives are equally given to vice. If there was licentiousness in the prophet's time, how much more is there today? If at that time the name of God had been blasphemed and people did not walk in fear of the Lord, is not such impiety greater than ever today? In the last year, how many have been admonished to return to God? Have you taken a single step towards Him? The majority of us would rather retreat from God. We see, then, that we are like the Jews. They are our mirror to show us our own rebellion against God. When God severely chastises us, will we say that He has not paid close enough attention to us, that we are not totally corrupt through and through? When we read today's passage, let us not condemn the Jews, but ourselves. Let us know that we are no more worthy than they. If there was such brutality among them that they did not serve the Word of God, today we are equally, if not more, brutal. When God warns us, let each be ready to reproach himself. Let us know that we cannot really placate ourselves by believing that our sins are "no big deal." God has reproached us for our sins and has sentenced us all. So let us throw away all those things that block us from God. Those who are married should live as if they were single. Those who have wealth should heed the passage: "If today God has given me joy, I must not think it permanent. I will cast it aside at once when God calls me." Those with great riches must not deceive themselves; they must be ready to become poor and abject to obey God. That is the second admonition.

The prophet says, "The mothers and fathers will die grievous deaths. They will not be mourned or buried, but left as shit on the ground to be consumed by the sword and by famine. Their carnage will be meat to the birds and beasts of the earth." Let us know that we can expect the same harsh treatment from God. The Jews are the sacred line; we are only miserable specimens.

They are the blessed root God chose, yet He punishes them so severely. When we see ourselves to be like them, let us know well that the God who exercised such vengeance against them has not changed in power or in will and so can well punish us. Now, as I have said, the world is as riddled by vice as it could ever be. With malice goes impudence. What must God do? Will God punish us as severely as in the time of Jeremiah? Let us think a little on this point: As our Lord had taken us by the hand, indeed by the arm (as Isaiah says), to pull us back to Him and yet was able to return only a few to God, would not God be just and equitable in punishing us a hundred times harder than before?

When the prophet says that they will have no tomb but will be meat for the birds and beasts of the earth, he is admonishing us that whatsoever happens in the world is the judgment of God. We know well, then, that there will be no tombs for us. God threatens the Jews that they will be shit because they are not worthy of burial. Now if one asks whether burial profits the dead, since they cannot feel hot or cold, it would seem that the prophet has omitted any mention of this in his recitation of God's threats. We have already seen that the tomb is a sign of our resurrection. Our bodies, though they rot away, sleep in the tomb; death is merely night; the day will come when God will awaken us. This is how a tomb is a memorial to the resurrection. The fact we rot in the earth does not mean we will not be resurrected someday. That is why the tomb was so honored among the patriarchs. Both Joseph and Jacob refer to the Kingdom of

God in their requests that their bones be taken from Egypt and buried in the Promised Land. Now there are many customs in the Old Testament that are not practiced today and would dishonor the Gospel if we were to adopt them again. Nevertheless, we retain this sign of the resurrection, by entombing the dead. Now the prophet tells them they will be denied burial, as if he were saying, "You are so wicked that you deserve punishment in life and in death. You have known His judgment against your sins; and after you die, you will face an even more severe judgment." That is why the prophet says that "they will be thrown on the ground." And afterwards, he says to the King that he "will be buried like an ass." The sepulchre of Jehoikam suffered no damage, but, still, it was a sign of God's vengeance.

We are admonished by today's passage to think beyond life in the present world. When we see men pass on, it seems that everything perishes and that death is the end of all things. However, let us not abandon the knowledge that our Lord left us a sign for hope in eternal resurrection. We must examine where God wishes to lead us by this sign. In Papism, there are all sorts of diabolical superstitions to seduce the world. On the contrary, we say only what God has told us about death, and God has told us all we need to know. Our Lord ordained burial in order that we recognize that we are not like a beast or dog, but go on to a better life after this one. We must bear this in mind along with Paul's statement that our body is only a clay hut. We, then, have good reason to moan and groan about life, not because our nature demands we be quit of the body, but because seeing what God has prepared for us in the afterlife, it is easy to be quit of all worldly things. Furthermore, we are taught that God's judgments are not reserved solely for this world or for our lifetime. It is necessary to look further than that. When God chastises us in our bodies and in our goods, we must recognize that a greater condemnation awaits us in the next world. Were this not true, many would escape punishment altogether. We must realize that not all God's judgments are executed in this world. God's judgment for evildoers is reserved for the next world. When God afflicts good people, in this world, that is for their benefit. God, then, leads us to consider the Last Judgment. However, when we see God afflicting us in whatever manner this may be, let us pose the question: If God punishes us today so harshly, how would we be able to bear his vengeance if He wished to treat us severely? Here we must note that God could well execute His sentence on evildoers. Just as we have to consider the severity of His punishments, we must also consider His bounty to console us. When God now gives us a taste of His mercy and paternal love, we did not merely sample them but can consume them fully.

The prophet says next, "Do not go into the house of mourning, do not lament or moan for them; for I have taken away my peace from these people, also my kindness and compassion. Both the great and the small will die in this land. They will not be buried and no one will mourn for them. Nor will anyone scratch and tear themselves for them. No one will break bread to console them for the dead. No one will give them the cup of consolation for his father or mother." By this, our Lord means that there will be terrible desolation everywhere: Each will be a hindrance to himself. When a man sees his wife die, he will not have the leisure to mourn, but will be so totally stupefied that he will forget all the duties of a husband. True, it is well that we are saddened when God admonishes us by death. But here we take advantage of God, because we assume that no one should die. We are never saddened enough to look inside ourselves and see our own sins. Here is our heritage from Adam at work, by which we are alienated from God. God is the fountain of life: If we alienate ourselves from God, we will die. This is not merely a matter of bodily death, but of eternal death. Whenever anyone dies, this is a warning to us, so that we must not wait upon a universal affliction before we see ourselves implicated. Whenever we see any affliction, let us not fail to realize that we ourselves deserve as much. Although we are innocent of the offense for which another is afflicted, let us mourn and know we deserve that punishment. That is why it is necessary to enter into the house of mourning. As Saint Paul says, "You must mourn with those who mourn." If you saw a beast in pain, your compassion would be aroused. Would you, then, not be equally compassionate when you see another human being suffering? God did not forbid the prophet to be compassionate; rather, in seeing such great desolation, one cannot say, "So-and-so is dead. Let us console his children." They will die not by the tens, not by the hundreds, but by the thousands. All were perverse, so all is desolate. That is what God means.

When he says that the children will die with their fathers, that does not mean that God is cruel. True, the iniquities of the fathers will not be visited upon the sons. Well before the time of Ezekiel, the Jews, thinking themselves innocent, complained that God punished them for the sins of their fathers. Our Lord said to them, "No, no! This proverb be stricken from among you; each will bear his own burden." True as this may be, the very moment God snatches back His hand from the fathers, the sons are already a poisonous seed that can do nothing else but provoke the wrath of God. If there is some good in us, it comes solely from the Holy Spirit, not from ourselves. There would be no good in man if God merely made him bigger. When God snatches His hand back from us, what will happen, save that our children will be like us? He has said, "I am your God and the God of your children." This means that our Lord shed His blessing both upon us and our children. On the contrary, when He snatches His hand back from us, our children bear witness to His wrath. That is why God punishes children, insofar as they are little serpents. Let us not, then, accuse God of cruelty; if we endure evil, it is because of our sins. That is the heart of the matter.

The prophet says, "You will make no cuts or scratches." These were signs of mourning, as we still find among the Papists, who have a Master of Mourning, whom some pay to scratch children upon the death of their parents. In the Orient, they shave their heads as a sign of mourning, for hair is a sign of honor. Some are not merely content with that but cut themselves all over with razors to show even greater mourning, so much is the world subject to such monkey business. Those who do not wish to cry will use various methods to feign tears to demonstrate some semblance of sadness. Our Lord forbid all this in the Law of Moses, for it is a custom fitting only to infidels. As Saint Paul says to the Thessalonians, "Do not cry as if you had no hope." Saint Paul does not forbid sadness; for it would be impossible not to be saddened when we see someone afflicted or dying. Yet we know it is God's punishment that those who gave us consolation be taken away from us. Saint Paul is not at all forbidding Christians to be saddened, but he is emphasizing that this must not be in the manner of infidels, who have no hope. Here is the consolation God gives us: If we look above, we see God has called us to hope. Now, how would mourning in the manner of Pagans serve the hope God has given us? Thus our Lord forbid all this cutting and scratching. Because He did so at the time of the Law, that is even a stronger reason why we must avoid such practices: The Jews do not have as strong a testimony of the resurrection as we; insofar as in the person of our Lord Jesus Christ, we have a sign of the resurrection ordained for us. It is certain, then, that we have a hope greater than the patriarchs. When we become desperate and enraged, we injure God. We curse God in ways that would shock even the Turks! So let us note well, then, that our Lord has forbidden in the Law that we resort to such desperate measures. We must grieve in moderation. When the Lord says, "You must not make cuts," it is as if He were saying, "Although I have forbidden you, you have not listened to me." As we have seen there is a mundane glory in this way of mourning: There is a great mourning and there is a lesser mourning. Those in the house of great mourning conduct themselves one way; those in the other, another way. When God wishes to humble us by taking our parents or loved ones from the world, it seems we wish to vex God by our ceremonies. This is why our Lord said to the Jews, "Although I have forbidden it, you have not listened. You have not the time to do so; for you face total desolation and so will have time to bury." God will spare us nothing. The reason, as I said before, is that the people were given many warnings and did not heed them. There is no way to escape the wrath of God. Consider this example: After we have been hardened against His Word, His wrath and vengeance will come down horribly on our heads. The Lord today still waits upon our repentance, so let us not make matters worse. If God exercised a terrible vengeance on these people, He will do the same to us. He will submit us to even more severe punishment yet, so far less excusable are we.

In order that we enrage God no further, let us pray that He not permit us to harden ourselves. Let us pray that out of true love for His honor we come to Him to glorify Him in all our life. May we always look to the glorious immortality He has prepared for us after our death, in which we will not perish, but be protected in the tomb until Lord Jesus Christ comes to resurrect us as He promised. May He shed His grace not only upon us, but upon all the peoples and nations of the world, etc.

* * *

All-powerful God, because you are pleased to teach us by your Word, that we experience not the eternal severity of your punishment: Give us the grace to accommodate ourselves to your teaching. May we not displease you by our vices. May we not provoke your wrath more and more, May we be in harmony with you. Support us through your mediator, that we have recourse to your mercy, until purged of all our filth we are received in your heavenly kingdom. May we stand before you there in all purity, which we so lack. May we enjoy the heavenly glory acquired for us through the blood of your Son, our Lord. Amen.

(10) Tuesday, July 9, 1549

Do not go to the house of feasting to sit and eat and drink with them. For the Lord of armies, the God of Israel says, "Before your very eyes, in this place, I will make cease the voice of joy and the voice of mirth, the voice of the bridegroom and the voice of the bride." Jeremiah 16.

Yesterday, we saw the great desolation that fell upon the land of Judah. God said that neither will the son have time to mourn for his father nor the husband for his wife. There will be only fear, war, pestilence, and famine. Now the prophet is forbidden to eat and drink in the banquet house. Yesterday, we saw that he was forbidden to enter into the house of mourning, in order to more thoroughly convince the evildoers, who did not take seriously his warnings. Our Lord ordained that what He said to the prophet be committed to paper. The prophets were a sign, as we said of Isaiah. The prophet reminds us what God said yesterday, to prompt us to do what God has admonished us to do.

It would be enough that the prophet merely spoke, were it not for the fact that we are so hard to spur along that the Word of God must be confirmed by example and that He must show that the evil He has ordained must happen. God reproaches our obstinacy when He makes the prophet abstain from what was otherwise legal, to show his teaching is valid.

Because we are so hard that we do not hear the Word of God, we must take pains to correct this deficiency. We expect that God will use all possible means to make us hear. He accommodates

Himself to us insofar as we are so sluggish. True, He could reject us and say, "It suffices that I have spoken once." But what would that accomplish? He supports us and provides examples with His Word.

Now we come to God saying, "You will not enter the banquet house," as if He were saying, "I will bring an end in your time to all mirth, weddings, and the like." The prophet must not go to the banquet, in order to signify that each must reflect upon himself and upon the punishment at hand. When God threatens us, does He intend to bring an end to the daily order of our lives so that we no longer live in the world? No, He intends only that we be terrified enough to repent. It is sufficient that we examine our faults, ask for pardon, and have a strong desire to return to the path of righteousness. When all that is accomplished in us, God will be content and the preaching of His Word efficacious. But why? If He calls us to sackcloth and ashes and we do not forsake rejoicing, would not this be out of spite for Him? When we persist in our vices, does this not mean that we pay no attention to Him, to His goodness, or to anything that is good? Thus God wished to make known through His prophet that He wanted to return to Himself this abomination which was Judah. The prophets cried out to the people, "The enemies come. Were you to have the whole world to help you, still you will feel the hand of God upon you. Do you think that God is called judge of the earth in vain? Must He not levy terrible vengeance against you? Although you are called His people, you are worse than the

Pagans. How can you hear Him when you are so nonchalant?" However the prophets cry out to them, they say, "Let them cry out as much as they want. We will not leave aside our feasts and become contrite. It is not their business to punish us. Their threats are threats that scare only little children. Let us eat, drink, and have fun!" Such was the resistance in these people. That is why God says to the prophet, "Because they have not heard my words, you must not go to their banquets." It is not that rejoicing in itself is bad, but that it is a curse to rejoice when we should groan. That is why the prophet must not participate in their merry-making.

It is not, then, merely a matter of merry-making, but of contempt for the Word of God, which is so much the more common today because it is forbidden. Are many touched by our exhortations? Most turn them into jeers, as if the whole thing is a farce to them. We are impious people; what Jeremiah said in his time was written down for ours. In as much as the world is given to enjoying itself out of spite for God--even though God shows more signs of His vengeance--so much the more are we grieved. There will be no laughter when the day of reckoning comes for all these merry-makers. God has sworn by his name as living God that their iniquity will never be pardoned. The people, abandoned to vice as they are, say, "Well, the prophet will have much to cry about, for we will not abandon our merry-making." But God says that He is a living God and will not pardon their sins. We cannot afford to be cheerful. There is no question about it. One cannot be attacked more readily than when he is merry-making. Each, then, must reflect upon his sins and be contrite. As each of the faithful bemoans every time God reproaches him and makes known His judgment, we must shun the company of the mockers who make fun of all God's threats and admonitions. If we mix with them, we will share in their condemnation. If we mock when reproached for our faults, this is an uncalled-for blasphemy against God. Those that share in such behavior will all be condemned. Those who attend banquets are condemned. The meat will suffocate them, not in body, but in spirit. They will know terrible punishment because of their obstinacy. But if we associate with them, must we share in their torments, for we are under a different condemnation? Yes, it is certain we will. We must stay away from them, showing no indication we wish to go to their banquets. It is certain that we will vex God by attending; for they will make an example out of us and consider themselves to be semi-justified.

This is especially said to the prophet in order that the levity of ministers does not become an occasion to mock God's teaching. What would happen if, after a minister preaches, he goes out to have some fun? Would not this be taken as an example that each should abandon himself to vice? What authority would his teaching have then? His teaching is intended to educate us so that we see the iniquities that must be surmounted and so that we are constrained to announce the judgment of God, which is hanging over our heads. We must speak from the heart; we must bear witness to our teaching, by our works. The prophet was no confederate of those who preach and afterwards go out for an evening of debauchery. Now some fine pastors of the Church hear of the lechers in the whorehouses and taverns; they reprimand them severely and most ungraciously; then, like shameless whores, they go to them to vomit forth their blasphemes. The prophet would be no friend of such pastors. After we proclaim God's warnings, we must be penitent, demonstrate that we have felt the majesty of God, and be all the more shocked when we see the evil ones mocking God. May this be as a mortal wound to us. Let us pray that God not permit His people to go to ruin, that He at least protect His own. When we reprimand vices, let each think on himself, that God have occasion to treat us in all mercy and bounty.

Our passage continues, "When you have announced to the people all that I have said to you, they will say, 'Why has the Lord pronounced such great evil against us? What iniquity and what sin have we committed against Him?' You will say, 'If you wish to know, listen well. Your fathers worshipped idols. They abandoned me. You have had evil fathers. You say that you are not like them? Ha! True, for you are even worse. You have not the same superstitions, but you are totally given to iniquity. The one takes up evil practices. The other is like a savage beast ready to devour his neighbors. You are full of all licentiousness and yet you say that you are not like your fathers! However evil your fathers were, so much the more inexcusable you are. You will be embarrassed before God and before angels, and there will not be one creature who is not ashamed of you.'" How true this is of us. The answer is always there before the question: "Why does he cry out after us? What have we done?" It is necessary, then, that God read the charges against them, as a judge would to a criminal going to the gallows. If men are so unfortunate as to ask, "What is it we have done?" God will make public every detail of the charges. First, we see the hypocrisy in men. This did not begin now, but is an inherent characteristic of the human species. Men always search for some excuse to say: "Hah! We are not like our fathers." True it is they dare not say that they are innocent, but it seems to them that they must be excused for their faults and so must be spared. Although they cannot claim complete innocence, they wish an easy reconciliation with God. They think it penitence enough if they just say a few brief words about their sins, just as the Papists think themselves discharged of all responsibility when they say a "mea culpa." Evangelists do not make the sign of the cross; but they think they can get God off their backs by prayer alone, so that all they need to for repentance is to say, "Alas! If I err, I now regret it." But Scripture says, "You are sadly mistaken if you think that you are superior to the devils and that you can wipe away the stains of your sins as a common whore wipes her mouth off." If these words do not move us, we are not Christians. Hypocrisy has always reigned and reigns among us more so today than ever, Men do not know their vices; their hearts are poisoned; their villainery seems good to them, just as a pig does not smell its own stink. Although there is not one creature who does not see the villainery of man, he denies all culpability, as if he were totally innocent. We should not be shocked today, when we hear all this grumbling against God and His ministers. Why? This vice is nothing new; as we saw, the Jews rose up against their betters and waged war against the prophets. We are well advised, then, to wage war against those who seek to justify themselves by condemning God. Furthermore, evil is so pervasive that it is right under the noses of men in their impudence to ask, "What have I done?" If only the prophets had known how to answer! But they did not know where to begin, seeing that evil was so rampant everywhere. What is our situation today? I confess, I, that I do not know where or how to begin. Men are so shameless that they try and make God think they are not as evil as one might think. But how? Are they so shameless that they can ask God, "What have I done?" when every creature knows their depravity? When we act like such small children before God, He will justly punish us by making us so much the more aware of our own depravity. Let us continue.

God says, "You will say to them: 'Although your fathers abandoned me, says the Lord, and followed after strange gods, you are even more wicked; for you walk according to the evil inventions of your heart and you do not listen to me.'" This means that so much the closer God is to us, so much less are we excusable for turning away from His Word. The Pagans, who are alienated from God, are not without excuse before God. Those who sin without the Law were not permitted to perish without the written Law. Now if they are without excuse, what are we, to whom God has shown the way, saying, "Follow me, I am your God. Love me"? When God shows us the way and we abandon Him, is not our iniquity doubled? We must well think on this, for God does not shed His grace on others as He does on us. How many are there who ask only to serve God and yet only blaspheme? Do we not see that God has given us the grace to know Him whereas the Jews and Pagans remain in ignorance? Is it not ingratitude on our part that we turn from Him? Would He not find it necessary to punish us so much more severely? We are well advised to keep our ears open to hear Him when He speaks to us. That is what is meant in this passage, where it says, "Your fathers abandoned me"; for it presupposes that they knew His teaching. Those who have not heard one single word of truth will be without excuse, for their consciences will bear witness to their stubborn persistence to remain confused. Although evil ones view truth as no more than a fable, God gives them a remorse that pierces through them like a burning brand. Now if these poor, ignorant ones will be condemned for abandoning God, what will happen to us?

God adds, "They have abandoned me, following idols." Here God is saying that as soon as we mix in some superstition with His service, we abandon Him. True, this is not the intention of idolaters: The Papists say that they have saints, not to abandon God, but because it is necessary to have an advocate to obtain grace before God. "When we build a chapel or go on a pilgrimage, God will be pleased," they say. But, on the contrary, the prophet says, "When you take up with idols, you abandon me." Why? God abhors what is done without His commandment. When we go to search for God through Saint Claude, we wrong God. That is what all the Papists do to God, for nothing they do is found in Scripture. Do not think that our Lord will tolerate our abandoning Him. "Indeed, but we wish to have God as well!" they say. Yes, but as Saint Paul says, "What accord is there between Jesus Christ and Belial?" Do we think that God will stand for being mixed in with idols? No! He will abandon us, for we have already abandoned Him. We must serve God according to His Word if we wish Him to accept the service rendered to Him. Do we wish to please God by our service? We must follow His ordinance; for, as soon as we follow our fantasies, God will proclaim that it is the Devil we serve and not Him. If we then invoke the name of God, that is a double condemnation. When the Jews killed their children and offered them as a sacrifice to God, He abhorred that and condemned them for having abused His name by applying it to such iniquities. If we invent all that seems good to us and if we turn all His ordinances into our own inventions, will God let us go unpunished? No! We must hold to His Word.

Now we find another useful teaching when God adds, "You do not hear my Law." Here God shows us that when we falter it is because we have not kept to His Word. Men always try to cover themselves by saying, "I did such-and-such with good intentions." This strikes us at once as a good excuse. But why? God proclaims that we dishonor Him by pleading ignorance when He speaks so clearly. God does not speak so over our heads that we cannot understand Him. We are ignorant because we reject His teaching out of premeditated malice and then we try and sooth ourselves by our ignorance. That is why men are without excuse, whatever ignorance they may feign. Let us note diligently the passage where it says, "Your fathers turned away from me." God is assuring us that if we have His Word, we know how to serve Him. Be attentive, give ear to the sermon, and you will not be deceived. True it is that we do not have ears by ourselves. This is why it says so often in Scripture, "Let him who has ears, hear!" to show that the office of Christ is to open them. However this may be, if we do not understand God's teaching, that is the fault of our own malice. When we come here to be taught, we must pray that God does not permit that the preacher spreads his sound in vain, since the Word of God is good seed. Let us pray that He cultivate us so that this seed bear fruit and that we strive all our life to serve Him. God presents Himself to us in such a way that the evildoers are without excuse. He speaks clearly, not from the bottom of a bottle, but like gold refined by fire, as the psalmist says. If we do not refuse to be taught by Him, He will teach us all we have to do. If, however, we follow the example of our fathers, who were sinners, we will be enveloped in their iniquities. As Scripture says, "You measure up to your fathers!" This is how it comes about that evildoers have the sins of their fathers hanging over their heads. This is not contrary to Ezekiel saying that "the son will not bear the iniquity of his father"; for if we follow those who set a bad example, we are culpable along with them, as if we made a compact to be supporters of Satan and declared that we wished to be unified with him to be members of his body. The church of sinners is a body just as is the Church of the faithful. If we follow in their wicked footsteps, we will also share in the vengeance due them. Those who have lived up to their fathers' iniquities, those who now spill the blood of the faithful are responsible for the blood of the prophets, of the Apostles, and of the martyrs, insofar as they have conspired with evil ones who have spilt the blood of the innocent. It is therefore necessary for them to share in one and the same condemnation.

The prophets say, "Your fathers abandoned God." Can we say we do not follow in the footsteps of our fathers' iniquities? Hezekiah did not follow in the footsteps of Ahaz, his father. Although his father was wicked, Hezekiah was a good king and so holy that he was a mirror of sanctity. Josiah did not follow the wicked ways of Manasseh. But if the sons had followed the wicked ways of their fathers, they would have all been enveloped in the same condemnation. You follow in your father's footsteps? Come, come, see your armor and your blazon. Your fathers were disloyal and falsified their faith in God. That is your noble lineage. The iniquity of those who raise up against God will be made manifest to all creatures. Note carefully that those who appear to be Christian will be less excusable than the Pagans, for ignorance will not excuse them. Our Lord has delivered us from Papism, but where is our obedience? Do we not see that there are those among us who have no scruples about abandoning themselves to all sorts of villainery as if they were beasts? Not since the time of Papism, I say, have things been as muddled as they are today. Wash ourselves as we will, we all wash in ink. How we search for subterfuges and foolish excuses. Let us know our faults; otherwise, we will be more deserving of condemnation than the idolaters.

Following this holy teaching, we prostrate ourselves before the face of our good God, in knowledge of our faults. We pray that it please Him to touch us to the quick, so that, if up to this hour we have not truly repented, He no longer permits us to remain incorrigible. May we be fully converted to Him to adhere to Him all our life. May He not reproach us because we have not always listened when He wished to inform us of our salvation. May He not only shed His grace on us, but on all the peoples and nations of the earth, etc.

* * *

(11) Wednesday, July 10, 1549

You have done worse than your fathers; for each of you walks according to the inventions of his evil heart, in order not to hear me. I will chase out of this land into a land which you know not, you and your fathers, and there you will serve strange gods day and night. You will find no mercy. Jeremiah 16.

We saw yesterday that it is not enough that idolatry be cast out of our midst; it was shown that we are worse than idolaters if we have idols while we lead seemingly Christian lives. Our Lord reproaches those who say that they do not follow the idolatry of their fathers. "Indeed," He says, "your fathers abandoned God. After He called them to His knowledge, they did not stay with Him, because they did not wish to hear His teaching. This was their great iniquity. But you, look to your own life. You do not have idols, but each walks according to the malice of his perverse heart. You have entered into a conspiracy not to hear what is said in my name. Do you not live up to your fathers?"

We must carefully consider what is our life and what is our government. Because God presents His Word to us, it is time to listen. When we conspire not to listen, this is a murderous iniquity that demands God's vengeance. Do we not see this conspiracy? Not only is each content to turn a deaf ear to the Word of God, but each delights in his vices, although they will say they do not approve of the iniquities which reign among us: "Let no one take delight in his evil." But they really do not mean business and will lose their temper with God and say of the ministers, "Let them yell as much as they want!" Although we speak quite loud, we do not pierce the ears of those filled with such blasphemies. During the sermon, they sleep off yesterday's wine or drink anew. The taverns are closed, but the throats are open. All is in confusion. Let these poisoners of souls take care that they be not surprised when one warns them of the judgment of God, for they are far from the sermon and close to the tankard. The prophet speaks of those who do not practice idolatry but are yet even more evil: "Let us not listen to God!" they say. "If we have been wicked up to now, let us be even worse yet!" Now if it seems at first glance that our Lord does not raise His hand against them, do we think that His Word is powerless among the iniquitous? The punishment which will befall the wicked will make our hairs stand on end. We are admonished above all not to harden our hearts and say, "Let us not hear our Lord!" Satan has hardened us to turn us from the path of righteousness; but Christ through His grace admonishes us; let us receive and hear in all humility what He has to say. It is not enough for us to be merely an audience which says, "Here is a good teaching." Christ speaks to our hearts, not to our ears: We must receive the Word in our hearts. The Word of God must have its seat in our heart and reign from there. We surmount all idolatry when, having His Word, we reform ourselves and are not foolish enough to reject His Word of salvation, for that is His intention.

Let us turn to the punishment of those who continue in their wicked ways. God says, "I will chase you out of this land into a land you know not, and there you will serve strange gods night and day, and you will receive no mercy." In the first place, He proclaims that they will be chased out because they have polluted the land given them for their heritage. If God gives us a land and sustains us there by His grace and we disgrace Him, is it not without reason He chases us out? Is not God's great bounty evidenced when the earth opens her breasts to nourish us? If the glory of God is everywhere evident and if now we pollute and snuff out this glory, do we not think that the earth will demand vengeance for the sacrilege we have committed against the goods she has given us? She reveals the glory of God when she opens herself so that we can take nourishment from her entrails. Now when we pollute her, rebel against God, and are ungrateful for all that we have received from her, is it not necessary for her to demand vengeance? When the earth is dry, she opens her mouth to receive water and God answers. Now if her requests are always granted by God (as Scripture says), indeed even what she requests for us, and if we are such unworthy ingrates, is it not without reason that her request be granted when she demands vengeance upon us? Here the prophet says, "You will be chased." It is necessary the people be chased into an unknown land, to pay for their iniquities. But why? If God sustains us in a land, and if this land is known to us, is that not reason to know God? But if there is no longer any knowledge of God, if we have forgotten Him and no longer wish to pay Him homage, is it not without reason that he sends us into a strange land? That is how our Lord renders payment fitting to the evil of men who no longer know Him. Therefore if we wish to eternally rejoice in the land God has given us, let us know God. Why is it that the earth, insensible creature, knows us, nourishes us? Why is it that the heavens, so far from us, rain upon us? From where comes this knowledge the earth and heavens have of us? From the commandment of God. Does not the earth have knowledge of God and obey Him to lead us to Him? If we turn from God, is it not without reason that the creatures who have fallen in with us now turn their backs on us? Although they have no emotions, they nurture us because we have the image of God and are of the house of God. Just as nothing is refused to a child in his father's house, so the earth is the house of God and nothing is refused us, who are the children of God. But if we erase the image of God within us, the creatures of God will no longer know us. It is not without reason that we will no longer rejoice in the good things of God when we decline to bear His image. The prophet says, "I will chase you from this land." This means that the creatures of God will find us strange when we no longer know God, who reveals Himself such a good father in all and by all.

The prophet adds, "There you will serve strange gods night and day and you will find no mercy." This is a second condemnation, for they will be forced to serve foreign Gods and will find no consolation. Now it is certain that it would be better to die of hunger than to be in the miserable state of being forced to serve idols. It is a matter that God wishes to deprive them of the true live and punish them in a way more grievous than death itself, namely, that they serve idols night and day, without cease. All their gestures will be watched. It will not be enough that they accommodate themselves only temporarily to the idolaters. There can be no more grievous fate than to be forced to adore idols. When God wishes to show the severity of His vengeance, He says, "You will serve strange gods." We see, then, that this is the greatest misfortune that can befall us. Here God submits us to extremely severe punishment. Let us note that this punishment not only befell the Jews, but also befell upon our fathers at the time of Papism. Why is it that there is more disorder in Papism than there is among the Pagans? Because of the wickedness which reigns there. Why is it that Papism, although it had knowledge of God, is so overrun with superstitions? After the Word of God had been received, Papists parted from it, thinking that it was given only for a few men. Because of this, God permitted a great confusion befall upon them. If the people do not wish to be subjugated to the truth, they must be subjugated to lies. Do we think things go any better with us? When our Lord enlightens us by the clarity of His teaching, who goes out to greet Him? Who says, "Lord, I am here to do what pleases you"? No one! We abuse His grace and fixate upon Satan. What can we expect, then, save that God will send a confusion upon us greater than that among the

Papists, or rather a brutishness that already we can perceive? Let those with eyes look at the world, not merely at the Papists, but at the places where the Word of God is preached; let them see how lawless and given to vice are men, who listen to nothing they are told. In Papism, God is served according to certain customs. Although one may not approve of them, still one obeys the rules. But where the Gospel reigns, there is such chaos that no doctrine has any authority. It is nothing new that the wicked reign. No more needs be said about them, save that they wish to take in people and will say, "Should we serve up prophecies? It is no longer the season." Take the case that Jeremiah is not preached: It is necessary that their wickedness and the vengeance of God be publicized, despite themselves. Let us fear when we see the vengeance of God upon them. This is a punishment they deserve. God says, "Because you did not wish to serve me, your true God, I will make you serve strange gods." Since we are in a place where we have the freedom to serve God, let us show we are not ungrateful, out of fear that He puts us in the unhappy circumstance of being forced to serve strange gods, as has already befallen us for our sins. What will happen now that our sins are so much the greater because we know the Word? Let us guard against defying His doctrine; for He will not fail to avenge Himself by sending us to unknown lands to serve strange gods. To better understand matters, let us examine what life was like for us when we were among the Papists. We were on the go incessantly, night and day, without a break, as are the poor fellows still with them. After we got up, we had to go to mass; next we had to worship an idol and another right after that. If you confessed once, you had to go back and confess again and again. And this is not all; for there was always this guilty conscience that you are going to go to Hell. I say this in regard to those who fear God, for there were plenty of mockers who cared about nothing. True, once a year they would participate in some stupid ceremony, but they would be quit of it for another year. But those with some fear of God were made to serve strange gods day and night. Since we have experienced all this, and since we are delivered from the service of strange gods, let us subjugate ourselves to God, so that we do not give Him occasion to return us to this torment, which He will make worse than ever. Let us pray that He give us the grace to obey Him and remain under His yoke, for He is gentle and His burden is easy. Why? He bears it Himself. Let us return to Him out of fear that we will be returned to this death where we have been, where our fathers were, and where the Jews have been. We will experience this death again if we do not receive His Word and honor it as is fitting. This is the sentence the prophet pronounces on those who conspire against the Word of God, saying, "Let him yell as much as he wants, for we are deaf. We will either be at the tavern or off on wicked ventures; or if we come to hear the sermon, it will be only to sleep and snore and to slander the Word to make it stink, so that one will find it distasteful!" Let us know this menace, so that we are not infected by these devils who strive only to pervert everything.

Because these menaces are so harsh, our Lord adds something sweet and enticing for the faithful, as was the custom of the prophets to mix in some promise of God among His menaces, to console those of good heart, by saying, "Behold"; that is, in the midst of afflictions those who serve God with good heart look to His promises and see their salvation as present. "Behold, the Lord says that one will no longer say, 'The living Lord who delivered the children of Israel from Egypt,' but one will say, 'The living Lord who delivered the children of Israel from the northern land and from all the lands to which He chased them. He returns them to the land He gave their fathers.'" This means that although it seemed that God had exterminated the Jews, that all was lost, and that there was desolation without remedy, nevertheless He preserved a residual of the good seed of His elect. Although they were in death, He delivered them in a telling way from this northern land. The prophet says that He delivered His people in such a way that one will no longer mention the deliverance from Egypt, but will say, "How did this happen? The God of Israel delivered His people from the tomb! We see well, then, that it is God who must be adored." "I will be glorified for this deliverance," says the Lord, "more so that I was for delivering my people out of Egypt by the hand of Moses." We see, then, that when God menaces us we must not become desperate. Why? He always adds promises to His menaces.

Indeed, the children of God never lose their taste for the Word of God. Although it seems that all must be destroyed, they do not find the Word distasteful, but they are instructed by it in fear. True it is that many are shocked when God menaces us; but let not be like so many who say, "This lesson is not fitting for us." Let us not have such audacity to exempt ourselves. Let us know that when our Lord examines us, He will find sufficient reason to punish us. When we hear of God's menaces, though we seem innocent, let us be moved and know that we are deserving of a chastisement, even of a second and third. God's menaces are intended to arouse His children, not to shock them; they are intended to inflict pain, to mortify their flesh, so that they may say, "Alas, I am far from ready to receive the Word." Because they are intended to awaken them to knowledge of the bounty of God, that He does not wish the to perish, so much the more are they intended to humble them. This is why the whole of Holy Scripture shows that whenever God flails people, it is in order that the evil ones cannot excuse themselves by saying they were not warned and also in order that they serve as an example to humble us before God, to teach us to despise our flesh and to enjoy His promises. This is how it is that those armed with the promises of God will never become disgruntled and come to hate the Word, despite the fact they encounter so much hardship. Now let us turn to the fact that the way God will redeem His people will surmount their deliverance from Egypt. First, we must note that God does not wish their deliverance from Egypt to be forgotten. On the contrary, all the prophets since the time of Jeremiah have spoken of it. Although we are not of Abraham's race, we represent these people, so we must not let this deliverance go in one ear and out the other. It is of use to us as a comparison by which we can know that the deliverance from Babylon was a much greater deed than the deliverance from Egypt. As the prophet says, "When God delivered these people from Egypt, they spoke only of that. But God will bring about another deliverance that will be so marvelous that only it will be spoken of." That is the view of the prophet. Now it is certain that God did not perform as many miracles when He delivered the people from Babylon as He did when He delivered them from Egypt by Moses. But the prophet is referring to the feelings of the Jews, for they considered themselves to be dead. The prophet strives to bring them to rejoice by saying, "My friends, your captivity will last only seven years." Now the people did not believe this. The prophet's consolations were to no avail, so he says to them, "No, no, do not measure God according to our sense of time. Put your confidence in Him and do not think that He works in the manner of men, for He works in a way totally incomprehensible to us." The prophet does not stop here, but wishes to lead His people even further, namely, to the universal deliverance accomplished through our Lord, Jesus Christ; for the deliverances from Egypt and from Babylon are merely the precursors of this. That is the true intention of the prophet, indeed of all the prophets. The prophet is not speaking of one small work, but of the total restoration of the Church, as it is written in Malachi. The key to understanding the prophets is that they are not tied down to these people, but dedicated to the deliverance of all the faithful through our Lord. When it seems that all is lost, let us not fail to hope in God; for He will not fail to save the remnants of His people. Furthermore, this will be a deliverance so marvelous that we cannot apprehend it the least by our senses. So let us not fail to invoke God in the midst of our afflictions, saying, "Alas, Lord, you do not fail to console those who remain your own and faithful to your Word."

Following this holy teaching, let us prostrate ourselves before the face of our good God, in knowledge of our faults. We pray that He grant us hope. We pray that, in spite of all our afflictions, we come not to doubt He will aid us and make known His bounty, as He would wish us to have assurance. Thus we say celestial Father, etc.

* * *

All-powerful God, because we incessantly provoke your wrath against us and yet you incessantly call us to repentance, give us the grace to be prompt and amenable to your commandment. May we not despise your gentle remonstrances, by which you invite us to return to you in the hope of obtaining your pardon and mercy. May we not come to condemn your menaces, that we may profit in your Word by being warned of your judgment. May we be inspired and conquered by the sweetness of your grace. May we be totally dedicated to you, that your wrath turn away from us. Render us capable to receive your grace, which you offer to all those moved by true repentance and who desire to be reconciled with you and to have your favor and grace through Jesus Christ, our Lord. Amen.

(12) Thursday, July 11, 1549

The days are coming, says the Lord, when one will no longer say, "The Lord lives who delivered the children of Israel from the land of Egypt," but will say, "The Lord lives who delivered the children of Israel from the northern land and all the lands to which He had chased them." I will return them to the land I gave their fathers. Jeremiah 16.

We have begun to proclaim the redemption of the Jews from their Babylonian captivity. The prophet says that it will be so marvelous that no one will speak any longer of the deliverance from Egypt. We have shown that this prophecy was not for the immediate future, but refers to the coming of Jesus Christ. When we speak of the deliverance from Egypt, we see our Lord has a strong arm for miracle making. He not only transformed the staff of Moses into a serpent, He also changed the waters into blood, sent rains on the earth, sent locusts, sent darkness after He had sent pestilence upon the beasts, and killed the first-born of the Egyptians, all in order to make Pharaoh release the people of Israel. Next, He parted the Red Sea to give passage to His people and engulfed in it Pharaoh and all his army. Then, for forty years, He nourished the people in the desert with nothing to eat but manna from the sky. Afterwards, He rolled back the waters of the Jordan to give passage to the people of Israel. Next, the walls of Jericho came tumbling down. How God worked to bring these people to the land of Canaan, which He had promised to their ancestors! This is what all the exodus from Egypt entailed, and God accomplished it all in fifty years.

The deliverance from Babylon entailed not only that the people were removed from there, but that the Temple was rebuilt and that all was put back in order. It is certain that in building the Temple, they worked with a sword in one hand and a trial in the other. The kings rose up against the people, but God preserved them miraculously. So many murders are committed whenever superstitions are rejected that the people retreated among the beasts and were sustained by God. Are we astonished not only that God gave the people freedom to return, but that by a miracle a pagan king paid to have the Temple restored? Furthermore, the walls were rebuilt. God had always sustained these people and He will fulfill His promise in that not only will there be men in His Church who have been delivered from Babylon, but that all the peoples will serve God. Thus the prophet says that God's act of deliverance will be so great that the deliverance from Egypt will be nothing in comparison to the way He will deliver His people from Babylon, where they were as dead and yet resurrected many times over by Him. The world is bound to be overwhelmed by admiration for this act of God. It is not for a mere day but until the end of the world that we must glorify this work of God. Although it may seem to the world that all is ruined and that the Church is finished, God preserves it through His Son, Jesus Christ, in order that He reveal Himself to us as He is named: Savior. Our Lord has drawn us into His Church, that He be honored among us.

We are compelled to say in the same breath that His virtue is admirable and that this deliverance is beyond our capacity to understand. Let us consider what our condition was before God had delivered us. Our Lord exalted us from beyond the heavens and sustained us with the promise that He would come to take us by the hand to give us entrance into the heavens. Have we not, then, reason to say, "God is living!", especially as He delivered us from Babylon? And it is not merely once that He has delivered us, for from our birth we were damned. What was life like for us when we were detained in this evil Papism? We see how He delivered us from it by His grace. When this comes to mind, must we not say that "the Lord is living!"? Not just once but day and night we must recall the gracious acts He has performed for us; for it is beneficial to us to remember the grace God shed upon us by taking us so far away from our captivity that it seems this was nothing but a bad dream, as the psalmist says. The faithful say we have been as dreamers since we left Babylon, for we do not know what is truth and what is a dream. When we depart from such abysms, we are ever so astonished; for we thought that we were banished from the land promised to our heritage. When we finally see this land, it is such a novel experience that we cannot tell if it is true or not. When we come to know His power and that this is no idle dream, we are overwhelmed in admiration for Him.

Now the hypocrites tried to turn this promise to their advantage, for it seemed to them that they must share in it. Therefore our Lord returns to His previous menaces and says, "I will send many fishers, that they fish them. I will send many hunters to chase them from each and every cave, for my eyes are upon their ways." This passage is commonly understood to refer to the Apostles and other preachers of the Church, for our Lord says, "Come, I will make you fishers of men." But the interpretation of the Jews is more correct: God calls the Babylonians hunters, for He adds next that "the sinners will not be hidden from them." Our Lord has spoken of fishers and hunters; insofar as the people have offended Him, He will send the Babylonians to chase them. When He speaks of the caves, he means that He will incite the Babylonians to drive them from their strong places. He speaks of hunters and fishers to signify that if He does not punish them one way, He will another. Because we rejoice when we think to have escaped some punishment, He adds, "You will not escape from my hand, in which I hold you. When you think you have escaped, I will fish from the ones and hunt after the others, so that in water or on land I can well find you." That is the true meaning of the prophet.

Now let us apply this to what I have already said. When our Lord grants salvation to His own, He reveals that He is kind and has pity and therefore aids those in affliction. But this does not hold for hypocrites or for those who take His name in vain. If we wish the promises of God to benefit us, we must prepare to receive them by repenting. When we hear the promises God makes to His own, we become so hardened that we do not believe that He is addressing us. If we persist in our evil ways, it is true that God will console the faithful by saying that He will never punish His own with such severity, but does this pertain to us? No. If we continue to offend God and if we wish God's promises be addressed to us, we must be so moved by our sins that we ask for pardon and have recourse to His grace. When God blesses His own, He begins to threaten the evil ones to show that His promises are not addressed to them. Let us know our faults and be displeased with them, that we have recourse to His mercy.

Furthermore, God does not reiterate His threats to banish all hope of salvation from us. We must remain faithful to the end, as we will see at the end of our text. Let us think on God's reprisals. Will any be able to find a bed to sleep soundly in? After we have endured one form of punishment today, tomorrow He will treat us as severely, if not more so. There is no end to God's punishments, save that we bring an end to our iniquities. After He has struck us with one rod, He will strike us with another. Search for subterfuges as we will, we must come to grips with our situation, if it is only to forestall God's punishments by humbling ourselves.

Let us turn to the prophet saying, "Their abominations are obvious to Him and their iniquity is not hidden from His face." This seems a superfluous way of speaking, for it would seem sufficient solely for him to say that their iniquities are obvious to God. Why, then, does He speak of the eyes and the face of God? This is not without reason, for it seems to us that we can fool God. True, we never say so, for that would be an unpardonable blasphemy; but when we give ourselves license to offend Him, do we not believe that He does not see a wink of our evil doings? True, we would not dare say so, but there is much that we would not dare to do before a mortal that we do before God. If we know that God sees all our works, are we not ashamed of what we do? Certainly. We are compelled to assume, then, that when we give free reign to our concupiscence, it is as if God does not see a wink and so does not see our evil deeds. This is why the prophet says, "Do you think that your iniquities are hidden from me?" He uses such repetitions to show we are all so very foolish, believing that we are hidden from God and that He cannot see through our deceptions. We will be brought to account before God, and what was hidden will be manifest before Him. Men may deceive themselves into thinking that vice is virtue, but God's justice will always have its own way and cannot be manipulated according to our fantasies. That is the very worthy admonition of the prophet.

Our Lord, after having spoken of our abominations, turns specifically to the idolatries people have committed on earth. "Indeed," He says, "do you not think that the stench by which you have polluted the earth does not reach me?" Here the prophet wishes to emphasize how contemptible God finds idols to be. Scripture is accustomed to speak in such a way. When we defile the service of God, we think this no great thing. This comes from not having God as we should; for it is certain that then we would have a much stronger desire to serve Him. But why? Men are of the ambition to value themselves more than they are really worth, so that serving God means nothing to them. The prophet is showing that the honor of God is a far greater price than we are willing to pay. Regarding sacrifices, he says, "They have filled my heritage with carcasses and abominations." The sacrifices made to idols were no more an abomination than those made in Jerusalem, for they were made with the same animals. If one is an abomination, then so is the other. But if the sacrifices made in Jerusalem are dedicated to God, He approves of them as if He had ordained them. This is why our Lord sanctioned them. What is sanctified by God is holy and has nothing that must not be esteemed; but when we serve God as we would wish, that is an abomination. This is why salt must be used in all sacrifices, to show that they are being done without God's consent and are only so much stench and pollution. On the contrary, if we sacrifice as God has ordained, that will smell sweet to Him. Let us note, above all, that what is not ordained by God is only shit and stench. Why? Nothing makes our works good, save the ordinance of God. Knowing this, we dedicate and consecrate all our works to God. Papism, then, is only so much stench. When we say that the mass is a sin against nature, we use the very words of Scripture; for God has said as much of the sacrifices made at Bethel, which were far more beautiful than the mass. Do we not have with the mass a beautiful cover-up? When God said, "Go to your sodomy!" it is as if they went to live among the asses and the beasts. Nevertheless, if we say as much, the Papists will reply, "Are you speaking in the Spirit? How? Do you have to say that?" How men wish to correct the Holy Spirit: Let us not trust in our own judgments, but in what God says, for He alone is sufficient. God says that all we do without His consent is a sin against nature. God, out of His contempt for idolatry, will address us in language that will make our hair stand on end. All that men invent is nothing but an abominable stench to God. Men may well mask the odor, so it would seem, but what God has to say to them! God is not content merely to enumerate their abominations; He uses much stronger language than that. When we hear God speaking this way, let us be circumspect. When it is a question of serving God, let us follow all His ordinances; for all that His Word sanctions is holy. Now if someone says that such-and-such applied only to the time of the prophet, he is deceived. If someone says that only stinking carrion was offered up to God, he is also deceived. Why? Animal sacrifices were made in Jerusalem, yet they were a sweet smell to God. Why, then, is it that the others are a stench to God? What is the difference? There is no answer, save that the one was approved of by God, the other by man. Whatever humans invent is only a stench. Now let us see if anything in Papism is founded in the Word of God. Where is mass founded? Where are pilgrimages founded? Where is the invocation of the saints founded? Where are the holidays that one must observe founded? Where is the determination of meat-eating days founded? Where are the priests founded? In brief, where are any of their ways to be found in the Word? It is certain that nothing of Papism is founded in the Word. We must conclude with the prophet that Papism is only so much stench.

We should not be surprised, then, that God lands His vengeance upon man, for the earth cries out to be revenged because she has been polluted. Our Lord says, "They have polluted my earth by their shit and filled my heritage with their abomination." It is not that the earth is His, but that it is called His heritage because He always held it together and gave it to the children of Israel; but He always retains His domination over it. He wishes to be served and honored by these people; for He is not known anyplace else in the world," although all the earth and all that is contained in it belong to Him," as Psalm Twenty-Four says. The first verse of this Psalm shows that in all the world there are no other people who serve God. Because the infidels have no knowledge of God, it was necessary to bring these people to this mountain and to draw a line to separate Judah from the other nations. That is what the prophet refers to when he says, "I have separated out the people of Israel, that they be my heritage, and they have polluted it!" Their crime is so much more magnified by this circumstance. The Pagans are without excuse and will be punished for their idolatry; that is why they were placed outside the land of Judah.

But as God consecrated this land, and as the people have polluted it, so much the more severe will their punishment be.

What was said at the time of Jeremiah is addressed to us. God has abolished this separation. There will no longer be any mountain called Zion. God wishes to be worshipped throughout the entire world and to have His seat in our souls and to have our bodies as His temple. As it is written in the fourth chapter of John, God wishes to be "adored in spirit and in truth" and "the faithful will no longer worship God at a certain place, but throughout all the world." Because our Lord wished all the earth to be sanctified, it is certain that once we become idolaters we will pollute God's earth. Although the Papists have polluted the earth where they live, God will sanctify in a special way the land where we live; for He has shown us how He wishes to be served. If we turn from Him and follow after our evil spirit, we will be so much the more culpable. Let us look to ourselves; for the prophet not only preached this teaching for those of his time, but wrote it down to instruct us. Wherever God is known, He must be honored, not in part, but in whole. Let each look to himself. Because God has blessed the land where we live, let us guard against polluting it. True, the prophet speaks of idolatry and superstition, but we must guard against all sins. He who was forbidden idolatry has also forbidden lewdness, greed, grudges, enmities, and all other manners of sinning. If we wish to be consecrated in His honor, we must guard against all that He has forbidden. Then the earth will be without pollution.

The prophet adds, "O Lord, you are my strength and my power and my refuge in the time of tribulation." The prophet is terrified like a man lost; for he does not speak of wonderful things but of God's judgment when he says that "God will send hunters and fishers." This is enough to terrify a man of pure conscience. True, the hypocrites will not be surprised; but those of a clean conscience who fear God will be terrified when God makes such threats; for if we are truly Christians, we know in our hearts that "it is a terrible thing to fall between the hands of the living God", as Saint Paul says. Let us think on His judgment, which is not the judgment of men; let us think about His strong hand and His wrath as they are revealed in Scripture. Then we will know that it is not without reason that Saint Paul says that "it is a horrible thing to fall between the hands of God." When the hypocrites mock his warnings, he stands his ground saying, "Alas what is this?" He cannot express the distress he is experiencing; he can say only, "Ah! Lord, you are my refuge." By this, we are admonished that whenever we speak of God's judgment, we should be touched to the quick by the example of the prophet. We should read Scripture as if God were talking to us. Do not think God's threats are so much hot air, see His punishment as present. Look not to vengeance in this world; look to the day when the evil ones will stand before God and experience how unbearable is His wrath. That is what we must glean from this passage. Furthermore, let us not lose courage, though we are threatened with God's judgment. When we see all in confusion, let us not be so shaken up that we forget to say, "Lord, you are my refuge, indeed in time of affliction." The prophet says "in time of affliction"; for when we are quit of our troubles and the sun is shining, we have no recourse to God. When, then? When we see only affliction. This is a teaching common among the prophets. Joel says that "the earth will tremble when there will be a world war." In this we see the wrath of God, " but whoever invokes the name of the Lord will be saved." I do not say that the earth will bring forth its fruits. Joel is not speaking of an orderly world; rather, he says that "the earth will tremble so that it seems all must perish. All will be in total chaos, but "whoever invokes the name of the Lord will be saved." Jeremiah says the same thing; he proclaims that it is not in vain that he says all will be troubled, but he concludes that he will not fail to return to God. We must take all our consolation in His bounty, which we never lack.

Following this holy teaching, let us prostrate ourselves before the face of our good God, in knowledge of our faults. We pray that He grant us greater knowledge of our faults. We pray that He permit us not to flatter ourselves by our hypocrisy. We pray that if we merit teaching by one rod, He sent yet another, to doubly insure that we learn our lesson well enough that we no longer need fear Him. May He shed His grace not only on us but on all, etc.

* * *

All-powerful God, you are not content to give only one small corner of the earth to your servants; you are pleased to extend your kingdom to the ends of the earth and make your home with us through your only Son in whatever place we are. Give us the grace that we may offer ourselves to you in sacrifice. Give us the grace to arrange our lives in obedience to your Word, that your name be glorified in us and by us, until finally we are made participants in the eternal celestial glory acquired through your Son, our Lord, Jesus Christ. Amen.

(13) Friday, July 12, 1549

O Lord, you are my rock, my power, and my refuge in the time of tribulation. Men will come from the ends of the earth and they will say, "Truly our fathers inherited lies and vanity, which are to no profit." Jeremiah 16.

Yesterday we began to examine how the prophet provides us with a good example of what it means to have recourse to God. When we see that things are so confused and when there is no longer any hope, this is the hour to retreat to God. Even if we were to see the sky mix with the earth, let us know that the hand of God is ready to aid us because we have invoked Him. That is what the prophet teaches us. When he is so afflicted and so oppressed that he can stand no more, it is then that he doubles his hope. It is then that he realizes that the true opportunity to return to God comes only when there is extreme confusion, as he has shown.

He reveals an even greater faith when he says that "the peoples will come from the ends of the earth," for we must note the circumstances of his time. It seemed that God had rejected the Jews. Where would He establish His Church? For, as I have said, it seemed that His small Church was about to perish. What could be concluded, save that all was lost? Nevertheless, the prophet said that people would come from the ends of the earth. This had never happened before. However the Kingdom of God flourished at the time of Solomon, only Israel obeyed God; and it was so afflicted that it counted for nothing. The prophet, then, is about at his wits' end; he can say nothing, save that this small Church is lost. Nevertheless, he looks beyond the world and says, "Men will come to you from the ends of the earth." That is the kind of hope we must have more than ever when it seems all is lost; for our faith must not be controlled by what we see; we must look beyond the world; we must hope in what seems unbelievable. We saw that Abraham "hoped beyond hope," that is, he did not hope in the promises of God the way he hoped according to the appearance of things and to human judgment. Although God seemed to promise him impossible things, he had faith. He paid no attention to the appearance of things. He looked only to the fact that He who made the promises was faithful. He looked only to the truth of God, which exceeds all human truth. This is what the prophet shows us not, for he looks only to this small Church. Although it seems that all will perish, for the people are in captivity, he says that people from all the regions of the world will come to Zion. Zion will be razed, that is, the Temple there. Nevertheless, he says all the peoples of the earth will come to Zion. He honors God by believing in His promises and sees people coming to God from the ends of the earth to be His Church. Nobody but the prophet had such faith. This example is shown to us insofar as we have been unable to attain this perfect faith.

We cannot attain faith by things in this world, but must look beyond this world to the sole power of God. Our faith must be like an anchor, which is small and unseen when thrown in the water but which nevertheless holds the ship and all that is within it. We must ground our faith, not by looking down, but by looking on high, where it has its immutable foundation; our Lord has promised that when the sun and the moon will be in the sky that we will not doubt that there is a Church on earth. If we saw that there were only two men on earth who wished to serve God and that Satan had imprisoned all the rest, let us maintain faith in God and say, "Although I see that all is perverted and annihilated and that your Church is no longer, I am confident, Lord, that you sustain a people to serve you, indeed that you will deliver them from these abysms. You will be served and your name invoked." Because this has come, let us acquire the faith we must have. It seems that this small Church of God is about to perish because of our sins. Let us return to God. Although this Church seems almost nothing, let us have faith that God will see to it that there will always be people to serve Him. Let us conclude, then, that as long as God is in the heavens, there will be a Church on earth. As long as He reigns from above, He will have His body down here. Indeed, the prophet says, "Lord, the peoples will come to you from the ends of the earth." He also says that the Church will be the seed of Abraham and that the peoples will be united with this seed. He is not speaking according to his own belief on these matters. Nor does he have the foolish presumptuousness to dictate law to God. Where, then, does his faith come from? He speaks according to the Word and will of God. God does not reign according to our thoughts, but according to what He has judged and proclaimed by His word. The prophet finds his assurance in the Word because God has spoken it.

He adds, "And they will say, 'Truly our fathers inherited lies and vanity, which are to no profit.'" This confession must be made first in order that when people come to God to serve Him. Terrific change was taking place, as God was then known only in Judah. When people come to Zion to be united with the people of God, they must renounce the doctrines in which they have been raised and confess that they had been as poor, misguided beasts. Because it would seem strange that people would renounce the doctrines and laws they had been brought up in, they add that their laws were nothing but lies. They are saying in effect, "Lord, as you can create out of nothing, so you can reform the thoughts of men to win them over to your service and you can return to yourself those who have been like errant beasts. You can reform those who in their wickedness effaced your image in themselves. You can illuminate those who have been blind all their lives." Thus the prophet shows us what must be done if people given to idolatry are to come to God. If we have been blind we must not be ashamed to confess it, even in public; for it is a crying shame when men try to hide from others what is known to God and His angels; they will be convinced of our good intentions, when our lips are opened to reveal our secrets. Those who try to evade shame will have their sins discovered and made public. The prophet shows what are the fruits of true repentance. Because we have been so evil, we must confess that we and our fathers inherited only lies.

Now there is one other matter: Children must make a confession for themselves and for their fathers. Today this is unpopular among many sons, who use their fathers as an excuse for their sins: "Why do we sin? We were taught to do so. We follow in the ways of our fathers!" They think this excuse sufficient reason for them to persist in their foolish ways. They wish to remain as their fathers raised them. But the prophet says that we must not persist in our sinful ways under the cover of our fathers. Is it not enough that they failed, without our using their faults as shields to make war against God? Nevertheless, we hide behind these shields, even though we are culpable. When we say that our fathers offended God, we proclaim their iniquities. We, then, cannot excuse ourselves by our fathers. Let us know the one we must serve. When He has spoken and when all the world is against Him, let us follow Him without contradiction. Let us adhere to the Word of God. Let us be like Noah, whom God commanded to build an arc and who remained faithful ever after. It is said of Noah that "he condemned all the world" because he held firm to the Word of God. Saint Paul tells us that we would condemn even the angels. That, of course, is an utter impossibility. But if it were possible for us to condemn them, we would certainly do so. Let us not deceive ourselves by putting our faith in men, in whom there are only lies. Let us not throw off God's grace. Let us not delude ourselves by pitting men against God to see who will win.

We are also admonished that we need not search into antiquities and be able to say, "It has always been this way," for we need only look to the immutable will of God, which was before the world was created. If we seek lies, we will have no trouble finding them. Why? Our fathers inherited them. Our father Adam sought lies and he was filled with foolishness and shame insofar as he rejected God's grace. We, who are the descendants of Adam, we are full of nothing but lies and shame. It is no surprise that we are so ignorant most of the time. Antiquity is of no use to us, for men have always been liars. Let us not be as the superstitious ones who assume it is enough to say simply that their religion is from antiquity. Let us agree with the prophet that whenever we see the lies of our fathers, we say, "Lord, we have failed."

The prophet, in this passage, is referring to all the religions there have ever been in the world, for they are nothing but lies if they are not founded upon the Word of God. Let us know, through this one word (lie), that everything founded on the Word of God is immutable. If we do not find this foundation, then it is a lie. Our God says that He is truth. If we search for truth outside of God, we will find only a powerless idol, for it has lost its foundation. The prophet, then, condemns all religions not founded on the Word of God. The Egyptians had a secret theology, such as the Papists have today. The prophet says it was only foolishness. Why? It was not founded on the Word of God. Let us recognize that there is no religion, save that it is founded on the Word of God. Not only is a religion ungrounded in the Word of God false, but all its doctrine, which is contrary to God, is from the devil; for God will not tolerate His Word to be disguised. Christians, when they found themselves on the Word of God, not only have sure and certain faith, but can condemn all Pagans. It is a great consolation to know that we cannot be destroyed, because we are founded on eternal truth, and that all the rest is just so much shit because God disapproves of it.

Here we see the poverty of the Papists, who are grounded only in their own beliefs. What will happen to them in the end? The prophet says that "all will be found to be only a lie and of no use in the end." When Papists torment themselves so much in their services, what will this profit them? True, when a man has been a zealot all his life, it seems that God should amply reward him. But when his conscience stands before the judge, when he is near death, he will say, "What has happened to all my Our Fathers and all my other mumbling about? They have all gone up in smoke. What did I profit by them? Nothing." Men may flatter themselves that all they do is approved by God; but in the end, when they see it was all to no avail, they become desperate. Let us know, then, that nothing will profit us, save what God sanctions. In Isaiah, God mocks those who spend their food money for things of no value, to teach these bigots a lesson. It is as if someone bought a fancy gilded table but had nothing to put on it or bought a beautiful cup but had not one drop of wine to put in it. Certainly such a person would be considered a fool and we would poke fun at him. For his fancy table and his beautiful cup, he dies of hunger. That is what will happen to those who amuse themselves with badinages and superstitions. That is the kind of reproach that will be made against them. Let us stick with what God approves and we will do nothing foolish.

By the words "vanity and lies" the prophet is referring not only to idolatry, but to man-made ways of serving God. We have spoken of the idols made by Pagans, which the Papists call "the books for idiots." Why? Because they cannot read the Scriptures, they go to pray to their little chaps, the saints. Their school is nothing but a lie, according to Habakkuk's reproach to them. So we see how they corrupt the service and glory of God into ignominy. It is as if someone threw shit in a man's face. The same is true when one makes visible images of God. Furthermore, as I have just said, the prophet not only wishes to speak of idols, but of all superstitions forged by man. It has been some time since the Pagans have had idols, but they do not fail to abuse the service of God by their addiction to superstitions. Idolatry does not consist solely of the making of images: Whenever one invents some manner of serving God, there is no doubt one is already steeped in idolatry. That is what the prophet means.

He asks, "Will men make gods for themselves?" This refers to the audacity in men to forge idols. What are we? Nothing but fragility. Yet do we not make gods according to our fantasies? How man will be the creator of the Creator! How man is like a grasshopper: As soon as he is created, he wishes to jump high. As soon as he is in this world, he wishes to forge a god suitable to him. There is only fragility in us. Someone remonstrated us in this way, there is not one of us who would deny that it is true and that all this lunacy is mere deception; but when we make this confession, the world just passes us by. The Pagans, who are quite intelligent, were insane enough to make gods. They even confess in their writings that these gods are nothing but lunacy, yet they wished to make greater gods than those of all the other peoples. What deceit! This is how man becomes possessed by Satan and is rendered culpable. Not only were the Pagans deceitful, but in all of Papism, there is nothing but deception. The Pope does not call the images gods, but patrons. The Pagans said as much; for they knew well that there was only one God over all, but the gods they made were their small gods. The Pope prays for the deceased one. Soon, torches will be used rather than candles, beautiful tapestries instead of mortuary drapes. Presto, a canonized saint. Next this little chap will be placed on an altar, and they will chant masses in his honor. That is how the Papists manufacture saints just as the Pagans make gods. The Pope runs the business of the house of God as if he were the Grand Master. That is the shame of Papism. If we come before their grand god, we find an even greater abomination. They take a piece of bread, blow on it, and it is their god. When we return to the prophet, we find that this is an example of the deceitful thought that man can make God. The Papists allege their practice is by virtue of Christ's words "Here is my body," but He did not say that the bread is His body. We see clearly, then, that this is only a human invention. When God nourishes us through His supper, He is not transfigured in the way the Papists imagine. Here is mortal man trying to make a god. What can be said of the little chaps can also be said of all the ways man invents to serve God. Whenever I invent some way of serving God in my head, it is as if I forged a god. God has given us the rule for how we are to serve Him. When we abandon that, we abandon God. We are then saying, "I do not wish this God, I wish to make a god suitable to me." When we wish to serve God otherwise than He ordained, it is as if we deposed Him. If we do not wish to be reproached that we attribute to insensible creatures the honor that belongs to God, we must lock ourselves into His Word.

The prophet continues, "I will reveal to them that my name is Eternal." Here God is saying that the Pagans will be converted; that is, He will open their eyes and make them sense His power! We could live a hundred thousand years and always be hardened in our imaginations, were it not that God transforms us. It is the proper office of God to inspire us; otherwise we would persist in our ignorant ways and evil would be more and more augmented. We must well note this passage, for here God declares it is His office to enlighten us. We have been deceived by Papism. Now that we know our poverty and the way to God, and now that we are assured by His Word, let us attribute all this to His bounty and not to our human wisdom. Let us not say, "I have outgrown Papism. Why? I have such good sense." Let us guard against that. Let us know that it is God who delivered us by His bounty. If we had an ounce of superstition before, we would now have a whole pound, save that God opened our eyes. We must bear this in mind above all when we come to the passage where he says, "I will make them see." This seems a bit odd, since up to that point God had allowed the Pagans to walk in ignorance. It also says that "He will reveal to them His hand and His power." This means that it is not enough to have doctrine, for we do not understand a word of it. Although God has His Gospel preached all over the world, the majority of people do not understand it. His arm will not be known by all. Many will be unable to say, "It is God who speaks to us, to whom we must accommodate ourselves." It is not enough that God delivered us from Papism; it was necessary for Him to reveal His arm and His might, of which the prophet speaks, to us.

Following this holy teaching, we prostrate ourselves before the face of our good God, in knowledge of our faults. We pray that He touch us so that we know well to condemn our past life, recognizing our poverty. May He accomplish in us all that He promised by the prophet. May there be only one fold and one shepherd, one rule by which to serve Him. May all the peoples accommodate themselves to His Word. May He shed His grace not only on us but on all the peoples and nations of the world, etc.

* * *

(14) Saturday, July 13, 1549

The sin of Judah is written by an iron pen with a diamond point, engraved on the tablet of their heart and upon the horns of their altars, so that their children will remember their altars and the woods by the flowering trees in the high mountains. Jeremiah 17.

We wish to erase the memory of our sins, but we have not the means. God has told us that if we wish to be absolved of His judgment, we must condemn ourselves. If we wish Him to forget our faults, we must remember them. We cannot do this, save that we delight in evil. We wish God to forget our faults, although we have no repentance! Nothing is more deceitful than to believe that God will forget our sins while we become complacent in our faults. The more we try to cover them up, the more He will find them and reveal our shame.

That is why the prophet says that "their sins will be written with iron pen," for the Jews, sinful as they were, wished to persuade themselves that God is content with them and that the prophets did not have to cry out after them. Therefore the prophet says, "Do not think that your iniquities are erased, for they are written with the point of a diamond to reveal to you how deceptive it is to think that God no longer must think of your sins. No, no, for they are engraved before Him." He says that they are written on "the horns of their altars," to show their works make manifest the evil hidden in their hearts. The prophet, of course, is speaking according to ancient custom.

Whereas we write with a pen, they used stilettos to cut into wax. He says that their sins are written with the point of a diamond, to reveal that they cannot be erased as one can erase something written in wax. As we know, what is engraved with the point of a diamond can be erased only with great difficulty. It seems strange that God says their sins are irremissible; for in all of Scripture, He promises that if we are touched by repentance, He is ready to receive us in all mercy. It seems contradictory, then, when He says that sin will not be erased from Judah, that is, from all the people. The solution is that the prophet condemns them without remission because they are so hardened; for if they had any true repentance in themselves, they would have remission. Their stubbornness is the reason why the prophet says they are without remission. Whenever one is unwilling to accept being corrected after having offended God and wishes his wickedness to be esteemed as a virtue, whenever there is such obstinacy, it can well be said that his sins are engraved, indeed with the point of a diamond. That is how the prophet says nothing repugnant to the Scripture. The prophet, as we have seen, is speaking to those who do not wish to obey God. It is reasonable, then, that they hear their sentence. God threatens and strains us in order that we do not come to damnation. But when we are stubborn, it is necessary for us to be condemned without trial; for the sentence is already pronounced and God is seated as judge to punish us. Because He warns us and yet we remain obstinate in our wicked ways, damnation must befall us.

We are well advised to prevent His judgment; for if we wish to contest it and play the fool for whatever it will gain us, we would have to hide our sins; but then we would be "all wet", as they say. The prophet says that our sin is engraved with the point of a diamond and that however we may hide it for a time, God will find it in the end. Let us not abuse the patience of God. If He does not punish us as soon as we have offended, let us not assume that He has forgotten our faults; for they cannot be erased, save that we repent.

Note that the prophet says that "the sins of Judah will be engraved in the horns of their altars." Here the prophet proclaims that it is not necessary for God to produce witnesses, letters, or other instruments to testify against us; for it is enough that our works be brought forth and that He uncovers our thoughts to make manifest what we are. Here, then, is our trial: God will produce what was hidden in our hearts and our works will be brought forth. By this we are admonished stronger than ever not to ensnarl ourselves in our hypocrisy by trying to hide our faults to the extent we believe that we have none; for in the end our faults will be made known further than we thought. However our faults may be hidden within our hearts, God will bring them forth. Let us not deceive ourselves. Let us listen to the prophet when he says that God will bring forth our works. He says this because we wish to have hiding places, not only to hide our faults from men, but to hide them from ourselves. But this does not fool God. Why? He can see far more clearly than we.

Indeed, we see that sinners try to conceal themselves, but that God stabs them with remorse, although they stave this off as long as possible. In spite of themselves, they sense this repugnance, though they are so cunning in justifying themselves. Here we see the greatest subtlety: Whatever cunning spirit we have, we employ to justify ourselves. Nevertheless, our conscience brings forth all that we have hidden. Our conscience is like an executioner who declares that we cannot escape the hand of God. Now if our conscience can bring forth all that was hidden, what will it be like when Jesus Christ will sit in judgment and not in a human fashion? Our consciences will be manifest and laid bare before Him, and all that has been hidden away will be brought to light. This day is called The Great Day, for all will come into play. That is what we must think on above all else. Furthermore, he speaks here of our hearts in order for us to recognize that if men have good reason to condemn us, God will have even far more than they. Now there is not one among us who does not know how easily he could be condemned by men. How, then, do we think that we can hide when we come before God? True, we can well flatter ourselves; but all the flattery in the world will not enable us to escape God's judgment. Let us think on the proceedings instituted against us by the prophet, namely, that the record of our sins be before God and that our works be evident.

Now there is yet another point, namely, that although we appear innocent, although it is not evident that we have offended

God, nevertheless our sins are engraved within our hearts. Let this not deceive us into thinking that our sins are not manifest; for we are condemned for our evil intentions as if we had carried them out. Indeed, God has said that "whosoever thinks of evil will be condemned before me as if he had committed this sin before men." The fact that men do not perceive of our sinfulness does not release us from God's condemnation. God is called "the judge of hearts," for it is He who sounds their depths. When we are before the throne of God, it will not do for us to bring a pretty painting or mask; that is to say, it will not do for us to put on a good facade. Let us hear Scripture when it says that God is of a purely spiritual nature. He will not judge us in a human way, but in truth. Let each regard not only what he has done, of which he will be reproached before men, but also the thoughts in his heart. To be culpable before God it is not necessary that I rob; it is only necessary that I wanted to rob, for me to be culpable before God as if I had in fact robbed. If one given to adultery covets the daughter or wife of his neighbor, though he does not carry out his will, he is as culpable before God as if he had. If a man hates his neighbor, although this be hidden, he will be as culpable before God as if he had killed his neighbor. Because not one of us is inculpable or innocent, let us go to God and pray that He swallow up our faults by His bounty. When God comes to erase our sins, we will know well the imprints they have made in our hearts. When a man is cauterized, he feels this in his flesh. Now the remorse of our conscience serves to cauterize us in order to awaken us. After we are so awakened, we come to our Lord, having forestalled His judgment by knowing our faults; for He will have erased them, so that we are no longer culpable.

When the prophet speaks of the "horns of the altars," that signifies the idolatry committed by the Jews under the guise of good intentions. It was not their intention to offend God when they employed their goods to build chapels and other things at the Temple. They thought they were serving God. Nevertheless, the prophet reproaches them, "The horns of your altars will witness against you, for your iniquities are there written." Let us not deceive ourselves by our good intentions. Let us follow the Word of God and know that however the Jews intended to please God, this was no excuse. The same holds for all the services we invent. He adds that "their sons will remember their altars," or rather, "they will remember their altars as their children." That means they are as carried away with their foolish superstitions as is the adulterer with his adultery. They are incessantly driven by a foolish love. Scripture sometimes calls idolatry adultery; for just as an adulterer is consumed by his foolish love, so too are the idolaters consumed by their superstitions. Once Satan has baited a man into idolatry, he is carried away by foolish love. Let us look to how it was when we were yet among the Papists. Without being pushed, we ran about here and there. The poor Papists employ their goods in baptizing chapels, paying for ornaments, and in making beautiful glass and other things. They certainly are not lacking in ambition: One must give to a temple and then to a foundation. After hearing one mass, he must return to hear another. After dinner he must return to vespers and Compline. After supper, he must return for the benediction. In short, he is never finished. That is how it goes with idolaters. God says that "all they have done is like adultery with wood and rock." That is what the prophet means when he compares them to "horses who neigh." He says that "they will remember their altars as their children," to signify that they love their children no more than their altars and idols. They are so in love with their foolishness and superstitions that they forget their children. That is why they are condemned. Their example serves to condemn us. If we become carried away with idols and cold as ice towards God, will not our zealous ignorance serve to condemn us? Let us look to ourselves. Let us examine how we deceive ourselves by our foolish inventions, which we think will please God. God will not be impressed by our inventions. All they will do is augment our condemnation.

Furthermore, if we consider that God "will remind the children of their altars and of the woods by the flowering trees in the high mountains," we see how their evil is augmented. The prophet says that the Jews not only have polluted this earth, but that they left this heritage to their children, so that idolatry remained after their death. This is a more grievous sentence upon the Jews, for they have brought up their children in their vices. By this we are admonished to make it our duty to instruct our children in the fear of God. It is enough that we merit condemnation for serving Satan and not God, without the lives of our children being brought in to augment our condemnation. If we take a good look around, we will find that most people are condemnable by the sentence of the prophet. How many fathers take care to instruct their children in the fear of God? Not only do fathers neglect to teach the Law of God, but they wish their children to be a credit to them, namely, that the children be worse than they. If the father is a larcenist, he hopes his children to surmount him in that. If the father is an adulterer, he hopes his sons will be ruffians in whorehouses. If the father is licentious, he hopes his children will be a thousand times more so. When the fathers see that their offsprings are given to evil from their youth, it seems to them that their children ennoble them and already bear their blazon. That is what we see today. The fathers wish their children to follow their footsteps in ignorance, adultery, greed, licentiousness, and all other vices. Indeed, they wish their children to surpass them. Now if this is not obvious at first glance, certainly it is apparent that vice is common everywhere. Why? If the fathers are cunning enough to deceive and trick their neighbors, and if they see their children given to this wickedness, they are well at ease. Fathers send their children to school for the sole purpose of sharpening their wits so they can be more deceitful. Thus we see that the prophet spoke not only for his own time when he said that children will remember the altars of their fathers. This was to reprimand the fathers that all they taught their children was superstition and idolatry rather than how to serve God.

The prophet adds, "O my mountain in the fields, I will give away all your substance and riches as pillage to tyrants and enemies." When he speaks of the mountain, it is certain that he means Zion or Jerusalem, as if he were saying, "Here is Jerusalem, which is the place of assurance", for it is a strong city, and God Himself is said to be its protector. If the people allowed God to reign there, it is certain He would sustain them. But how could He? Their foolish pride led them to abandon themselves to evil and to pollute the Temple. Now, God can live only in a holy place and for this reason He says, "My mountain, you will be like an open field," as if He were saying, "You trust that you are impenetrable, but you are not. Your height is of no use to you, for you will be exposed to prey." We are admonished, then, that if we do not walk with a clean conscience before God, all our means of defense will serve us nothing, for God can well knock down all our bastions and ramparts when He wants to punish us. Let us not trust in the deceptive ways of man. Let us make it possible for God to dwell in the midst of us, that our bodies and arms be consecrated. Then we will be safe-guarded and fear not on battle fields, for He will put His hand out in front of us. He calls Himself a "wall of iron and steel" when it is a question of protecting His Church. But if He does not dwell among us, we have a big hole in our ramparts. God can well give the enemy easy access. He can throw him through the air at us as if there were no obstacles before them. What has been said of Jerusalem, we must apply to ourselves.

Let us note carefully that He adds, "You will be stripped of the inheritance that I have given you and I will give it to your enemies in parts of the world you know not." Now we know that the Jews were commanded to rest on the seventh day as a memorial to God and that God ordained that the earth was not to be worked every seventh year. Now the prophet says the people will be stripped of their heritage because that did not let the earth rest as God so ordained. The Jews were ordained to rest solely because God did not wish their labors to interfere with His reign among them. Because creatures were ordained to the service of man, it was ordained that the earth rest every seventh year. The prophet warns them, "You will rest insofar as you have not allowed to rest the land which God gave to Abraham as his heritage and you will be chased afar, that the land might rest from your labor." What we must glean from this passage is that when we wickedly exploit God's creatures, when we injure them by our greed, they will serve us only with regret and are oppressed by us.

It is not that creatures have feelings or the capability to tell us that we oppress them. They cannot make us understand what they wish to say, unless they could speak in the manner of men. But when one sees a poor horse who has been worked so overloaded that he cannot take another step, there is an oppressed creature. Why do animals nourish us? It is not so that God's glory might shine through all? If, on the contrary, God is blasphemed by the scandalous behavior of evildoers, are not the creatures offended and the order of nature perverted? That is what the prophet means by saying that God will make the earth rest. The prophet is not standing on ceremony, but is referring to the truth that we share with the Jews. If we wish creatures to serve us peaceably, we must be at peace in our conscience. Also, we must not overburden those things that God has ordained to our service, but we must use them so they serve us of their own good will; and that is when we use them as God so ordained. When we use them graciously, the creatures will be in accord with us and serve us willingly.

The prophet adds, "And you will serve your enemies in a land which you know not." This brings to memory what we touched upon last Wednesday, namely, if we do not wish to serve God in peace, He will send us to an unknown land where we will not have the leisure to serve Him in peace. Why is it that He maintains us in a certain place, save for us to serve Him in all holiness? On the contrary, when we will have perverted everything, is it not the case that the creatures will no longer know us? Yes, for when we obey God, a melody exists between all creatures insofar as they are all in accord. There is peace when we serve and honor God. On the contrary, when we no longer honor God as is fitting, not only does confusion reign among us, but all the creatures become confused by our ingratitude, and this in turn has an effect upon us. When we see that God has so well ordained all creatures, when we find that we always have occasion to praise whether we look above or below, and then when we see how we have brought chaos everywhere, are we not deeply ashamed of ourselves? If we wish to keep everything in order, we must strive to honor God throughout all our life. Then there will be order, and all creatures will be in harmony with us. They wish only to follow God's ordinance. They are, then, always ready to serve us. Whenever we have some calamity, tempest, pestilence, war, or other such torments, let us know that we have troubled God's creatures and therefore they know us no longer. Insofar as we do not know their Creator and ours, it is necessary that they no longer know us and that they are avenged of us by the glory of God in punishing us.

Following this holy teaching, let us prostrate ourselves before the face of our good God, in knowledge of our faults. Let us pray that He make us know better our faults, that we be touched with repentance and so no longer held culpable. May we not only strive to serve Him, but may those who succeed us. May not only we sow good seed on the earth, that we share in the promise He made our fathers to bless them and their children. May He shed His grace not only on us, but on all the peoples and nations of the earth, etc.

* * *

All-powerful God, because you invited each of us so sweetly and humanely to repentance and because you revealed that you are always ready to reconcile yourself with us, give us the grace that by our rebellion we do not reject your good will towards us, which we can never esteem enough. May you subjugate us and not be displeased in our vices. May we be touched by a true desire to serve you in all holiness. May we have no other desire or intention in our whole life than to strive that you will find us worthy in our service. May your name be glorified by us and may we, in the end, share in the celestial and eternal glory, which was acquired for us by your only Son, our Lord, Amen.

(15) Monday, July 22, 1549

Cursed is the man who confides in man and who makes flesh his arm and whose heart departs from the Lord. Jeremiah 17.

It is not without reason that Scripture strives to snatch us back from trusting in creatures and that it condemns this so strongly; for not only are we deceived and inflated by vain conceit, but this keeps us from going forward. Not only will he who puts his trust in creatures be deceived and inflated by conceit, but he will fight against God as if he were assured of winning. That is why the prophet speaks of this matter now. Up to this point, the prophet had warned the people, indeed even to say that God will chase them into a strange land because He was not known in this land where they live: "Because you have not honored me in this land which I have given you, I will send you to a land which you know not."

Now He says that "woe is he who trusts in man." Why? Men have confidence in their neighbors. Now the wretches only mock when they are remonstrated and they delight in their vices, thinking that they will go unpunished. When we put our confidence in men, not only are we presumptuous, but we are also abandoning ourselves to evil and therefore hardening ourselves. That is how one evil leads to another. We see now why the prophet made this statement and it is necessary to well note this. It is not enough to hear what the prophet says; it is necessary to examine why he said what he said. Now let us examine his purpose in saying, "Woe is he who trusts in the flesh and in creatures." Why? Because his heart departs from the Lord. This is not to say that men who put their trust in men and in God are exempt from this curse, for here is a double condemnation. When we put our confidence in things down here, we no longer have any access to God; for it is impossible that our confidence be cut in two, so that part is in God and part is in man. No, no. The prophet shows us what a mockery that would be. Therefore, if we wish to put our confidence in God, we must put all our confidence in Him; for if we put the least drop of confidence in creatures, that will pervert all.

Here is what the prophet teaches us. In the first place, we are told what kind of confidence we must have in God: It must be in God alone; otherwise, we go round and round in circles, trying to find certitude; for we can find only vanity when we turn from Him. That is why we so torment ourselves. Although we strive all our lives for certainty, we cannot govern ourselves such that we do not fall into decline one way or the other. So much the more, then, must we put our confidence in Him, not in part, but totally. That is what we must do in the first place. Now, there are several things which can turn us from God. Sometimes it is superstition that pulls us away from God, as is the case with those who trust in the saints. True, they wish to trust in God, but they stray from Him. What is the cause of their straying from God? Although they know that God alone is sovereign, nevertheless they think He can have companions. That is what turns them from God. Let us not walk according to our imagination; let us fix our eyes upon Scripture. Besides superstition, there is this audaciousness by which we think that we alone are wise enough. Then there is our incredulity. However God assures us that He will sustain us, we simply cannot believe in Him. For this reason, if we wish to remain faithful, it is necessary to restrain ourselves from our fantasies, from self-indulgence, from deceiving ourselves by creatures. All these things must be done away with. To yet better understand the prophet's message, let us note that he distrusts flesh. Now, that means ourselves. We must not trust ourselves. If I trust in myself, I deceive myself and therefore do evil. The prophet does not say only that we are not to trust in others, but that we are not to trust in ourselves. Who is cursed? Everyone. As soon as God departs from us, we are given to all evil. The prophet speaks to us from the standpoint that all of Adam's sons are inclined to trust in creatures; but Christ wishes to correct this imperfection and perversity and convert us to Him. Nevertheless, we will always be inclined to this vice until God batters down all confidence we put in ourselves and in creatures.

Now that we know in sum what the prophet wishes to say, he turns to how we should apply his teaching in practice. In the first place, whenever and wherever God speaks, let each look to himself and let us not deceive ourselves by thinking that we have the arms to defend ourselves against Him and therefore can protect ourselves against having to obey His remonstrances and fearing His judgments whenever and wherever He threatens us. Note that this is the essence of his teaching. In brief, unless we are purged of all ambition and trust in creatures, we are not able to receive this blessing. That is the first point. Furthermore, in order for us to trust in God, our confidence in anything other than God must be battered down, for these are two incompatible things. Do we think that we can mix fire and water? Hah! That would only make a mess and we would have neither one. So it is when we put our trust in creatures. Do we wish to do evil knowingly? We cannot flee from the prophet's sentence; for he spoke in all earnestness. When he says that "cursed is the man who makes flesh his arm," let us guard against becoming poor wretches willingly. If we wish to escape that fate, it is necessary, as I have said, that we throw down all trust in creatures. Now, to begin with ourselves, let us examine how it is that we come to trust in them. We do so whenever we think we possess some virtue or we expect to be aided by creatures. In brief, man cannot trust in them that he is not instantly inflated like a bladder. As soon as it is pricked by a pin, it goes flat. When the bladder is all full of air, it is so shiny. If there are two or three peas within it, it makes a great racket. But, as I have said, it is necessary only to prick it with a pin and its racket stops immediately. So it is with those who trust in themselves or in creatures. Since this trust is mere deception, let us learn to recognize that we have nothing except what God has given us. When we come to know our indigence, we will no longer have reason to glorify ourselves. But this cannot be accomplished without effort. Until we come to know God, it is impossible to know our faults; for we are in darkness, like men who cannot discern night from day. It is as if our eyes are bandaged so that we cannot see our turpitude. When God begins to enlighten us, then we begin to know our infirmity. But it is impossible for us to put our trust in God until we have totally battered down all trust in ourselves. Now once we have come to distrust ourselves, we must also come to distrust all that is around us. That is the prophet's point. The Jews, admonished of the approaching punishment of God, say: "How will we defend ourselves?" They build ramparts, they search for aid here and there. They not only trust in themselves, but they trust in others. We cannot trust in others that we do not trust in ourselves. That is why the prophet curses the man who trusts in men; for then we are separated from God and, being separated from Him, we are always cursed. You ask, "If God created creatures to help us, why should we not trust in them?" True, God created creatures to serve us and we profit by them; but if we put our trust in them and therefore withdraw it from God, we display an overwhelming ingratitude. Now we may say that this is not to withdraw our trust from God. But the prophet says that one cannot trust in creatures without abandoning trust in God; for one cannot depart from God in one direction, only to approach Him from the other. How is it that our confidence will not be in creatures? Whenever creatures fail us, we must not abandon our trust in God. On the contrary, when we have all the ways and means, and when the sky and earth offer themselves to us, let us know all this would serve us nothing, except that God blessed it all. We must bear in mind two things. The one is that it is truly nothing for us to have all creatures to ourselves. The other is that our heart must not abandon our trust in God. When we are denied all help and do not know which way to turn, let us know that, although we are helpless down here, God has a hand strong enough to deliver us from our enemies.

Now it is not enough to know that we are cursed because we trust in the flesh. We must also have this blessing, which is the second major point of the prophet's teaching. I say that it is not enough to know this trust is cursed, for even the infidels themselves would confess that. But why? They are so confused that they can only confess their curse and therefore know no remedy for their misfortune. Therefore it is necessary that we add into our reckoning the prophet's statement that "all who trust in God will be blessed." Now to really taste this blessing, we must not force ourselves to trust in God. We must do so of our free will. As I have said, infidels will confess that it is folly to trust in creatures, but they are not forced to break this trust. We should not force matters; but the Word of God should have authority over us so that immediately we quit ourselves of all things, whatever resources they provided us. Because God condemns trust in creatures, we must do likewise. We must do so willingly. We must not fear the execution of His sentence, but we must immediately throw down all our carnal fantasies. This is how we are unlike the infidels. We no longer find compelling our arguments to trust in creatures. A second difference is that after having received this teaching in obedience, we do not doubt that we have His blessing. On the contrary, if God has said only, "You will be cursed, you who confide in creatures," that would have surprised us; but He adds this blessing, as soon as the faithful are brought down and humbled, to say, "Indeed, you do not know who rescues you? It is I who will lighten you." We see, then, that God rids us of our trust in creatures not merely to augment what we already are and have; for we have only foolish opinions and are easily intoxicated. As we read in the ninth chapter, "Let not the mighty glory in their might, neither let the wise glory in their wisdom; but let them all be glorified that they know God." Now when we see that we have no glory, we wonder if God has omitted this from us. No, He wishes to cloak us in His glory. That is why, after the prophet declares that we are cursed for trusting in the flesh, he adds that "those who trust in Him will be blessed." This is not said to cause us anguish, so that we say, "How could we possibly attain this blessing?" No, it is not to make us languish, but it is meant to say, "Poor wretches, do you wish to do evil wittingly? Come to me and I will reveal to you the love I bear you. Receive my promises and do not doubt that you are blessed."

This trust must not be for a day, but eternal. After he says that "cursed is the man who makes flesh his arm," he adds, "He shall be like the briar in the desert and shall not see when good comes and he shall remain in the dry desert, in an uninhabited salt land." Briars have little greenness and do not bear fruit. Since he is saying that those who trust in the flesh will be cursed, it seems fair to compare them to briars. But he is claiming much more for man than can be claimed for briars. Although they have some greenness, one does not expect them to bear fruit, for they have none. When men blossom a little and when God permits creatures to smile on us and we are consoled, we come to trust in ourselves and think ourselves capable of bearing fruit. But how? God will lay His hand on us and we will realize that what we thought to aid us is of no benefit to us. That is what the prophet means by the dry lands and briars.

On the contrary, God consoles those who trust in Him. "They will be," he says, "like a tree planted by a river. When the sun warms it, it will not fear draught." Why? It has water under its feet. Thus it remains strong and green despite the heat of the sun. We must note, in the first place, that the tree does not trust in creatures, however it may appear, for there is no support in sand. We have a poor foundation if we wish to found ourselves on creatures by trusting in them; for we will find that sand is always sand and that we cannot take root, save that the earth is thick and fertile. If there was no natural nourishment in the mother's belly, the infant could be neither conceived nor nourished. Likewise, it is necessary that the earth offer forth its entrails and that there be nourishment in them, or the tree can neither be planted nor grow. Trust in creatures is only so much sand. Despite the fact that it seems we have a root deeper than three lances, we have none, as we will see in the next lecture. Here, then, is an example of the fact that we cannot take root, save in God.

Furthermore, it is said that if we are faithful, He will enable us to "spread our roots like a tree," meaning that our knowledge of God will profit us more and more, enabling us to spread our roots. We cannot trust in Him as is fitting and yet be always unfaithful. What must we, then, do? It is not enough that we take root. We must plunge ourselves deeper and deeper into God. If it were enough to be given knowledge of God just once, we would not need the Gospel. "Oh!" some will say, "It would serve to support this knowledge!" Yes, but though we trust in Him and are planted in Him, this is still not as it should be. God has called us to Himself in order that we profit more and more. However we have taken root, Satan knows well how to shake us, were we to take even deeper root. When God reveals His bounty to us, it is as if He were bringing water by a subterranean canal in order to give us room to spread our roots. Here we should note that the prophet says that the tree extends its roots to the water's edge.

Again He says that "when the heat comes, the tree will not feel it." Although we are planted in God, we will not fail to feel the heat and must not think that we are delivered from the miseries of the world and no longer subject to temptations. No, no! We must be tested. Being well-planted trees, we will nevertheless feel the heat as if we were about to burn up. But why? God can well remedy that. If we put all our trust in God, and even if God were to rain down such punishment that it seemed to the evildoers that all is lost, we will not be shaken up by this, provided that we have taken root underground. I say underground because in winter it seems the tree is dead, whereas it blossoms in the spring. We must draw our strength from under the ground. We must be assured that God will never fail His own. That is why it is said that we will not fear the heat, provided that God is there as our remedy. This is our sole consolation.

Now we see that those who are wicked are inexcusable. Why? God has pronounced sentence against them. But insofar as the prophet has not pronounced sentence against them, are they still inexcusable? Yes, for the curse does not come when it is spoken; for the matter itself bears this curse, namely, that one trusts in creatures. Why does God proclaim it? To rescue us from our trust in creatures. There is no need to say, "I wished to walk, but did not know the right path." That will not get us anywhere. God is manifest enough, not only as a fountain, but as a river. That is why we are inexcusable. He takes us to Himself only if we have His blessing. When we put our confidence in God, we are taught enough to know that whenever we are afflicted we must not search for excuses but immediately recognize our own faults. Once we know His grace, we will remain with Him.

Following this holy doctrine, we prostrate ourselves before the face of our good God, in knowledge of our faults. We pray that we come to know them better, that we no longer persist in our evil ways but convert to Him. May we be taught to draw upon His grace to profit more and more. May we fear all our stumbling blocks to God, specifically our rebellions, which occur only because we have turned from Him. May He shed His grace not only on us but on all the peoples and nations of the earth, etc.

* * *

## (16) Wednesday, July 24, 1549

The heart is perverse more so than anything else. Who can know it? I sound the heart and test the reins, and give each according to his ways and the fruit of his labors. Jeremiah 17.

We have seen in what our well-being consists, namely, that we put all our trust in God. On the contrary, it was shown that whenever anyone strays from God, he will become wicked and evil. We are subject to so many miseries in this world; but we have our Lord as a river to refresh us, in all our temptations.

There are those who do not agree with this. But how many among them trust fully in God? On the contrary, each looks out for his own self-interest; and the majority, feigning trust in God, do no less than that. Because the prophet finds so few trust in the truth, he says to the heart that "it is deceptive above all things," as if he were saying that the heart of a man is the patron of all malice. The heart seems beautiful, but if one sounds its depths, one finds only contradiction. What does it gain a man to deceive those with whom he interacts? Nothing. If there were a hundred thousand times as much profundity in his heart, God would know it all. Therefore, no one can escape this condemnation when the prophet says, "Cursed be the man who trusts in himself!" After we have heard the trust we must have in God, we must remember that he adds that "if a man thinks he has a pure heart, let him look within and he will find only lies." Let us not be deceived by our foolish confidence. Let each test himself to see if he has the kind of trust God wishes.

First of all, let us note that he is not speaking of the hearts of one or two men, but of all of us, and that he says he finds only cruelty and perversity. These are the two virtues the prophet attributes to man. I say virtues to signify the contradiction! Men always wish to be big: "Yeah! The prophet gives us two qualities: Not only are we full of cruelty, but all manner of perversity dwells in us." Any one of them would be enough to lead men astray, but the prophet gives us two. Let us note, then, that God finds nothing in us, save that which would totally condemn us. Therefore, I say that those who trust in themselves are well deceived. Because our self-love blinds us, let us come to the mirror the prophet shows us. Before man sees himself, all the world mocks him. When he comes to see himself in the mirror, he hides himself, there where previously he wished only to be seen. Let us come to the mirror. There is no use complaining to God that He will show us we are full of rebellion. Let us confess at once that we are such as He pronounces. As I have said, not only do we deceive others, but we deceive ourselves. We do not see what we really are, until God tells us that. Let us hold to what He says. It is true that our hypocrisy does not readily reveal itself; but if we examine ourselves closely enough, we find that it is not without reason that God calls us all hypocrites and perverts; for man will feign goodness and be taken as such while all along he is full of venom. That is the primary way our hypocrisy reveals itself. Now if this is our general state and none are exempt from it, what is to be done? There is no other remedy than for us to become totally dissatisfied with ourselves. The Papists deceive themselves with their free will and think that there is some virtue in themselves. But let us know that there is only evil. God is not content merely to say that there is some perversity in man, but that when one searches high and low, one will find such rebellion only in the human heart. We must conclude that we are all full of perversity, that there is nothing else in our heart. The Devil has so filled us with evil that we are all full of it to the brim. Let us not search for any good in us; for it has all been smashed down, insofar as God has pronounced this sentence upon us. When man knows this, it is necessary that he search for a remedy for his evil; otherwise, he is not truly dissatisfied with himself. It is not enough to simply reply to this doctrine by saying, "Let us be quit of evil." That is not God's intention in speaking to us. Rather, we must become so dissatisfied that we seek after a remedy and beseech God to heal us. This is why the prophet says that "God sounds hearts." It is to warn us that we must not expect God to come and examine us. Instead, each must accuse himself, then condemn himself, and then seek the grace of the Holy Spirit to be converted as is fitting. This is God's intention: In true humility, we beseech Him to pit us, that he purge and subdue our malicious, perverted heart. When Scripture says all this about God, that is not only in order to make us aware that God is such a demanding ruler that He can only find fault with us, but also in order that we realize what is lacking in us and seek after it with the realization that there is no other way than to go to the fountain. We are full of lies, so where is truth? We are full of rebellion, so where is the rule of all doctrine? In Jesus Christ. We must seek and fetch in Him. That is what God strives the hardest to teach us. He reveals our condemnation to us in order that we learn to be dissatisfied with ourselves. As I have said, in our natural state, we are true enemies of God. We wish even greater evil than our rebellion and malice. In brief, when we remain in such a state, it is impossible for us to be in God's grace. Now as much as it would seem that God must change and accommodate Himself to us, the truth is that we must change and accommodate ourselves to Him. God strongly insists on this point if we are to return to Him, for He holds to no other way. If you do not understand what I have said, it is certain that you are far from God. Satan strives to make men believe that there is some good in themselves in order that they trust themselves and find God distasteful, just as the Papists make men believe that there is some good seed in their nature which will lead them to God. They believe that the fact that there is great infirmity within us does not mean that we do not possess some virtue to lead us to God. We see, then, why it is necessary for us to understand God's teaching. Satan incessantly whispers in the ears of men to make them believe they are not as evil as one might think, that they possess some good seed in themselves. On the contrary, God strives to reveal to us that the whole of our nature is corrupt through and through. The whole of Scripture is full of this doctrine, so be aware that God does not take it lightly. Let us hold to this doctrine. Let us know that we will well profit from realizing that there is nothing but evil within us.

Now, as I have said, by these two words, perversity and malice, the prophet denotes all the evil that can reign; for when we know all the evil that there is in us, we can reduce it to these two, namely, perversity and malice. When men have the audacity to cover up their faults, that is malice. Our obstinate refusal of God, that we cannot tolerate His yoke around our necks, and all our concupiscence is denoted by the word perversity. In our natural state, we are an abysm of evil. True, this may not seem obvious; for God holds our emotions in check, though we be the force of chaos! Nevertheless, we do have this malice and evil in us such that man is like a sea wherein all evil swims. True, it is difficult to persuade ourselves of this fact. That is why the prophet says that "God sounds hearts," to reveal that however much we may disguise evil as good, all will be made manifest when the books are opened.

The prophet wishes to emphasize two points here. If we are to be children of God, we must accommodate ourselves to Him as soon as possible, that He purge us of this malice and rebellion. He wishes to ratify the condemnation of those who feign being righteous while they are nothing but hypocrites. The prophet shows that they will have to bury themselves deep in the earth, for God can well find them. As it says in Isaiah, "Woe to them that seek to bury their iniquities so deep that God will not see them, for He will bring all to light." If we are to have recourse to God, let us pray that it please Him to remedy our faults such that the faithful are not encompassed by this curse; for, as Saint Paul says, "they bear the sign of God, justice, and truth." When the prophet says that "the heart is deceitful and wicked," it is certain that the faithful are included in his remark. We have borne all malice, from the belly of our mothers. God must step in to correct us. God not only corrects those evildoers we know, but He sees further than we. As Saint Paul says, "Although I do not sense myself culpable, I am not justified." By this the means that while he can see only goodness, God can see much further. What will happen to men who are not as illuminated as Saint Paul when he said this? What will befall men blinded by their own self-love? It will come to pass, as Solomon said, that "a man will think himself right, but God does the weighing." This means that God will find their weight and measure false. Let us stick to this doctrine, namely, that there is only malice in us and that it is up to God to convert us. Let us go to Him and pray that He be pleased to subdue this rebellion, that He convert our hearts of stone into hearts of flesh, that they bend easily to His Word. On the contrary, let us pray that those who wish to remain obstinate know that their sentence is already passed, so it is not necessary for the prophet to pronounce sentence upon them to condemn them.

In this world, the hypocrites hide themselves so well that nobody knows who they are, but they will be uncovered before the Judge. There are two kinds of hypocrites. The ones are taken to be little angels. But what will that profit them when the books are opened and their iniquities are made manifest? Although they make up all kinds of fictions about themselves, they are not such good painters that God cannot dry out their colors. The others are so impudent that they have lost all shame and mock God. These are even among the pillars of the Church: adulterers who are like dogs chasing after a bitch in heat, drunkards, pigs at meal times. If they are discovered and reprimanded, they have at their fingertips their shield of righteousness: "Oh, I am a righteous man, I am so respected." They have such good credentials that everyone is deceived by them. What will become of them? They will be sent before the Judge, as the prophet says. Isaiah says, "Cursed are you who bury your iniquities." Following the prophet's example, we say, "You got away with everything because nobody knew who you really were. To the Judge, to the Judge, with you. May you be convicted."

But let us know, on our part, that God will reform our hearts in His image. He sounds the hearts of the faithful and of evildoers, but He sounds them differently. The physician examines a man's illness in order to cure it. When the physician sees that the patient has an injured brain, he does not give him a crack on the head. When he sees that the patient has a damaged lung, he does not tear out his entrails. He always tries to cure them. Now it is not this way with a judge. He inquires into the deeds of evildoers in order to send them to the executioner. God sounds us as a physician to help us. On the contrary, he sounds evildoers in order to condemn them. Let us turn to God and beseech Him to be our physician.

How do we go about this? Through the office of doctrine, which, as Saint Paul says, is "to argue, reproach, teach, and correct." Whereas we were in darkness, God illuminates us through this office. Let Him sound the depths of our hearts, for we have a serious illness there. If we follow God's prescriptions, He will bring us around so that our heart is enlightened and we follow Him willingly. God uses His office of physician to convert our lies into truth, when He reforms us in His image; for we bear the image of the Devil, Father of Lies. If we bear the sign of God, it is certain that we bear His image and present our hearts to Him in total obedience. Now, this must not be only for a day, but for our entire life. Therefore, when we come to hear sermons, let us assume that God has recommenced His examination; for Satan recommences his work in us every half day. The Devil is like a spider who immediately goes back to work on his web after we have broken it. God has to reform us hour by hour, so let us daily drill on this doctrine. God also sounds the Devil's recruits. He has already begun by giving them the shakes so that their teeth chatter whenever they are reproached. God will examine them, not to reform them in His image, but to expose their turpitude to all the world. While our sins are pardoned, the evildoers are shamed. Choose now which way you like best. If you wish to share in the grace of God, you must discover your shame; but God will be there to bury it. On the contrary, if you wish to cover up your malice, God will exercise His office as Judge of the world.

The prophet adds, "to render to each according to the fruits of his labors," for he has said before, "Who is it who will sound the heart of man?" By this he shows that not only are we ignorant about other men, but that we are deceived about ourselves. He says that we must come to God, who can well sound our depths and who will not condemn us according to our imagination or deeds. But He will hold culpable those who reject his doctrine. The prophet gives an example to show that God will get through to those who paid Him such little homage. To confirm his statement, he says that men trust either in themselves or in other creatures. Thus, when they amass great riches, they vex God, for they are not subjugated to Him. He says that they are like the partridge who tries to cover those she did not hatch. The little ones know well who their real mother is and so flee this robberess. The partridge is so audacious that when she loses her own eggs through her ignorance, she steals from others. Nevertheless, the little ones have the nerve to escape and run back to their mother, just when this robberess thinks she has succeeded. So it is with the evil ones who have amassed great wealth. They may enjoy their wealth, but soon they will be tormented; for just as the little ones fled from the robberess, so their goods shall flee from them, knowing that they were not justly acquired.

We have here an example of what the prophet is saying, namely, that we are deceived by our trusting in ourselves or in creatures and that if we wish to put all our trust in God, we must be emptied of all else. Those who have wealth can use it well, provided they are not outrageously greedy. On the contrary, those totally abandoned to greed, who trust in things, will find themselves to have been deceived in the end. God wishes to reveal by the example of the small partridges that He can well give spirit to small creatures to condemn the foolishness of man. How is it the nature of creatures to follow their mother, whatever spirit there be in the eggs? God puts this nerve in beasts to show that those who strive to amass great wealth will be frustrated in their attempts. It may seem to them that they are rich, but insensible as the light might seem, God has given it the power to flow through the fingers of those who acquired it evilly. God reveals that the creatures cannot bear that men go wild, grabbing from here and there. True it is that creatures will be subjugated to them for a time. But soon, one piece of earth will take its leave, then another. Why? Because God so desires. Now this matter requires further treatment. For the time being, let us take up again our theme that unless our hearts are purged of all evil, we are not ready to come before God. Furthermore, seeing our hearts full of malice, let us search for the remedy, which is in God alone, for only He has the cure for our illness.

Following this holy teaching, let us prostrate ourselves before the face of our good God, in knowledge of our faults. We pray that He reform us, that in our lives we show ourselves to be His children and know His as our Father. May we remain with Him and not turn away, as we are wont to do. May it please Him to fill us with His Holy Spirit, that we come to offer our prayers to Him in saying: Celestial Father, etc.

* * *

All-powerful God, because we are nothing, indeed less than nothing, give us the grace that we know and recognize our poverty and indigence such as they are. May we renounce all the trust we have had in ourselves and our world, that we return to you in total humility. May we be seated in you, such that our trust be in you alone, and that you alone be glorified for all the goods we have received in this world as well as for our eternal salvation. May we remain fixated to you throughout all our life. May we persevere in invoking your name in total humility. May we, in this way, receive your aid and help not just once, but may we be assured that you will always assist those who invoke your name in good conscience, until finally we be filled with the plenitude of those goods assigned to us in the heavens above by Jesus Christ, our Lord. Amen.

(17) Thursday, July 25, 1549

As it is with the partridge who sits on eggs she did not hatch, so it is with him who amasses riches, but not by right. He will lose them in the midst of his days and will be found a fool in the end. Jeremiah 17.

Today we consider to be very smart those who know how to make big profits. This opinion is not unique to our day; for from all time those with great success in their affairs have been admired. The key to success is not to walk in simplicity, but to run with the wolf pack, if you can, so that absolutely anything goes. On the contrary, the Holy Spirit reveals that although those who amass great fortunes are much admired, they will be ridiculed, frustrated in their efforts, and will not enjoy the booty they acquired by evil means. God lands a double punishment on those who take the sustenance of others for themselves: They will have no joy; and however it is their intention and however it may seem that God is bound to let them enjoy themselves, they will be frustrated in their efforts, and time after time God will make manifest their shame. They are like the partridge who covers eggs she did not hatch. Why? Our Lord reveals that creatures, although they have no feelings, know well to escape from the hands of robbers, as the small partridges know well that it is not their mother covering them and know how to escape back to their own mother. Thus, the partridge, who took such pains to cover eggs not her own, believes to have possession of the small ones and does enjoy herself in that; but soon, she becomes upset, seeing that they leave her. That is what happens to those whose only passion is to possess great riches. Although they believed they would take great delight in the riches that they amassed fraudulently, these slip through their fingers and escape from their hands. But how? Why? We believe nothing, unless we have experienced it. Well! We certainly do see that however hard they worked to amass a fortune, God will carry it off immediately. Or, if they live to a ripe old age, they never have any contentment. When they have amassed as much as possible, they are famished and feel that they are lacking things. And they dare not use anything that they have, because it is necessary to conserve on this, it is necessary to conserve on that. They are like a man who has bread before his face but dare not eat it. We can say to them, "Sit, partridge! Sit and watch while the others sleep. You will never enjoy your goods!" Besides all this, it is necessary their folly be discovered: Those who amass great fortunes put their own necks in the noose and those of their children as well. They give their children reason to go sour, for there will always be men after them who make them believe that they are idols. They will become spendthrifts, so that soon their fortunes are all depleted. Because they have neither the knowledge nor the skill to earn their own livelihood and because they do not wish to work, they will become robbers and brigands. That is how the children will make quick work of the goods their fathers worked so hard to amass. And not only will their fortunes be gone, but they will be syphilitic and full of evil, and, as I have said, they will rob. "To the gallows, to the gallows!" That is how those who were so ardent to gain great wealth will be embarrassed before men and before God. When one sees them, one will say, "Is it not a great pity that these men worked so hard for the ruin of themselves and their children? If they had not been so obsessed, God would have put His blessing on them and their work. Yet, they worked so hard. And all this because God put a curse on them!" The prophet gives us this example of the partridge in order that we heed this warning early and wherever and whenever we see that riches are the occasion of ruin, both to those who amassed them and to their children, and also in order that we come to recognize how obsessed men are with their greed. God put this curse on them to teach us to be content with His own good will. Let each of us live in all modesty. Let those who have much realize that this is nothing unless God blesses it. Let them know that God gave them goods to aid neighbors and not to devour them. Let those with hardly anything at all know that it is still enough for themselves and their children. Let us all recognize that all the goods in the world amount to nothing unless God blesses them.

After the prophet reproaches the Jews that they could not be harder, he says, "O Lord, your glorious high Throne from the beginning is our sanctuary, the hope of Israel. Those who abandon you will be confused," as if he were saying, "God has revealed Himself to us and has His Throne in Jerusalem. But what good is all this if the men are cursed? Is it not fitting that they are such brutes? In this the prophet shows that the condemnation of the people will be so much the greater in that they do not honor God as they should. Today, since God has His Throne among us, just as He has His majesty in the heavens above, He wishes to be honored by us. Let us not be guilty of such a curse as the prophet speaks of. Let us diligently attend to the words of the prophet, for we see today that this curse is within us. God does not have a material throne. Nor is He to be found in a certain place as He was in Jerusalem. It is by His Gospel that we know He is our sovereign King. The Throne of Heaven refers to the fact that our Lord does not wish us to be bound to the earth. He gives us His Gospel because He wishes to take us on high. That is why the Gospel is called the Kingdom of Heaven. It is a solemn consecration in order that He may reign in the midst of us. Although there is no material temple as in Jerusalem, there is a greater one. Although there is no consecration as that made by Aaron and Solomon, we have the blood of Jesus Christ. Trust in God alone! If we run after creatures and are deceived by corruptible things (although God reveals He has the perfection of all goods and neither profits nor gains from us), what does this mean, save that we are culpable? Will this not be occasion to say among ourselves, "O glorious Throne, those who have abandoned you will be confused"? One could certainly say of us, "They wished to have this honor, but they threw it away by their malice. Worse yet, they are addicted to all sorts of filth. Where is this consecration?" All the honors that God has bestowed upon us will become the charges in our trial in order to set the sentence of condemnation upon us. Let us pay God homage as our King. He wishes to have such eminence among us, not only because He wishes His Gospel preached, but because He wishes to consecrate us by washing away the pollutions of this world. Let us depart from the filth of this world as well as from our evil cupidity, so that He may multiply His grace in us. May His eminence be as radiant in this world as it will be on the Last Day.

The prophet says, "Lord, those who abandon you will be confused, for they have abandoned the fountain of living water: You, Lord!" He has said that the Throne of the Lord was glorious and that it was called the Sanctuary. To show the great perversity in those who abandon God, he says, "They have abandoned you, who are the hope of Israel." In this, he shows us that having God for ourselves is reason for us to be content, for we have the Throne of Glory. We have the same will of God towards us as had the Jews. In brief, "we are the true Israel," as Saint Paul says. Of what benefit is the teaching you have listened to all these days, save that you become fully rooted in God? Let none say, "I am looking hither and yon because I do not see any salvation!" Alas, we cannot say that, for God has not abandoned us. Showing that we have good reason to stick to God, he says, "Those who turn from Him will be confused and unhappy." Thus the prophet speaks of "the hope of Israel" to emphasize the great ingratitude of the people. Infidels who have never been taught are not inexcusable in their infidelity. If they lust after creatures, they are condemned. Our condemnation, then, is double: If the infidels are punished, what will happen to us who have done as much or even more evil than those who never sensed God's love? The prophet says, "They will be confused." Since we heard in another passage that those who have never heard of God are without excuse because nature taught them well enough that there was a Creator, we know that those who turn from God to follow after superstitions will be condemned. Furthermore, are not those who abandon God after knowing Him worse than those who never knew God? Let us drink in well the words of the prophet when he says, "Those who have abandoned you"; for we are perjurers and disloyal when we turn from His doctrine.

The prophet says that "they departed," to emphasize more strongly their ingratitude; for if they departed from God, they were once close to Him. Saint Paul says that the Jews had an intimate relationship with God. This is why the prophet says, "Lord, those who departed from you." Note, then, that the more we know God, the closer we come to Him. It is not enough to take one step towards Him; we must take a second and a third. We must aim that "God be all and in all things," as Saint Paul says. Let us harken to the words of Saint Paul: "I look to the things before me, forgetting past things and looking to what is approaching me." Will one not mock a man who thinks that he has marched far enough and stops to rest in the middle of the road?

Nevertheless, that is what men do. After hearing the truth, they turn from it and go astray. Why? They knew not to profit at the opportune moment. Let us not make this same mistake. When we see evil, let us not participate in it. Does it not seem that we have conspired against God? Why does He give us preaching, save to attract us to Himself? He holds us in His hands, as Isaiah says. But each of us is obsessed with his own glory in this and that. We do not bother to remember God's teaching after we have heard it. Many do not wish to give ear. Even though we are here for the purpose of instruction, our minds wander off the topic and build castles in Spain. Instead of approaching God, we distance ourselves more and more from Him. God sustains us, but we abuse His patience. If we do not wish to fall into the confusion the prophet threatens, let us strive to approach Him closer and closer; for those who stray from Him "will be written in the earth."

The prophet gives the reason, saying that "they have abandoned the river of living waters." Do not those who reject the living fountain before them merit dying of thirst? Is it that after we come to know God as the fountain of living water, we wish to dig cisterns for ourselves? Why? These are such leaky containers. If we turn from God, who is the fountain of life, and look to our cisterns, we will find only mud; for although there was some appearance of water in the beginning, it all leaked out. Let us attend to our task. Now, as that has already been addressed, let us move on. Our Lord is called a fountain; but this is not a title He shares with other fountains; it is unique to Him alone. When God refers to His majesty, that applies to Him alone. That is what we must note in the first place. He is called the fountain of living waters because He will never dry up. Each who comes to the fountain will be nourished and there will always be more. God's grace does not grow or diminish in itself, but it appears to grow before our very eyes. Now this fountain was not put under ground or hidden. All can get to it. The prophet admonishes us to search for God in all that sustains us in the world and not elsewhere. His hand is as extended as the sky is large. When the sun shines, that is due to no other reason except that God has His hand there. When the waters give fish and the earth gives fruit, it is God who has His hand there to give us what we need. Because we must search for all our goods in Him, He is called the fountain of living waters. Let us not fear that God becomes depleted in His goods when He gives us more. Let us not imagine God to be like men, who, when they give much, have little left to give. It is not that way with God. Let us not doubt that this fountain will persevere for us in life and in death. Not only has He goods enough to sustain our lives, but--and this is the third point--He does not wish His waters to be hidden. True, if we searched for God in His majesty, that would refer us to an underground source; for who can climb high enough to God to find Him in His majesty? Why? Has He not revealed Himself in Jesus Christ? That is why it is said that He is from the beginning the life and that He has the plenitude of all goods, so that all that we have was taken from Him grace by grace. Although God is always manifest by His Word, He has appeared to us in Jesus Christ, so that we do not say, "Where must we search for His grace? We must have wings!" No, no! All we must do is open our mouths, that is, give God entrance into us through our faith. God wishes to enter only by His teaching. Let us give Him entry there. When our Lord says that He is the fountain of living waters, that does not mean that His goods are hidden from us, but that they are given us, provided that we search for them in Jesus Christ.

When the prophet wishes to magnify the ingratitude of those to whom God revealed Himself, he says, "O Lord, heal me and I will be healed. Save me and I will be saved, for you are my praise." This signifies the temptation of the faithful when they see people turn from God. What will happen here when men turn from God's teaching? The faithful are in danger of following their example. The Word of God is to be preached, not in a single place, but everywhere. Yet the Papists are such enemies of the children of God that they wish to destroy them all. The Word of God is to no avail in them. And in us? The majority of us are hypocrites who mock bitterly the Word. Those who did show some zeal for God for a time are now wilder than brutal beasts. We have the same scandals that the prophet had in his time. We would decline, save that we have recourse to God, as did the prophet. That is why we must say, "Lord, heal me and I will be healed." When we see a pestilence we pray to God for the care of our bodies. When we see the earth deluged by iniquities, do we not fear that our souls are infected? Yet how many truly have this worry? Why? They see no need to pray to God that He not permit them to be led astray by these scandals. Jeremiah, who was as an angel among men, who had no other care then to lead all to God and to exalt God, knew that he was a fragile man who could be tempted by such scandals. If Jeremiah had this fear, what is the situation with ourselves? Let each look to himself. If the prophet saw that there was only disloyalty in men, that those who received knowledge of God turned from Him, do we not see this even more so in ourselves? Our Lord admonishes us by the signs of our times that we take shelter under His wing; for if we venture forth the least, we will be lost immediately. Let us pray to God, saying, "Lord, heal me," for Jeremiah himself was not exempt. Who among us can claim to be exempt from temptation? Although God has subdued natural imagination, it still has a grip on us. God must continually sound our hearts and continually purge us. First God sustains us and then He heals us, just as a physician gives a patient preservatives to keep him from falling ill again. That is how God works with us, for He is our spiritual physician, and even the most perfect among us are subject to temptation. God sustains us in order to heal us by His salutary remedy. Let us pray, then, as Jeremiah did. When Jeremiah beseeched God to heal him, it was not by fiction that he assumed God has what he needs. If we pray that God sustains and heals us, what happens with the free will of the Papists, Pagans, and all infidels? We see this free will is nothing but deceit. If we had a free will, we would be able to keep ourselves in good health. We would not hear the prophet saying, "Heal me and I will be healed." If man cannot help but fall, how can he raise himself up again? It is sheer deception that men will not bow their heads to subjugate themselves to God, thinking that they have the wherewithal to sustain themselves and to protect themselves, however God may protect them. The prophet attributes everything to God and confesses that we have nothing. When he says that "you are my praise," this signifies that if we wish God to protect us, we must not trust in ourselves. Let us go to Him, knowing that it is He alone who sustains all and so will sustain us.

Following this holy teaching, we prostrate ourselves before the face of our good God, in knowledge of our faults. We pray that, knowing all our goods are in Him, we will be inflamed to approach closer and closer to Him. We pray that He attract us by His Holy Spirit and preserve us from all the scandals today, which tempt us to infidelity. May He shed His grace not only on us but on all the peoples and nations of the earth, etc.

* * *

All-powerful God, may it please you to teach us to subjugate ourselves to you so that rich or poor we confess that our sole happiness and perfection depend upon you alone. May we cling to the salvation you have already let us savor, until we come to total joy of eternal rest, when we will share in the glory acquired for us by the blood of your only Son, our Lord, Amen.

(18) Friday, July 26, 1549

They say to me, "Where is the Word of the Lord? Let it come now. I am not too forward to be a pastor following you and I do not desire to see the day of affliction, as you know. Jeremiah 17.

It is a pity that we relish what God curses. We desire good, so it would seem, but we choose evil. Instead of our hearts being in the heavens above, we put them on earth. Each is inclined to some vice, as we know all too well. When God wishes to rain down severe punishment, He says that "the men will be written in the ground." Do we not see how deceived we are? The prophet says that "those who turn from God will be written into the ground" and that they will be as brutal beasts; for what we have on earth, we have in common with the beasts. God calls us to the heavens above. If we do not wish to go there, let us remain on earth with the dogs and other beasts. If we do not wish to approach God, we must remain on earth with the brutal beasts.

The prophet shows that men do not have the good sense to depart from the earth and cling to God. Indeed, men mock and vex God, as if they had nothing to fear from Him. They say, "Where is the Word of the Lord? You have said that He will smash down Jerusalem. Hah! Where is the Word? Let it come quickly!" It is an unpardonable blasphemy that men raise up against God. Yet the prophet saw this in his time. This pride still reigns among men today. Men still have the audacity to provoke God. If they do not say so, their life shows as much. Every day we are told the reasons why God is angered by our rebellion, but what has this led to? Has it not led us to vex God by not taking into account His Word? Yes, for if we believe His Word, we would be terrified. Why? When we do not take His Word seriously, it is a sign that we attribute no more importance to God than to a barking dog. We fear the dog might harm us; but here God speaks and we do not hear Him in our hearts; the sound of His words never reaches our ears. God has been defied from the time of the prophet until today. What is worse is that we have these mockers, or rather these vomiters of unpardonable blasphemies. When they are warned that God will tolerate no more from us without avenging himself, they poke fun and mock, saying, "Let them yell as much as they want. What authority have then to oppose us? Indeed! as if we spoke purely for ourselves and had not drawn upon the Word of God. True, those who vomit up such blasphemies think they are talking only to men, as they did at the time of Jeremiah; but they all know that they are speaking against God. We see their contempt for God when they try to provoke him by saying, "Let Him come,let Him come! What does He have to really show for all that He has to say?" This awful hardness and stubbornness is still with us today. When they are told it is with good reason that God will avenge Himself on them, they think that this will amount to nothing in the end. This admonishes us to be more reverent towards the Word of God. Whenever we hear His threats, let us be as frightened as if this had already happened. Let His Word carry weight with us as if the thing is present. If we do not do these things, let us heed that Jeremiah's sentence is laid upon us; for he proclaims that men to not fight against him, but against God. When we hear His threats, let us tremble before the Word, as Isaiah says. When God wishes to put His sign upon His children, He says that they tremble at His warnings. That is what we must do.

The prophet says that he "has not been too forward to be a pastor following God." Although this passage is not accurately translated, it carries the true meaning of the prophet's actual statement: "I have not hastened to be a pastor following you," as if he were saying, "I do not interfere in matters according to the whims of my imagination, but I follow only your vocation." He uses the word "pastor" to denote the charge he was given; for he is His prophet whom He wishes to exercise His charge and office, indeed without opposition, or rather by him demonstrating that he is not opposed to the Word of God. Here, then, is the prophet's intention: It is to demonstrate to those who hold his teaching in contempt that it is not only with him that they will have to reckon; for God will take matters in hand, insofar as he does not serve men but God. Let us note, then, that if we bear the Word of God, and if there is contempt in us, we will regard mortal men as those we wish to hurt, but that God is always their guarantor and will feel it is He that we wish to wound, for He is wounded in His Word when it is rejected.

Furthermore, we see here what is the office of a good governor: He does not interfere in matters on his own accord, but follows God, namely, his vocation. Now when the preacher is called to follow God, he is not merely called to preach, but to faithfully exercise his charge. After he receives the Word of God, he proclaims it and adds nothing of his own. When we are called in this charge, we have our charge through prophetic writings. We have only this commission to proclaim His Word; for when He ordained the Church, He ordained prophecy in order to instruct the people. It is the task of ministers to draw upon prophecies for warnings and corrections. That is the charge of pastors, that is, ministers. Those who exceed charge are no longer pastors; for who can say, "I am beyond Jeremiah and so have more to say than he"? Let us follow the Word; otherwise God will disavow us and we will not merit being heard in His Church. In brief, we have a beautiful passage here to distinguish between ministers of God and those who falsely usurp the title. If someone calls himself a prelate and does not preach the Word of God, he is not a pastor. All he will proclaim to us are lies, and what prelature is there in that? Prelates are condemned by the sentence of Jeremiah. Why? Where does the doctrine that they proclaim come from? It seems beneath their dignity to preach! When they do speak, what is it that they say? All lies! Insofar as they have a doctrine totally askance from the prophets, they must be rejected. Although such evil ones usurp the office of prelature, we will not be deceived; for if they teach the Word of God, they are prophets.

Furthermore, ministers must obey the Word of God. We cannot fight against them or reject them that we do not battle against God. Let us follow them in all humility. Whosoever does not wish to do so, let him understand that his business is not with a mortal man, but with God. Some will say, "Oh! We do not know if they lead us to God." That is all their fault; for the prophet proclaims that he serves the living God, that he is faithful to his office, and that you must know it is God with whom you must deal. It is a too frivolous excuse, then, to say, "Oh! I do not really know if they lead us to God"; for it is your malice and your ingratitude that block you from knowing. If you do not wish to open your eyes and look to God, can you really claim ignorance? Is this not rebellion? It is all our fault if we do not know whether the prophet speaks for himself or for God. If a preacher is faithful to the Word of God, we know that God sent him. If he abuses the name of God, we must reject him. God not only reveals to ministers what is their office, but He also reveals to all what ministers must be heard. If we are certain of all this, we will be much more obedient to the Word of God. Jeremiah and the other prophets all tell us that when we read their teaching, we must not take it as from men; for God inspired them in order that they lead us to Him. That is how prophetic teaching is assured, for Jeremiah speaks not only for himself but for all the other prophets that God commissioned.

Jeremiah continues, "Lord, I have not desired to see the day of affliction, as you know." In saying this, he is protesting that he foresaw his worldly state would be full of hate. He who is in the office of ministry must prepare for war. Even those who loved us come to have a grudge against us when we reproach them for their vices; otherwise, we would not be servants of God, as Saint Paul says. If we wish to lead men to God, we must do them violence, which is repugnant to our nature. That is why the majority will be angered by us as if we did them a great wrong. In sum, the Word of God bears with it this reality: If we are faithful to it, we will be persecuted. Indeed, we see this persecution today; but it is the case not just today but always. The prophets, apostles and martyrs were all persecuted. Although the evil ones do not always have a sword specifically designed to destroy the faithful, they have always raged against ministers of the Word of God. Those who seek the office of minister are sadly deceived, for they seek war against themselves. I mean, those who seek this office because it seems like easy work are deceived. Saint Paul said that whoever desires to be a bishop must work as much as possible and will be paid by grumbling and threats. When God loosens the bridle on evildoers, he must put up with it. Regarding reason, the situation is all too obvious: You cannot faithfully serve God without turning topsy turvy all the wisdom of the world and all the sanctity claimed by men. Men are of the foolish presumption that they know how they must be governed. On the contrary, God says, "Listen to me, for you are only beasts." We bear the Word of God, and He wishes it to be heard in all modesty; yet men are quick to defend themselves by professing their seemingly good intentions. That is how men always respond against the ministers of the Word of God. It seems to them that God is well taken with them when they mumble about all morning. We preach to them that, on the contrary, there is no way to come to salvation than by knowing their confusion. We say, "Look to the grace of God and pay no attention to yourselves." Because we stand against the sanctity of the world, that is to say, against its hypocrisy, we will always have these battles.

Then there is the matter of our evil appetites. Some say, "Indeed, we must obey God. But why?" Those given to avarice, those given to adultery, those given to drunkenness do not wish the minister to speak of their vices. If you cry out against adultery, the adulterers will rise up and say, "Oh, are you speaking to us when you cry out against adultery?" If you cry out against evil dealings, another group rises up. If you cry out against licentiousness, that you would rather be dressed in sack cloth than to be adorned by vices, another group will rise up and say, "Hah! Does it not seem that he has a grudge against us? This is too much!" This is how a thousand enemies come to be against the ministers of the Word.

The prophet says that he "has not desired to see the day of affliction." Why? He is referring to the stubbornness of the people, who say, "Oh! He has always threatened us and yet we are safe, which goes to show that he has no power against us!" The prophet says, "Lord, I have not desired the day of affliction," as if he were saying, "They hate me because I proclaim your judgment. They blame everything on me, as if I were the cause of all their troubles." That is how it is today; what we see today is a good illustration of this prophecy. When we cry out against the evils of the world, do not people respond the same way? Can we expect God's blessing when we anger Him daily by slamming the door in His face? Since the world is so depraved, all that those with the office of instruction can say is: "Look at what you have done. You have been warned for a long time and yet you get worse and worse. How you have abused God's long-standing patience." But the people will reply, "How they relish our destruction. Does this preacher of the Word wish that too? Should they not proclaim salvation and remission of our sins?" Nevertheless you see the threats of God before your very eyes and this makes you groan. You wish to blame us for everything. We can say along with the prophet Micah, "I am not the cause of your ruin; your sins are. Blame yourselves for your suffering, for I cannot help it. Far from being the cause of your affliction, I am the one who warned you, that God not avenge Himself upon you!" Let us examine matters from the standpoint of the layman. If we are iniquitous, is it not the office of God to punish us rebels? God does not fail to have his hand armed against us. When He threatens us, it is to return us to Himself. If we are such ingrates that we blame the evil that befalls us on the teaching and warnings of God, do we not anger Him? When warned of impending doom that must befall us, let us know to blame ourselves and not God's teaching. God would rather be merciful than to torment us. Let us take Him warnings as medicines for our salvation. Let us not rail in anger against Him, but obey Him, recognizing that we have failed Him.

Furthermore, the prophet says that "what comes from my mouth is before you." Now, there are two things we must note here. First, here is what ministers, who are charged with the office of instruction, must know in their hearts: God charged me with His Word, that I say nothing except that it comes from Him. I know that I am accountable for all that I say; I know that He has given me His Word for me to serve it in order that I and others profit by it. The second is that ministers profess a doctrine approved of by God. Now, God approves only what He says. Men must not mix in their own words with the Word of God, for that would be just so much pollution. True, God has not commissioned us merely to recite Scripture, but to reveal His will. When we apply Scripture to this end, we must be careful not to corrupt it by our glosses, as is the case in Papism, where they have made Scripture into a nose of wax, as they say, that they can twist and turn as they so desire. Here is an unpardonable blasphemy that not even Satan would dare utter. Nevertheless, this is a fundamental principal of their doctrine.

One can see, then, that all their doctrines serve only as means to lead men to Hell. Nevertheless, when one speaks of

Scripture to them, they say that there is no certitude and that one can make of it as one wishes. But God does not give us uncertainty; God gives us truth. If we do not reject His Word, we well readily know that He is saying and have a very facile exposition of Scripture.

Furthermore, let us recognize that the prophet does not speak only for himself; he condemns all those who rebel against his teaching and says that they will be without excuse before God. Why? Because he has not turned from his vocation, but exercises it as God so charged. He says this in order that men know with whom they are dealing, that they recognize that they do not stand against one man but against God. He strives to convince men that if they do not know the will of God, it is all their fault. He strives to eliminate all occasions of excuse making by saying, "Hah! How am I to now if he preaches the true doctrine of God?" It is not without reason that Scripture is called "the lamp to guide us." As Moses said, "Here is the true way." We see, then, the deceit of men today who think that by following the blind they will not fall, that they can falsify the passage in Scripture where it says that "if the blind lead the blind, both will fall in the ditch." Nevertheless, they would like nothing better than to fall, and it seems to them that they are exempt from having to confess that they are beasts knowingly. Why? "Since we have lived by this tradition up to now," they will say, "why will we not prolong our days?" We see their deceit. Since our doctrine is true, all those who go against us must be condemned. We know what value to place upon doctrines that come from men. It is certain that truth comes only from God, so we are certain that we must hold to it alone.

Furthermore, if we wish to make ourselves out to be wiser than we are, by mixing in the dreams of men with the Word of God, it is certain that we will not have truth but total corruption. We must hold to those things which our Lord taught us. He taught us truth, so let us hold to it. Furthermore, He taught us sufficiently for our salvation. Therefore, anyone who is discontent with His teaching or who does not hold with it shows that he is a rebel. Such persons would have it appear that God has not taught us our ABCs and that the Pope was the first expositor and more sufficient than God. They would give us a doctrine forged by the Devil himself. All those who would follow them are evildoers. On the Last Day, they will well recognize that God values His Word far more than all the excuses they bring.

Following this holy teaching, let us prostrate ourselves before the face of our good God. Let us pray that, because He wishes only to return us to Himself, He does not permit Satan and his supporters to lead us astray. May He give us the grace to hear His doctrine. May He give us the grace to recognize that we must adhere to His doctrine for our salvation. May He give us the grace to recognize that outside of His Word there is only His curse. May He shed His grace not only on us but on all the peoples and nations of the world, etc.

(19) Saturday, July 27, 1549

The Lord said to me, "Go and stand in the gate of the children of the people, by which the kings of Judah enter and exit, go and stand in all the gates of Jerusalem and say to them, 'Hear the Word of the Lord.'" Jeremiah 17.

Yesterday we looked at the prophet's prayer. He continues it, saying, "Lord, do not terrify me. Let me be not confused, but confuse my enemies." Let us note that the servants of God will always be terrified when they see the evil ones rise up against them, even though they know that God sustains them. Ministers of the Word of God are taught that they must do battle and that they would lose were it not for the fact that God sustains them. When we can do nothing more, let us arm ourselves with prayers and that will be sufficient. When we see ourselves so afflicted and about to lose because of our great infirmity, the only solution is recourse to prayer. This passage is worthy of careful note. One is willing enough to preach the Word of God before the blows land; but when the blows start landing, there is not a one who will not be lost. I speak of assaults, not only in terms of iron swords and matchlocks, but in terms of all the machinations thrown against ministers of the Word of God, which make them well wish to quit. Thus, as I have said, here is a passage worthy of note in order that none go to pieces when terrible things happen. Why? The prophet himself was frightened by these things. Since we encounter these` things in the service of God, we have nothing to fear; for the prophet says, "Lord, do not terrify me, for you are my hope in the day of my adversary." This must be our prayer; for the prophet is not driven by his own carnality; but, driven by the Spirit of God, he beseeches God not to terrify him. We are certain that God will grant us the victory over all opponents, provided that we stand upon His promises; nevertheless it is still necessary to pray. The promise God made the prophet is certain. Not only will we be defended so that we do not succumb, but the evil ones will be confounded, however it may have seemed to them that they could not be crushed. Let us wait in patience; for in the end, God will not tolerate that they battle against His ministers without avenging Himself. This assurance is not only for ministers but for all the faithful. God will fortify them in death such that they will be victorious. When the evil ones come to judgment before God, they will undergo a torment well different from what they force the faithful to endure. God sweetens the torment of the faithful in that they know that it is for His glory and for the certitude of their salvation that they endure such torment. The evil ones will feel the hand of God upon them and will be unable to dodge it. Not only do the ministers of God have what they need to arm themselves by confidence, but all the faithful can be assured that God will sustain them to the end, though they be in enemy hands. Is it not sufficient consolation that God promises to give us a glorious heavenly crown and that even in the midst of death He strengthens us such that we will not fail? In this, we have all that we need to console ourselves and to be comfortable in following our vocation.

The prophet reveals that the enemies he had were not Pagans, nor those who make a profession out of rejecting the Law of God, but the very people he was commissioned to serve as a prophet. He says that there was such rebellion that the people stiffened their necks and hardened themselves against what he had to say. Here is what he says about his situation: First, he says that he had been sent by God to the largest gate, by which the kings of Judah entered, in order that his public presentation was more solemn. From there, he had to go to gate after gate, that none excuse themselves by ignorance. In order that none could excuse themselves this way, he had been commanded by God to go from gate to gate, for then all his acts would be public. It is as if today someone were sent to all the gates of this city and then to the lands of Mollard and Fusterye. Now it is said that not only will the prophet speak to the people but to the kings and that he will say, "You, kings of Judah, and you, residents of Jerusalem, who enter by these gates here, the Lord says to you: 'Guard your souls; bear no burdens on the day of rest to bring them through the gates of Jerusalem. Do not venture from your homes with burdens on the day of rest, but sanctify the day of rest, as I commanded your fathers.'" All were reproached, for all were at fault.

For what reason does the prophet reproach them? They had not observed the day of rest. It seems like this is a small thing, but so much the greater is their ingratitude; for if we do not obey God in small matters, hardly will we keep His commandments in regard to important ones. The point is not merely to observe the seventh day, called the day of rest, but what truth is signified by this. To clearly understand this passage, it is necessary to know why God commanded the day of rest. God makes severe threats against transgressors, and we see in Ezekiel that those who had not observed the day of rest were sharply reprimanded. Why? Is it a greater sin to work on a holiday than to commit adultery? Now, as I have said, our Lord does not regard the ceremony but that which it represents, as He says in Ezekiel and in Exodus Thirty-One: "I am your God, who sanctifies you." Now it is no small matter that God reveals that He sanctifies us, that we will not perish with the infidels. Despite the curse which is upon all the sons of Adam, God put this sign of sanctification upon us. Despite Satan putting his mark upon the human specie, God gave us this sign of sanctification. Would it not, then, be an unpardonable ingratitude for us to reject it? That is why the day of rest is commanded. To violate it is to reject God's grace. It is to say, "We no longer wish to be His nor to be His Church." Now it is certain that this would be a greater evil than larceny, adultery, or any other vice. Why? Because it is necessary that the rest follow when there is no longer any knowledge of God. As God says through his prophet, "Blood will touch blood," since all have vomited blood and the larcenists have been without measure.

Now the point here is that all evil comes from the fact that there was no knowledge of God. To refuse God's sign is worse than committing adultery; for then one renounces God, and all evil is contained in this renouncement.

Now this word "sanctification" needs further explication. As I have said, God separates us from the other peoples when he sanctifies us, not that He takes us by the arms, but that He joins us to Himself. This is the sanctification which is signified by the day of rest. Scripture calls this sanctification the mortification of the flesh by which our chaotic appetites are abated and so no longer reign in us. God reforms us by His Holy Spirit, that we do no other thing than His will. That is the sanctification God works in us. We see, then, in sum, that this sanctification of rest consists of two things. The first is that our evil appetites no longer dominate. The second is that we no longer desire, but the Spirit desires within us and leads us there where we must go. That is the truth of the day of rest. Therefore, God said, "You will do no work whatsoever on this day." Yes, Lord, for we are yours! It was certainly work to go to the Temple and read the Law; but God does not forbid His works, only the works of man. This day was made for sacrifices, prayers, meditations on the good things that God has done for man, to edify one another. The works of God are not a stumbling block to the sanctification of the day of rest. The Apostle says that it is "a spiritual rest, that man abstain from work." It is necessary for God to continue His works, but we must cease ours. When we see what is the meaning of true rest, is that no small consolation? When we see ourselves to attain such perfection, does that not move us for more? It is certain. That is why God rested the seventh day. Therefore, He commanded us to sanctify this day of rest, when men mortify themselves and try to eliminate all stumbling blocks to God's working in us, for there is a resistance between man and God as between water and fire. If men are employed at their tasks, God is rejected. If God is to reign, man must be abated. Now we see that the day of rest must be a spiritual observance, in which man no longer gives himself the liberty of doing what he wants but accommodates himself to God in order that He have dominion over all. That is what is signified by a day which has been called the day of rest. Since this spiritual remorse should be observed every day, why has our Lord sanctified only the seventh? It is not necessary that the symbol correspond exactly to the truth; and God in this day wished to signify to us eternal rest, as if He were saying, "In this day, you will not be given to yourselves, for I will lead you by the Holy Spirit, that you be led as is fitting." That is what God wishes to signify by the day of rest. We have good reason to rest from our works to allow Him to do His; for as long as we are in this world, there will be no perfection. Although a horse may be prompted to go when he is spurred, sometimes he is rebellious. So it is with us. Although we may want what God wishes, there will always be some resistance. Therefore, we will never be able to accomplish this spiritual rest as we should. That is why we must observe this commandment to rest on a certain day.

It is true that this symbol was abolished with the coming of Christ, as Saint Paul declared to the Colossians and the Romans. If we are locked into this custom, that is by lack of intelligence. The matter is more fully stated in Colossians: God has brought us out of the shadows because we have the truth. Saint Paul says that we must abandon these symbols, for we are no longer children and these symbols were our ABCs.

Thus the observance of the Sabbath is not commanded as strictly as it was before the coming of Christ. True, we have a day of rest, but not like the Jews, even though they have Saturday, which was their seventh day. Why is it that Sunday is now our day of rest? It is to show the freedom we have acquired through Jesus Christ. But the crudeness of man makes this impossible to understand. It is very necessary to have a day of rest, not as a ceremony according to the Law but as a day of refinement. The Sabbath was not only commanded of the Jews to teach them mortification of the flesh but also to civilize them by their coming to the Temple to hear the Law. It is good that preachers preach daily, as in fact they do. But, because many do not come to Church on work days, it was necessary to ordain a day when they must assemble at the temple. This made it compulsory attendance for those stubborn asses who would not attend unless forced to do so. It could well be called the Day of Asses. It serves to admonish us that we must treat others in a humane and civilized manner, that we must not overburden our servants. God says, "Remember that you have been in servitude and God delivered you." This means that we must not be tyrants and treat cruelly our subordinates. Our Lord makes this commandment not only for the treatment of men but also for the treatment of beasts, and He ordains that we allow them to rest. Since we have the care of beasts, it is our responsibility to rest them. These are the reasons why these observances were commanded of the Jews as well as of ourselves; for the civilizing of man is perpetual task. The Sabbath is mandatory today in order to compel asses to attend temple and to admonish them to treat gently their subordinates, not only this day but every day; for God does not wish people to be overburdened. It is also mandatory in order that men do not have occasion to go astray. Although Sunday is the day of rest, we must make all our days Sundays. Although the other days are called work days, we must make nothing, however it is that we need work to support ourselves and our families. What would our lot be if we did not have Sunday?

Now let us compare ourselves with the Jews to see how these things pertain to us. If the Jews were reprimanded for not observing the day of rest, how much more will be condemned when each of us gives himself the freedom to do whatever he pleases; for the Jews had only a shadow. What does it amount to when we pollute the day of sanctification, which must be observed throughout all our life? It amounts to rejecting God, as we have said. When we have rejected God and do not wish Him to reign in us, what happens then? If we do not rest from the appetites of our flesh all the days of our lives, God will have reason to complain and His sentence is already upon us. What, then, must we do? Let each make his neck pliable to obey God and let each give ear when He says, "Hear me!" There is no Christianity in us until we renounce ourselves. We must not measure the commandments of God, whatever they may be, according to our standards and values. That which seems of no importance among us may carry great weight in the eyes of God. Let us not measure things, as I have just said, according to our values, which we are accustomed to doing. Let us confess that God commanded this day of rest and that we have done otherwise. Why? The commandments of God may seem like a small thing to us. But, as I have said, let us not measure it according to our standards. In the Gospel it says that "whosoever belittles the least of these commandments and teaches other men to do likewise will be called a transgressor in the Church of God." If we wish to do this, God will hardly be taken with us. Indeed, He will have good reason to belittle us because we have belittled Him. Now it is not necessary to attend to a commandment in itself, but it is necessary to regard who speaks, who is the legislator. Since it is God who speaks, we can be certain that the commandment is no small matter. Let us act accordingly, so that the commandments of God have great weight in our eyes and we hold back on our presumptuousness to think that what God says is no important matter. There is the remedy for which we search.

Now the Jews forgot this commandment, so it is certain they also forgot God. Indeed, if we think that we can get away with being nonchalant when we come to temple, we are deceiving ourselves; for it is not enough that we receive baptism and communion. No, no! Anyone like Judas could receive them, but what would this profit them? Absolutely nothing. True, the sermon is not the main thing. But will those who do not come to hear it be excused? No! They will say, "I did not go hear the sermons. I do not understand how those who do have the time for it." They think that this is a valid excuse. But those who do not come for the sermon or take communion show well that Jesus Christ is nothing to them. Their contempt for these signs shows their contempt for the truth. When the prophet reprimands the Jews, he is not thinking of ceremonies but of the truth. Thus, today, when the sacraments are held in such contempt, let us say as strongly as we can, and in as much as God has said so: "Indeed, you do not take baptism seriously? That is a sign you do not prize the blood of His Son. You do not take communion? That is a sign that you do not value the redemption He made for you." Not only will we be reprimanded for polluting the Sabbath but also for lacking reverence towards the sacraments. It pleases God to have this great assembly here, provided that it performs its functions. When we have a baptism here, some of you walk around, others chat with one another. This is a good illustration that we do not prize this sign, which also means that we do not believe in the truth of this sign and that the redemption Christ made for us is truly nothing to us. None of you can come to communion without having to be chastised for blasphemies and adulteries. Well we show that we do not prize the truth, which is Jesus Christ, when we hold this sign in such contempt. Therefore, we will be reproached that the sacraments were of no importance to us.

Furthermore, it is said that the prophet went "to all the gates," to show that it was necessary for him to speak to everyone. This means that God wished none to claim ignorance. When the clock sounds today, that serves to condemn all those who do not come hear the sermon. God wishes to speak to us, yet we do not wish to take a step! There is no doubt that we will be reproached before God. Why is there an ordinance to preach the Word of God every day at the same time and place? To eliminate all ignorance. Let each profit, so that none have complaint against us and so that we merit not condemnation.

Following this holy teaching, let us prostrate ourselves before the face of our good God, in knowledge of our faults. Let us pray that He not permit us to be hardened but that He make our necks pliable to obey Him. We pray that, insofar as all we do is blame-worthy, we learn to accommodate ourselves to Him and to obey Him. We pray that, as we say "His kingdom come," He give us the grace that we all desire to obey Him. May He shed His grace not only on us but on all the peoples and nations of the earth, etc.

* * *

All powerful God, because you were not content only to send prophets in times past but wish that daily your will be revealed to us, give us the grace that we may be instructed by you and accommodate ourselves to you. We pray that we bear your yoke so peacefully that your holy Word is received by us with the reverence it merits. May we be subjugated to you and made to understand your will through men, that finally we may enjoy the presence and sight of your glory, in which consists our perfect bliss. May we not only contemplate your glory face to face but may we also hear yourself speak, indeed in such a manner that we find our contentment in this sweetness that we wait upon in hope, through Jesus Christ, our Lord. Amen.

(20) Monday, August 5, 1549

"If you hear me," says the Lord, "and if you bring no burden through the gates of the city on the day of rest, and if you sanctify the day of rest, so that one does no work on that day, the kings and princes seated on the throne of David will enter by the gates of this city." Jeremiah 17.

We have seen why our Lord so strongly commanded the day of rest and have seen what this ceremony signified at the time of the Law, namely, that God revealed to the Jews by this day of rest that He sanctified them to be His own, as it says in Exodus and Ezekiel. The Jews, then, were separated from others, in order to be God's own. We also said that it was necessary for us to be sanctified and that we must not be governed by our own spirit but subjugate ourselves to God in order that He governs us throughout our entire life. Therefore, we see that this ceremony of rest was a great sign at the time of the Law. That is why God complains bitterly when it is profaned and violated; for this is a sign that we do not wish to live in obedience to Him. We have shown that if we are contemptuous towards the sacraments, which bear spiritual significance, we have not taken seriously God, who ordained them. If we hold baptism in contempt, we have not taken into account the blood of Jesus Christ and therefore do not know what it is to be a Christian. If we do not take communion as we should, we are as culpable of the death of Jesus Christ as if we have murdered Him, although his body and blood are not within our grasp, and we are also culpable of having dishonored Him. Now, it is true that the day of rest is not as strictly commanded of us as it was in the time of the Law, but that is because we have the truth which it represents. Let us, then, subdue our will and all our passions, is that God may reign in us. If we do that, we will be sustained and protected by Him, and He will take us in His hand. If, on the contrary, we wish to act like runaway horses and live according to our carnality, we can be certain that He will well chastise us and that we will pay the price according to the master we serve, namely, Satan.

Furthermore, although we do not have to observe the Sabbath, we are commanded to observe a day of rest. True, we must cease and desist from our own works everyday, but this is especially true on the day of rest. Nevertheless, there are so many nonchalant ones that will not come to the temple unless they are forced. Therefore, God wished there be a day upon which all Christians would rest from their labors to devote themselves to His service. It is not that God is served by our laziness but that He wished there to be a day upon which we would have the leisure to devote ourselves to prayers and orisons and to come together to confess our faith. God, then, ordained the day of rest in order that, not being preoccupied in our tasks, we could come to temple. Now, if we do not observe this practice, we show well that we do not take God seriously. When Sunday rolls around, those who were unable to leave the city all week because of their businesses wish to have a festival to show off their wares. Others, who did not have a chance to play all week, devote Sundays to pleasurable outings. They seem to think that the day of rest was ordained expressly for them to take up their favorite pastimes. When it becomes a question of sanctifying a holiday, we have not taken God into account.

Now, it is a very bad sign for us when we do not observe this regulation. Our Lord rested on the seventh day to teach us to sanctify this day of rest. He rested on the seventh day, not because He was tired, but to teach us to follow His example. Just as God made the world in six days, He incessantly works everyday to sustain and govern the world. Our Lord, Jesus Christ, said that if "God did not sustain the world, it would return to nothing." Christ, then, did not cease work on the seventh day because He was tired, but because He wanted to set an example for us. When we see the sky that lights us and heats the earth so it can produce, when we see the earth which produces the fruits for our nourishment, and when we see that God not only has care of us but of all the birds of the air and beasts of the field, we cannot help but be moved to praise Him, seeing all the care and love He bears us. This is how we must be motivated to know His bounty and wisdom. This is how we come to love Him and fear Him with so much the more passion. Our Lord rested from His works in order to arouse us to examine them.

If men stop to contemplate the works of God, they come to love Him so much the more. Now, if we do not do this, if instead of contemplating all the good things He has given us, we go off on the day of rest to take up our pastimes, our frolics and vices, it is certain that He will not tolerate this without avenging Himself. Thus it is said, "If you hear me and if you bring no burden through the gates of the city on the day of rest, and if you sanctify the day of rest, so that one does no work on that day, the kings and princes seated on the throne of David will enter by the gates of this city, and this city will be inhabited forever." When we hear our Lord make this promise to the Jews, let us pay heed that if we do not have the Sabbath, we have its truth. If we observe the day of rest, our Lord will multiply His grace in us. But, if we disobey His ordinance, He will consume us all in an inextinguishable fire. Now, after we have ceased all work, we must be careful to observe the regulations, namely, that God be served and honored among us. Let us frequent hold assemblies, attend prayer meetings of the faithful. Let us learn, I say, to observe this ordinance, which is to put us under the yoke of God. If we do so, we will not doubt that as we have received God's grace in the past, so we shall receive even more ever afterwards.

Furthermore, when our Lord says that "the kings will be seated on the throne of David" and adds that "people will come from the cities of Judah and from all the surrounding lands to offer sacrifices in Jerusalem," He had two things in mind, which are the basic principles of all mortal life. First, we must have magistrates according to His will. Secondly, we must have an ecclesiastical order over us, so that we are ready to obey Him in all matters. These are the two principal blessings that we should desire, so the prophet lumps them together here. It is not without reason that he says, "The kings will be seated on the throne of David"; for this is the kingdom God has sanctioned, as we know. Furthermore, there is one other consideration: This kingdom signifies Jesus Christ, for it was said that "until the coming of Christ into world, the Kingdom of Jerusalem had been in the hands of Judah." Now Judah was not the son whelped by Jacob. Nevertheless, God gave him this blessing. That is why this kingdom did not cease until the coming of Christ. That is why the angel says to the Virgin Mary that "the child you bear will sit upon the throne of David." That is also why the prophet says that "the kings will enter by the gates of Jerusalem and will sit upon the throne of David," as if he were saying, "If you observe and sanctify the day of rest, our Lord will fulfill the promise He made you that you will always have kings from the House of Judah, that no tyrants will come to usurp authority over you, but that you will have kings that God has elected to reign over you to guard and protect you from your enemies and to be as your shield against all others."

There are two things that we must understand from this passage. The first is that we will never have good magistrates unless God has elected them, as He had elected the House of David to reign over the Jews. The reason why kings, princes, and magistrates perpetuate so much evil is that they were not elected by God. Insofar as our Lord did not elect them, this means that they came to power by themselves. For this reason, they show that they have not come to govern but to destroy. True, tyrants always give some appearance of justice; but they exercise their cruelty against men in order that men come to think that their well-being and good government depends upon none other than the tyrant himself. That is the first point. The second is that God does us no small favor when He gives us good magistrates. People are often destitute. Why? The magistrate is not worthy of his office. Whereas we would be at peace if we had good magistrates, we have only tyrants who take pleasure in tormenting all and wish only to destroy everything. I say that if we are going to observe the day of rest, as God so ordained, we must have good princes and magistrates. But, we are so wicked that God, seeing our wickedness, permits us to have magistrates who abuse their office by all manners of cruelty. Why? It is righteous vengeance on the part of God that whenever we abuse His grace we are punished by those who should sustain us. Why? If God has given us good things today, He is always ready to give us others tomorrow. But when we so abuse Him, He snatches His hand away from us. We must be so much the more diligent to know His grace, that we be governed according to His will. When we enjoy some good thing, let us recognize that it a treasure of inestimable value given us by God. Let us be thankful to Him, to give Him reason to continue giving us good things. But, on the contrary, we flaunt our ingratitude. That is what we have to bear in mind. Indeed, God gives us all that we could ever want. Besides our health, He gives us possessions, riches, treasures, all manner of goods in abundance. In brief, He will give us anything that we have ever hoped for. Nevertheless, what would the world be like if there were no governments, if each lived according to his own volition, and if offenses went unpunished? It would be better to be struck dead at first blow. All the good things we have are of no real benefit to us unless we have good magistrates to keep us in order. It is not without reason, then, that the prophet says our Lord gave His blessing to the people by giving them Kings from the line of Judah. He did not wish them to use their office as they pleased. No, no. He wished them to know that they are called to office by God to administer justice, protect people, and maintain order. That is why God ordained persons of superior rank. That is why kings and princes, as well as those not kings and princes, must know that God called them to office in order that His ordonnance be observed by all the people.

Now we come to the point where he says that "people will come from all the lands to offer sacrifices at the Temple." By this, as I have said, the prophet shows that it is not enough that we have terrestrial police to maintain order. We must have spiritual police to insure that God is honored and that communal prayers are offered. The prophet say that even if we have everything we want, we would all be criminals unless God ordained that we serve Him. Saint Paul, in his First Letter to Timothy, Chapter Two, admonishes us to pray for the magistrates, not only that we support them but that "we lead a peaceful and tranquil life in all sanctity and honesty." Here, then, are the two duties of the magistrate: They must see to it that each accommodates himself the ordinance of God and they must chastise all scandal makers and maintain equity among us. Let us return to what the prophet says, that "people from all lands will come to offer at the Temple in Jerusalem." Now, we know that we can offer up beasts in sacrifice without compromising the truth of this sacrifice. What is this truth? It is what the prophet says next, "They bear offerings of praise in the House of the Lord." The sacrifice of beasts is not the main thing that God demands. As it says in Psalm 50, "Do you think that I eat the flesh of bulls or drink the blood of goats? Sacrifice praise to God and fulfill your vows to the Most High. Call upon me in adverse times and I will deliver you and you will honor me." God is not hungry to have beasts sacrificed up to Him; rather, it is a matter of us coming to honor Him. Gathering at the Temple was intended to bring the people together, to symbolize Jesus Christ, and to lead the people to Him. Today, now that we have the truth, the kind of sacrifice that God demands is that we come to praise and honor Him. It is a singular blessing that God wishes to be served by us. How is this to be accomplished? Through our use of His sacraments; for from them flow prayer and all the rest, namely, a Christian life, in which we strive for nothing save that God be praised throughout the world. That is why I say that if we are so ungrateful as to hold the civil police in contempt, so much the more contemptuous are we of the Christian life.

How should we go bout a confession of faith to show that we are united to Him? How important is this ordinance of the Church to have communal prayers? There are some who wish to abolish all this. When it is a question of sermons, they would annihilate them all. When it is a question of the sacraments and one administers the sacrament of baptism, the ones promenade about the Church, the others wait by the door to pay honor to men. By such honor, God is dishonored. Then there are some who do not come to the door until the sermon begins and leave as soon as it ends. Their rationale: "Is it not enough that we came to the door? What are we expected to do here? We will leave at the end of the sermon." What value do they place upon God's grace? It is "no big deal!", provided that they can go about their business and amass wealth from all directions. We see how God deprives them of His grace and permits them to be returned to their subjugation under Satan. If God sent a similar temptation among ourselves, it is certain He would find such impiety and more. There is grave danger that God will deprive us of one of the two basic principles of mortal life. We should most especially fear this, since God so deeply cherishes these. The prophet, wishing to reveal the greatest gifts we have from God, pointed to these two things in order that when we are stripped of them we will come to know our pride. Our father, Adam, after having been stripped of God's graces and after having had the leisure to meditate upon them, cried out, "Alas!" So it shall be with us. When we are stripped of these gifts and put under the thumb of the Turks and the Anti-Christ, we will have the leisure to cry our, "Alas." But this cry will be in vain. Now it is said and we are warned early on that God must be honored and that His spiritual rest must be observed such that His name is glorified. Let us take care that His Word is better received than it customarily is and that we do not come to the sermon merely to say, "That's all old hat to me!" but that we return home and meditate on the Word we have heard. Let us take care to thank God for the grace He had given us, that He have reason to multiply them in us.

Now we come to God's threat that He "will light a fire on the gates that will consume the palaces and will not be extinguished." We see that our Lord exhorts us every way He can in order that we are not slowed down in coming to Him. We have seen the promises He made by saying, "Come to me and you will know all goodness; I wish only to do good for you." But why? We do not take Him seriously and all this seems nothing to us. It is necessary, then, for Him to resort to severe threats because we do not take seriously His promises. We must pay attention to the caring He has for us. He is transfigured, in a manner of speaking, to make us better understand His love, and He shows us more than we could ever understand. On the other hand, we are warned of our own crudeness, seeing that God calls us so sweetly and speaks to us not only as a father but as a nurse speaks to the infant she is suckling. Whenever God calls us so gently, He threatens us by making us aware of our own crudeness. Does it suffice for God to open His mouth and speak to us? He must strike us with a hammer. Does He land His hammer on a docile head? No! Since God is unable to lead us to Himself by sweetness or by warnings, we must be harder than an anvil. That is why we should not find it strange that God threatens us so often. We are like a sick man with a high fever who thinks that he is well. Nevertheless, the physician knows his illness and prescribes a medicine. The sick man will consider the physician irksome, for he thinks all he needs is the medicine. Our Lord, who is our spiritual physician, knows our illness. Although we may think of ourselves to be healthy, He knows that we are near death. Therefore, He uses remedies on us to revive us. But by virtue of the fact that we do not think that we need Him, we grumble and feel that He is too harsh. Nevertheless, because He sees more clearly than we do, He does not fail to use threats as remedies to draw us to Him.

Now let us see if the prophet's threat is addressed to us or not. It is certain that it is. If we consider why the Jews are reprimanded by the prophet, it is certain that this is because of their avarice. The Jews think that there is never enough time for their work. Men are naturally obsessed with making a profit and never find time to serve God. Instead of coming to the Temple to serve God on the feast day, one brings his wheat, another brings his hay, and God is left behind. That is how the Sabbath is profaned. How is it with us today? After having worked all week, it seems a grievous wrong that we are called to the Temple. It would appear that Sunday was ordained solely to grant us the leisure to go out for a walk. Seeing that we are subject to the same vices as were the Jews, let us fear we will be punished in the same way. We have this day of rest to serve God. Let us take care that we do not throw this treasure away, and God will not exercise this vengeance He pronounced on them by His prophet. We know that we are not more precious than the Jews and that Geneva is not more privileged than Jerusalem. God has said of Jerusalem, "Here is my Throne and my dwelling place." Yet we hear the warning that "all the palaces will be consumed by fire." Men have looked only to themselves and to build their own homes. The House of God has been slighted. Therefore, their pride will be felled and their houses destroyed. Pay heed that this will happen to us.

After the prophet had spoken his sermon, he added that the people have been hardened. When we see such rebellion in people, we know well to condemn them; for instead of bowing down to God, they resolve never to turn to Him. When we understand this, we can say that it is right all these torments befell Jerusalem, that the King had his eyes put out and was led away into captivity. If this vengeance seems severe, nevertheless God was not too severe, seeing the stubbornness of the people. If we can well condemn them, let us pay heed to ourselves. Jesus Christ is our altar and He demands of us only spiritual sacrifices, namely, as Saint Paul says, that we serve Him in all sanctity, invoke His name, and look upon Him as the Author of all good things. Do we not, then, have more reason to serve God than did the Jews? If we can well condemn them, are we excused? No, certainly not! We must prevent His vengeance. But what way is there? It is the way the prophet proclaimed, namely, that we praise God. But let us pay heed that God is not praised by the mouth. It is not enough for us to sing His praises and say amen. We must praise Him with our hands, with our feet, with all parts of our body. Then the tongue will not idly praise Him. If, however, we have been negligent in our praise, there is the prophet's remedy, namely, that we do not harden ourselves but humble ourselves. If we pay heed to his remedy, it is certain that God will receive us in all mercy and that we will know that His bounty is without measure, providing that our ingratitude does not become a stumbling block.

Following this holy teaching, we prostrate ourselves before the face of our good God, in knowledge of our faults. We pray that He make us to know our faults better than we ever have. We pray that He permit us not to be deceived by our hypocrisy but make us know that it is right He punish us. We pray that He teach us His grace, that we praise Him not one day of the week but throughout all our life. May He shed this grace not only on us but on all the peoples and nations of the earth, etc.

* * *

All-powerful God, you have not ordained a certain day for us to witness that we are sanctified by you. It is your pleasure that we observe a holy rest throughout all our life and renounce the world. Give us the grace to meditate on this holy rest. May we crucify our old man, so that, truly united and joined to your only Son, we share in the blessed resurrection, to which He has shown the way. May we be assembled in the heavenly kingdom, which He acquired for us by His death and resurrection, after we have so struggled in this world, under your teaching, that you reign always in us. May you so govern and lead us by your Spirit that we have no other end for our life save to be governed by you until finally you are all and in all.

(21) Wednesday, August 7, 1549

The Word of the Lord was given to Jeremiah, saying, "Arise, go down to the potter's house, and I will make you hear my words." When I went down to the potter's house, behold, he was making a work on the wheel. The vessel he was fashioning out of clay was damaged in his hand, so he made another one as it seemed good to him. Jeremiah 18.

We see how we harden ourselves against the warnings God gives us. The reason is that we do not believe that God is powerful enough to punish us until He strikes us. But then it is too late. After God warned the Jews, He exhorted them in order that they did not think that the prophet was spinning yarns but that they take matters seriously. Our Lord shows us clearly here that we are difficult to convince that He is our master and we are in His hand. True, it is shameful for us to turn our backs to God's warnings. Yet, we are unable to believe them. Experience teaches us well that we are not moved when God reveals His wrath to us. It is not without reason, then, that the prophet puts before us this metaphor of the potter.

God sent Jeremiah to the potter's house and commanded him to see what he was making in his shop. The prophet sees him make a pot that breaks and from this same clay make another. The first pot comes to nothing, so the potter makes another, as seems good to him. The Lord says to the prophet, "You see that the potter has the power to make of earth that which he wishes. At the very least, I have as much power over these people. Although I promised their fathers to be their God and to sustain their descendants, I am well able to destroy them. On the contrary, if they return to me, though it seems they must perish, I will completely restore them. You will say this to them in order that when I warn them, they do not harden themselves but come to me." That is the crux of the matter.

Isaiah, speaking of this same passage, puts it another way: "Will a clay pot dare raise up against the potter?" Here God reprimands man's pride to rise up against Him; for although His punishments are always fair, men accuse Him of great cruelty. Therefore, the prophet says, "Cursed be those who rise up against their Creator, for man is like a clay pot. God can do with him what He wishes, just as the potter can do what he wants with the clay." The prophet wishes to reprimand this pride, but Saint Paul goes further yet in the ninth chapter of Romans where He says that the Lord will pity whom He would pity and be merciful to those whom He would be merciful, and to those destined for eternal death He says, "You will perish!" Before the creation of the world, our Lord elected those He wished to save and this without regard to their merits. He did this rather than abandoning them, although He hardened those whom He wished to perish. This astonishes us and we say, "How can this be? Is it the office of God to play with men as if they were a ball? If we do evil, why does He accuse us? Is He just?" This is how men raise up against God. Saint Paul knew well how to combat this pride. He focused especially upon the infirminity of our understanding. He rebukes them, saying, "How, poor wretch, can you talk back to God? You are less than a clay pot. You see that the pot allows the potter to make what he wishes. Yet you wish to challenge God." Here Saint Paul shears off our horns. True, God can satisfy our idle curiosity, but we are not high-minded enough to comprehend His works. We must humble ourselves, for all true wisdom consists of the fact that we humble ourselves and do not exceed our limitations. Furthermore, it would by overly presumptuous to assume that God is obligated to answer to us at our own beck and call. Let us close the door on all curiosity and be content with what He has told us. That is how Saint Paul understands this passage.

Now, let us return to Jeremiah. He reveals to us that the Lord has the power to throw us down into Hell in one instant and pull us back up again the next. Let us humble ourselves. Whenever He does something good for us, let us not assume He is obliged to continue. Let us pay heed that we sustain His wrath if we do not turn away His vengeance by humbling ourselves before Him and begging Him to pardon us.

To throw further light on this passage, let us not that he did not go to the potter's shop because he had work for him but because of the hardness of the people, who would believe nothing unless it were shown them by example. It was necessary for him to be able to say to the people, "God has revealed to me how it will be with you." Now, we do not see that the prophet refused God when He said, "Go to the potter's shop." The prophet did not say, "Why is it that God could not have spoken to me at home as well as He could by sending me to the Potter's shop? What am I supposed to see there?" He uses no such words, he obeys without question. This instructs us that it is not up to us to choose how God teaches us or what methods He uses. Let us find good everything He says to us. We are not wise enough to impose rules upon Him, as if He did not know the best way to teach us. Let us simply obey Him. Furthermore, our Lord teaches in very simple ways, in order to accommodate Himself to our crudeness. We are such brutes that if He did not do so, we would understand nothing He says. Sometimes we ask, "Why is it that God speaks to us in such an elementary fashion?" If we knew better, we would not ask such questions. If we obeyed Him as we should, He would need only raise His finger; but when we are like asses, He has to shout after us, "Hey, hey!" That is why he uses such elementary means; otherwise, we would not understand Him. Besides being so crude, we are cursed by being so delicate that if God speaks a little roughly to us, we are vexed and murmur against Him. If he speaks to us in an elementary way because of our crudeness, we say angrily, "He seems to be speaking to small children, but we are men!" That is how we become vexed when He does not esteem to be as wise as we wish. Let us note, then, that the prophet had no difficulty going down to the potter's house, as if he were going to school, there to be taught what he must do. Let us refer all back to Him and His works, which we would be more inclined to do, were not our crudeness such a stumbling block.

When we contemplate the fruits of the earth and the diversity of needs, we are compelled to look to the providence of God. On one hand, we must look to His providence in order to be humbled. On the other, we must look to His bounty in order to be infatuated by His love.

Now we come to the point where the prophet says that "we are in the hand of God just as the clay is in the hand of the potter." Whenever some prosperity befalls us, we must not assure ourselves that it will remain; for that would be to take matters into our own hands without consulting our Proprietor. Whatever good God has given us, He can take away. Let us recognize the frailty not only of our life but of our whole state. If we are rich God can soon make us poor. If we are healthy, He can send sudden death upon us. If we are honored, He can make us fall into dishonor and embarrassment. If we are flourishing, He can destroy us in an instant. That is the kind of power God has over us, just as the potter has over the clay.

Now this is not to say that God resorts neither to reason nor to order in governing men. That would be an unpardonable blasphemy. God does not play with us as if we were a ball. Although God is all-powerful, He will not do just anything; for the will of God is the standard of all correctness. We have no better rule, no better touchstone to discern good from evil than the will of God. If something pleases God, it is certain that it is good. If something displeases God, we are compelled to assume that it is evil. That is how the will of God is the true standard to discern good from evil. Do we not wound God when we put human reason above His will? That is as if we put the earth above the sky. What a muddle that would be. Let us always remember that although we are in the hand of God as the clay is in the hand of the potter to do with as he so desires, God always uses us rightly so. Let us remember also that whenever we rise up against us, He will always have a way to confound us. As it is said in Psalm Fifty-One, "whatever judgment He makes is always fair." Men will never abandon grumbling against God, but they will be embarrassed in the end. Let us guard against such presumptuousness. Let us recognize that since God cares for us, He is not an unlimited power; for all that He does is just and fair. Indeed, that is what the prophet claims; for he says that if we enjoy prosperity, God has brought about such a state, just as the potter makes such a pot as he wishes.

But how can we go about all this? Is it not necessary for us to be reassured that he will bless us to the end? Would that be an occasion for us to deceive ourselves and puff ourselves up? No. Our whole life is so fragile that, though we be in honor, He could change all this in the twinkling of an eye. But there is a reason for that: We abused His bounty. The prophet does not attribute to God the authority to do what He will with us by absolute power, as the Papists say in blaspheming Him. God condemns us because we have offended Him. But the Papists attribute two powers to God. There is the ordinary power of God, by which He governs in all fairness; but there is an absolute power, by which He would damn even the angels. That is the doctrine of the Papists. God permitted them to fall into such blasphemies in order to show us that they are nothing but the synagogue of Satan, where God is so disfigured that you cannot tell Him from Satan. If God's bounty were omitted from His works, what difference would there be between God and Satan? It was by God's bounty that we were pulled out of such an abysm. All the works of God are fair and just, but we would not know this if we measure God against our standards. We confess that the wisdom and power of God are infinite! How, then, is it possible for us to comprehend them by our minds, which cannot contain even one drop of reason? We wish to comprehend God, but that is impossible! We will never be able to understand why God did such-and-such a work. But let us realize that He had good reason. Let us not be as presumptuous as to measure Him according to our standards. Saint Paul puts well what I have said: "O man, who are you to talk back to God?" It is not that God has done something against us to cause complaint, but that we cannot climb high enough to know what He does in fact do. True, He will be revealed to us; but that will happen in the heavens above, when "we are like Him," as Saint John says. In the meantime, let us be content with what He has told us and leave all the rest to the Last Day, when we will have our eyes more opened and our vision more cleared to better discern what we cannot see now.

Let us return to what the prophet has to say. On one hand, he says that whenever God promises some good to a people and they turn from Him, He will immediately deprive them of what He had promised them. Now, this is not to say that God is mutable. True, Scripture says that God "repented of Himself." It is common for Scripture to speak of God in this way; for if it spoke of His majesty, it would be beyond our comprehension. Therefore, it was necessary for Scripture to abase God and speak of Him in terms familiar to us. We know our own crudeness when we see that God had to accommodate Himself to us in order for us to understand Him. Be that as it may, He is not mutable. The prophet wishes to show that we cannot take it for granted whenever God gives us some good, as if He were obligated to continue. How if God can deprive kingdoms and peoples of His promises, what will happen to each and every one of us? When God speaks here of His power to exterminate, He is not addressing one man alone; rather, He is saying that wherever a kingdom flourishes like a well-planted tree, He can instantly destroy it. If that can happen to whole kingdoms, could it not happen to ourselves? As Isaiah says, all God has to do is blow on us and we wither; for we are like the petal of the flower that fades as soon as one blows on it. Let us be humble. If God gives us good things, let us not hold Him obligated to give more. Let us recognize that it is nothing at all for God to destroy us. Let us know that in an instant He can turn riches into poverty, glory into embarrassment, and life into death. As we recognize this for each and every one of us in particular, let us also recognize it in general for all cities, possessions, and kingdoms; for it would be nothing for God to build up a kingdom in one instant and to destroy it in the next. This does not mean that God plays with the world, makes a game of tennis out of it. But it does mean that, as it says in the Psalm we chant, lands which are fertile will be instantly destroyed and turned into deserts (as happened to Asia Minor, which is now marred and uninhabited, whereas it had been grassy and fertile). God does not take pleasure in destroying lands. The inhabitants of rich, grassy lands rose up against God and therefore merited being deprived of His blessing, so the lands where they lived remain dry and unproductive. Sodom and Gommorah were lands abundant in riches, but their inhabitants so rebelled against God that in an instant all was destroyed. Why? Ezekiel says that it was because "the people were fat" and were given to all villianery. The wrath of God descended upon them, and the men were put to death and the lands remain uninhabited and unproductive. That is how God can well change opulent places into deserts. After the prophet says all this, he adds that God shuts up the foul mouths of mockers and evil ones who say that all is governed by fortune.

We learn how to live under the hand of God by seeing that those who had prospered for a time fall into calamity, those who had been powerful God renders weak, those who had been rich fall into poverty, those who had been healthy fall into illness. This is not to say that God takes pleasure in all this, but it is all necessary insofar as men go astray. Let us learn, then, to walk always in fear. Let us pay heed that we are always in the hand of God, that He can chastise us whenever He wishes, that He will sustain any good He gives us unless we turn from Him. If we do not wish to be emptied of God after we have been made a vessel of honor, let us accommodate ourselves to Him, that we be formed in His image; for there is no change in Him, as there is in things of this world. When God will have reformed us in the likeness of His Son, we will not be subject to mutation. True, this is not yet the case with us, but that is why we must return to Him in order to be reformed in His image. As Saint Paul says, "We must be clothed as members of Jesus Christ"; for those reformed by His Holy Spirit will not change, but will be assured that He will sustain them in His grace to the end. Now all this comes back to what the prophet says here, namely, that we must not take matters into our own hands without consulting our Proprietor. Those surrounded by prosperity think that they can use God. Saint Luke speaks of the poor fool who said, "Enjoy yourself, my soul; you have wheat and vines and all manner of goods in abundance." Immediately his soul replied to him, "Poor wretch, what is it you think? This night the devils will steal your soul." So it is that poor fools deceive themselves by thinking that their goods need them, whereas they need their goods. God can strip away all our goods, for He is not obliged to sustain them. Let us not deceive ourselves into thinking that we have no need of God. Let us recognize that if we enjoy prosperity, God wishes to extend His hand to us, but that He is not obliged to do so. Let us recognize that He sustains us freely and can change our lot whenever He wishes. If we recognize this, the image of Jesus Christ is in us and we will be sustained all our life.

Now, let us see what the prophet has to say on the other hand of the matter. He says that if God threatens to punish a kingdom, but if the people convert to Him, then He will withdraw His threat. Just as we have seen that the promises of God do not change, neither do His threats. Because His threat is conditional, there is a remedy. It is as if one were to say, "If we do not amend our ways, God will punish us." Now, this is not to say that God has resolved to punish us, for in that case it would have to be executed. Rather, it is to call us to repentance in order to prevent this calamity from falling on our heads. That is the intention of the prophet. What should we do? We see the evil which menaces us is not far off. If we look at our life, we see that God can no longer hold back on punishing us. Seeing His power and our frailty, we know we are clay pots in His hand that He can do with as He so desires. If this is firmly imprinted in our minds, then whether or not we have been deceived for a time, we would know that He is our Father, that He can well turn away the evil already upon us; we would know that just as He has the power to raise the dead, He can roll back the calamities that were about to fall upon us by virtue of our faults. If a potter is not blocked by the pot from making of it what he will, if he can remake it if it breaks, know that God has at least such power over us. It is of great consolation that although God may consider punishing us, He is ready to receive us in all mercy, provided that we allow Him to mold us according to His will. When we see that God is so kind and present to us, will we not well relax our obstinacy? Now, as I have said, the time has come to pay heed these matters more than ever; for if God wishes to focus upon our faults, it is certain that He will not put up with us, especially because we continue to abuse His grace after He pulled us out of this evil Babylon. We see what punishment He selected for those who were much worse than we. Although we have not come to our end, our ears will tingle, as we shall see. What must be done? Let us return to God. Let us pray that He continue to shed His grace on our bodies and souls. Let us pray that He make us so profit from His grace that we do not return to Him, knowing our misfortune.

Following this holy teaching, let us prostrate ourselves before the face of our good God, in knowledge of our faults. We pray that He return us to Himself, so that we strive to glorify His name throughout all our life, that in this way He be encouraged to continue His bounty towards us. Thus we all say: "Celestial Father, etc."

* * *

(22) Thursday, August 8, 1549

Now go speak to the men of Judah and to the inhabitants of Jerusalem, saying: "Thus says the Lord: I imagine evil against you and I have thought up a device against you. Return from your evil ways and make your ways and actions good." They will respond, "There is no more hope! We walk according to our thoughts and each acts according to the imagination of his evil heart." Jeremiah 18.

We have seen how God turns the wheel to mould us as seems good to Him. We have seen that whatever form He gives us, He can change in an instant, so that we are consequently changed. We have said that this is not a wheel of fortune, but that God governs all fairly. If He sustains us in equity, that is the work of His grace. On the contrary, when we are so evil that we abandon Him, He still turns the wheel, but He regrets the good He has done for us.

Although the prophet applies this to the Jews, it represents a general principle; for God does not wish His Word to be left hanging in the air; He wishes it to serve all, for our government belongs to Him. The prophet says to the Jews that God takes them in His hand, but that when they turn from Him, He can well throw them out. Therefore, he says, "People of Judah and you residents of Jerusalem, God sent me to the potter's shop for no other reason than your instruction. God said to me, 'I imagine evil against you and have thought up a device against you, always looking to the wheel, which I do not turn in vain. I am considering punishing you. What must you do? Amend your ways, and whereas I had considered punishing you, I will sustain you in your state.'" Now we have a clearer exposition of the doctrine we treated yesterday. After God has spoken generally, He does speak specifically because each is inclined to let His teaching pass him by. Men will say, "Oh! That is a good teaching, but it is most appropriate for others better than ourselves." When God's judgment is mentioned, they will say, "Oh! His judgment upon those people was well spoken, but He does not seem to have anything to say to us." To preach the Word of God, I must make an examination of my life, and my mirror is the Word of God. It also serves as a mirror for all of us. Before looking into this mirror, we think that we are beautiful and clean. He puts the Word before our eyes in order that we come to know our faults and humble ourselves. Let us follow the prophet's train of thought here, namely, that God directs all by His providence and that He can destroy His enemies and instantly restore them if they return to Him. The prophet says, "You and Judah," because they were the ones to whom he had been sent as a prophet. It is as if I were to say now, "You of Geneva," for we have the Gospel. When he admonishes them, each must look to himself and know the prophet is speaking to us and not to people far away from here. We see, then, the foolishness of these who wish that the preacher was speaking to people far away, for then how sweet and gentle he would be! But why? God's intention is totally the contrary of that. In brief, the Word of God is not a matter of chance. It has a certain goal. It is not to be left hanging in the air. It is to be applied to those who hear it. One could well preach with his eyes closed, that is, without looking at the people to whom he preaches. But what purpose would there be in that? God intends, as I have said, that His Word be presented according to what we are. Those charged with instruction must pay attention to their pupils. Medicines must be provided according to the vices of the people. A physician does not put all his remedies in a big pile to dole them out to just anybody, for then he would no longer by a physician. A physician carefully studies the illness and prescribes medicine accordingly. This is what we must do. This is what the prophet did.

The prophet says, "I forge evil against you." This means that God does not punish out of sudden anger, is not quick to raise His hand against us, although He does not forget our faults. No, He attends to us in all patience, for He is called "patient" in Scripture. This is not without reason, for we see the result: We fail and not just for a day or a month or even a year but continually over very long periods of time, and yet He sustains us all the while. Why? Do not think that because He closes His eyes to our faults that He cannot see a wink of them or that will go unpunished. The trial is over, the sentence is passed. The poor criminal knows nothing of this. Upon being taken from the prison, he goes right to the executioner. Think on this. Let us look at Sodom. The inhabitants mocked God and went further and further astray from Him. The Lord said, "I came down to earth to see what was happening, for their clamor reached all the way up to me." Now, as I have said, while the inhabitants of Sodom enjoyed themselves, their trial was conducted, but they were aware of nothing until their sentence was executed. However our Lord may close His eyes to our faults, the time will come when He will punish them. There are two things to note here: the patience of God and the fact that He does not forget our faults. Because He does not punish us as soon as we have offended, we know His paternal pity upon us. How? Make no mistake about it: His bounty does not block Him from making a list of our faults to call us to account whenever He wishes. True, God does not conduct a grant inquisition like earthly judges, who remain ignorant of our faults until they are so informed. When God says, "I have thought up a device against you," that means that we cannot know God in His majesty. Therefore, it is necessary to describe Him in a way that we can understand.

Our Lord spins the wheel to throw the Jews off the face of the earth. Why? To give them the leisure to repent, that their punishment be deferred. The prophet says, "Return, each of you, from your evil ways and make your ways and your acts good." We see, then, to what end God warns them. He does not say, "They must perish. That is final!" Rather, He speaks in order to warn them. Know, then, that all the threats of God are declarations of His love. He declares His love for us, not only in His blessings, but also in His threats. God's threats profit us, if we act accordingly. "Make your ways good," He says. Consider the situation of these people: Their ruin is imminent when Jeremiah spoke, although it had been a long time coming. I say imminent, because a long time had passed since the warnings and death of Isaiah. At the time He spoke, there was a treaty between Judah and Babylon. He told them that it was because of this treaty that their ruin would come, for such treaties cannot be manmade but come only from the providence of God. God warned them in order that they might return to Him. Even in His threats He has pity on us. Why does He carry out His threats against us? We flee from the proceedings against us. "Return to God," says the prophet, "for He will defer punishment. He delayed execution of your sentence to see if there was any repentance in you."

When he says, "Make good your ways," it seems as if there is a capacity in man to change himself without the grace of God. Indeed, the Papists use this passage to support their notion of free will, although they are forced to admit that God has the greater share of this power. Nevertheless, they give man a share of God's power. In support of their concept of free will, they say, "Here is what the prophets have said. Now, their statements make no sense unless man had some power in his own right." They have paid no attention to the teaching of Saint Paul where he says that the exhortations made to us are the power of mortal life, as if to say that God has sentenced us all to death unless we soften up enough to obey Him and receive what He says to us.

It is not enough for us to receive teaching from men as if it came from them alone. The prophet does not say, "You can go to God of your own free will." Instead, he says, "Look to your calling and not to your power." After God has shown us what we must do, we cannot say, "I cannot do that," for God has said it will be so. After He has admonished us, He then gives us the power to do what He commanded. Therefore, after having heard His teaching, we must go to Him and pray that it please Him to make us profit in His teaching. That is how we will receive nothing in vain. That is how Scripture must be received! When Scripture says, "Cast away the evil which is in us," this is not to say that fallen man has to power to return himself to goodness; for it is necessary that God takes him by the hand and pulls him up. Not only have we fallen into evil but we are destitute of all goodness; for Saint Paul says that when men fall they become enemies of God. Let us go and accomplish all of which the prophet spoke, namely, let us make our ways good. Let us go, then, to God and pray that He rule us such that we may receive pardon instead of angering Him and meriting severe punishment.

The prophet says, "All is lost!" He is not instructing the people but condemning them. He intends this to be a witness to their future. When God will have transported them to Babylon, they will know that is no longer any remedy and that this is not God's fault but the fault of their own malice. This condemnation, then, shows that God is just when He resorts to severe punishment. Why? If the Jews had failed, and if God had not sent prophets but had punished them immediately, we could well say that if they had been warned, they would have returned to God. Although God keeps silent, we have no complaint against Him and no cause to say, "Why had He not done such-and-such to warn us?" The eighteenth chapter of Deuteronomy shows us that God did not leave them without prophets to search out fortune tellers, but that in order they were not tempted by such curiosities, He gave them prophets. If our Lord had left the Jews without any prophets, we could well say, "Where are the promises which had been made to these people?" But after the prophet had spoken to them, they say, "There is no more hope! We walk according to our thoughts and each acts according to the imagination of his evil heart." They were saying in effect, "You will baptize us only with water, for we are resolved to do evil and worse. You will have ample reason to threaten us, for we follow the evil of our heart." When we hear the prophet's condemnation of the Jews, our hairs stand on end. We are all shocked when we hear the prophet speak of their rebellion, saying, "Although God has spoken to you for a long time, you have not ceased from doing evil and even worse. Nevertheless, He is ready to receive you if you return to him." They reply, "All is lost!" Look to ourselves. See that we do no less. How do these warnings benefit us? How have we profited from the fact that if we are touched by His bounty to return and convert to Him in total obedience, He will receive us in all mercy, notwithstanding our evil lives? We see nothing but rebellion within us.

Although we may not say, "All is lost!" we act that way. Let us look at ourselves, for this behavior is common to all men: When it is a matter of converting to God, everyone thinks that this is too much. But when it is a question of evil, not a one will say, "Enough!", according to Isaiah. He says in effect, "Do not doubt that God promised to sustain you, since He took you as His charge. But that you are so troubled is well a sign of your defiance. Do not think that God is powerful enough to sustain you!" Do we think this defiance remains unpunished? No. He adds, "Besides the fact that you lust after things God condemned, you have all these superstitions and yet you never say, 'Enough!' Whatever warnings you are given, you never tire of your evil doings." Although God chastised them that they had become obsessed with Egyptian ways, they never shouted, "Enough!" Who will say this? You are so inflamed with your won malice that you have no consideration for God within you! It is a vice common to all men that although God chastises them for their superstitions, they take the bit in their teeth like a mule, so that no one can control them. So it is with the poor infidels. Although God smacks them on the head, they only become angry and rebel against Him. They do not abandon their evil ways. We are so abandoned to evil that whatever bridle is put on us, we cannot be controlled. If it is a question of doing evil, we are never tired. If it is a question of doing good, we never have the time. We are incorrigible. This is very true of the Papists. Although God condemns all of them, they are so wrapped up in their idolatry that they can never do good and cannot fail to do evil. On the contrary, look at ourselves. It pleased God to deliver us from such darkness, for He wishes now to lead us by His Word. But are we as determined to follow the Word of God as are the Papists to follow their patrons and good intentions? Far from it! Although we have a good wind, we poop out soon enough. The prophets speak of our sluggishness, which we know well from experience and practice. We would not fall if we did not wish to, for our Lord holds us in His hand. Let us not become desperate and cry, "All is lost!" Let us not reject God's grace when He presents to us. Let us take care to constrain our nature, seeing that it is contradictory to God. When God shows us the way, let us continue to the end. When we have done good today, let us do good tomorrow.

Now, when the prophet says that each claims he "will follow his unbridled appetites," it is certain that he speaks in a manner not customary to Jews. Men always wish to be esteemed as righteous, though they are really worth nothing, and they strive to cover up their turpitude. The larcenist strives to hide his crime. The adulterer will say that he is a righteous man. They are so impudent that they wish to maintain this facade of righteousness. However the air may stink with their wickedness, they will say they are righteous men. It is unlikely, then, that the Jews would have spoken in the way of the prophet. Rather, they would have tried to justify themselves, saying, "What will we do? We will do as we have been accustomed to do!" The prophet says that they responded that "we will follow the evil of our wicked heart!" Why does he impute this to them? Now, as I have said several times, God does not regard words but truth. However they may have spoken these words, their actions show that it is so. The prophet sought to declare fact and truth. The prophet does not slander them by these words; but, as I have just said, he declares the truth. Why is this true of them? In that they had resisted God, what excuse do they have? The lesson we get from this passage is that God does not use our balance, our measuring stick, our standard of measurement. He judges us according to what is true about ourselves, despite our subterfuges. Today, the Papists try to cover themselves up by saying, "O, we follow the ways of our fathers," and they call their abominations "services of God"! Indeed, such an honorable title, but why? When they go to mass, they renounce the death and passion of Jesus Christ by worshipping a piece of bread. When they trot off on some pilgrimage, they worship some piece of wood or some saint. When they try and excuse themselves by these things, how will God receive them? All these subterfuges will count against them as if they had said, "We do not wish to follow God!" Why? That is what the facts show. These subterfuges are to no avail. God is not amused by them, for He looks only to the facts. This is also true of us. When we are admonished by the Word, we do not say, "We wish to follow the Devil." Instead we say, "Oh, I do not wish to be so oppressed. Oh, the Word will serve us nothing!" However we may whitewash our turpitude, God says that we have angered Him and that we have said we will walk according to our evil ways. Let us understand this well. Let us not be amused by our hypocrisy. Let us recognize that our subterfuges will do us no good when we come before the heavenly Throne.

The prophet continues, "Go among the Pagans and see if they have heard of such a thing. The virgin of Judah has sinned!" Here the prophet is following up the remarks he made in the second chapter; for he uses the same expression "All is lost!" and makes the same statements, namely, that one should go to the Pagans to see if they have heard of such a thing. He speaks more at length in the first passage: "Visit the Pagans. They are loyal to their gods. Although they are merely idols, they are loyal to them. But my people are not loyal to me. Is this not a monstrous thing?" Now he says as much in the later passage: "Look to the Pagans, if they have seen such things. Have they abandoned their religion? No." He brings in the metaphor he used in the second chapter. However, he states it in another way to bring matters to a climax. In the earlier passage, he says that they have abandoned the living waters and dug cisterns: "They work and they abandon me, who am the fountain of living waters." Now he says, "When a man will have water in his fields, he will go fetch the snows of Lebanon." This is foreign water because it comes from snow, yet the man is content with it and does not search elsewhere. Now, when God is present to us, not only does His grace flow forth to us but we are led to the very source. Jesus Christ is the fountain which is present to us. We will never need the cold waters of snow, for He gives Himself to us. We will share in the grace of Christ. Are we not, then, accountable? Are we not worse than senseless? The examples of the Pagans will serve to render us less excusable if we do not serve God. If we do not serve God, the Pagans alone will be sufficient to condemn us. This is also true, as I have said, of the stubbornness of Papists. They do not have true religion, but they will not abandon what they have, even though they have no assurance it is good and even though God condemns them. We see the Turks, who are as hardheaded about this law of Mohammed as they can be. We see the Jews, who did not know what God they worshipped, yet they went about their religious affairs with an inexpressible mania. When we see such obstinacy everywhere, do we think that what we do is pleasing to God? We do not take ourselves into account! We hear God, who calls us, we see Christ, the infallible truth who wishes to lead us, and yet we have no loyalty in us! Will we be excusable? Alas, no! Whenever we speak of the Jews of Pagans, let us examine ourselves. If at the very least we are not as loyal as they are stubborn, so much the greater our condemnation. However assured we may be of God's bounty, we have not wished to accommodate ourselves to Him. There are several other things to be said here, but they will have to wait for another time.

Following this holy teaching, we prostrate ourselves before the face of our God, in full recognition of our faults. We pray that it please God to give us the grace to know how obstinate we have been in the past. We pray that He give us the grace to be admonished and to profit from His admonitions. We pray that we incessantly profit from them, until we are stripped of all flesh and vices. May He shed this grace not only on us but also, etc.

* * *

All-powerful God, because you have held us from the beginning, so that we fall as it pleases you, we recognize our weakness and fragility. We are always mindful that our life is nothing but a passing shadow, that we are absolutely nothing. Give us the grace to rest in you and to be able to depend upon you and your good pleasure. You are the beginning and the end of our salvation. Give us the grace to humble ourselves before you in all fear and trembling. Give us the grace to persist on the path of our calling. May we continually invoke your name and throw out all our remedies from your bosom. May we do so, until finally delivered from all dangers, we assemble together in the blessed repose acquired for us by the blood of your only Son, Amen.

(23) Friday, August 9, 1549

Will a man abandon the waters of the snows of Lebanon, which come from the rock in the field? Will he abandon the waters which are cold and which flow? Jeremiah 18.

Yesterday, we began to examine the ingratitude of men. We saw that they are not content with God after He has revealed Himself to them, so that they search hither and yon for their salvation. This leads us to the following metaphor: If a man has good fresh water at his home, he is content and does not search elsewhere for water, even though he is not at the source. Although his water is only snow water from Lebanon, still he is content and does not look elsewhere. Now, our Lord does not give us His grace as a little stream but as a living fountain. If we are not content with this, do we not deserve God casting us out and making us face our own infidelity? Here is why the prophet cries out that "if one searched the whole world, one would not find such ingratitude as is in the children of Israel." The pagans are loyal to their idols, yet those to whom God gave knowledge of His infallible truth desert Him! God has testified in our conscience that we do not have a God forged out of our imagination but that it is the true God we worship. We have such certitude and yet we turn from Him to seek after strange gods. Is this not an unpardonable ingratitude on our part?

Every single word of the prophet pertains to us. We know that God appeared to us, indeed that He has been present to us for a long time in Jesus Christ. Not only has He revealed

Himself as the fountain of living waters, but today we have the Gospel, by which God calls us to Himself, that we might come to Him and have all our needs satisfied. This fountain is available to us alone, for God has not extended this grace to all. We see our neighbors dying of thirst while God draws us to Himself. All we have to do is drink. Because we have this fountain, let us take care that we do not abandon it. True, not all have their heads turned from God by idols; but we are all subject to wicked passions that do turn us from God. When the prophet spoke to the Jews, he did not speak only of superstitions; he says that their infidelity came from the fact that they went to Egypt for aid. Because we do not follow God, this accusation of infidelity is also directed against us and quite naturally condemns us. If we have cold water, we are content with that and do not search elsewhere. God gives us not only cold water but everything we could ever need. Listen to what Christ says: "Come to me and drink. Whoever will have his fill of these waters, not only is there enough for him but he can share it with others." Isaiah says, "Come and drink, he that has no money," and he adds that God will give him this water "gratuitously." When we hear all this, do we not see how terrible ungrateful we are? Pay heed to what God is present to us, for He calls himself the fountain of living waters. That is the place we must come to dwell. If we go elsewhere, it is by virtue of the fact that we are deprived of His blessings that he wishes us to have. Why are our tongues worn out with thirst, having not one drop of water to refresh ourselves? We have strayed from the fountain. Here God shows us a greater abundance of goods than He did the Jews. Knowing that He communicates with us, let us not draw back from Him. Let us cling to Him, so that we are not deprived of His grace. Let us hold to Him, so that our evil cupidity does not turn us elsewhere and we no longer drink at this fountain. If we have drunk our fill at the fountain today, let us return again tomorrow, in fact all the days of our lives. Continuing on, the prophet says that "the prophets (that is, the seducers, who abuse the name of prophet) had caused them to stumble. The reason is that "my people have forgotten me." I have already said what was the starting-point of their trouble, namely, those individuals who wished to seduce these poor people! There is no worse pestilence than when, instead of having good teaching, we are eaten alive by lies, when we have seducers and tricksters who would turn us from the path of righteousness. That, I say, is a pestilence. So we are admonished to recognize the grace of God when we have good ministers. Could you more tellingly point to us the folly of men than when they stray from the fountain of living waters after having been replenished? If we find this bizarre, and indeed it is bizarre, let us know, then, that God has done us an invaluable service by providing us with good pastors who lecture us in His promises. When we have this, God is among us.

Furthermore, let us make our task not to allow ourselves to be deceived by the pride of men. True, this will be very difficult unless God gives us a hand; but it is certain if we accommodate ourselves to Him and desire to follow His truth, He will open our eyes that we will never stray from Him. However the seducers may take on various guises, we will not turn from God or from His Word, for He has promised to give us the discretionary power to see through them. Therefore, the prophet says that if the Jews claim that they were seduced, they are not excused; he accuses them because they have been deceived. Men are not deceived unless they want to be. If we fully wish to adhere to the truth of God and hold firmly to it, we will never be deceived, not by Satan nor by his supporters. We will know well how to protect ourselves, provided that we seek God. Thus, the Jews are strongly reprimanded insofar as they had knowledge of God. Nevertheless, the trouble started with false ministers. Indeed, but only insofar as the people wished to be deceived. This how God punishes us. If we fall, it is because we did not wish to cling to Him. If God sends us false ministers, it is because we have abandoned Him. It is certain that if we had stayed with Him, He would have protected us. When God discovers there is only hypocrisy in us, He will permit us to be thoughtless. This is why Saint Paul said that "it is necessary that there be heretics, in order that those not subject to fantasizing be known." Although men can be quite cunning, we will be informed enough to know their fantasies, so that we will not be deceived by them. Let us, then, be on our guard and pray to God that He does not permit us to stray from His grace but that He renders us victorious in the struggle against Satan. It is in regard to this point that the people are said to have been deceived and yet be without excuse, for they were deceived by their own hypocrisy. Such temptation shows us that we have not loved the Lord with a true love.

He adds that "they have turned from their ancient paths to walk in paths which were unfrequented." Here the prophet is showing that for a long time God has been admonishing the Jews that they must accustom themselves to serving Him. We have a God who was revealed to our fathers. We do not have a God who is an invention of today. We have a God who is from all time. On the contrary, the prophet says that they let themselves fall and stray, for there is no longer a road or path when we abandon God. Now, he calls the path to truth the "Ancient Way." This renders the Jews doubly culpable, for if we came to have knowledge of God only today, still that would not be reason for us to abandon Him, however we might wish to declare ourselves inculpable. Because God has given us His grace such that from our infancy we have been instructed in His Word, and because our fathers had been so instructed, it is certain that we will be so much the more condemnable if we reject this truth that He had made reign for such a long time among ourselves and our fathers. That is how the prophet multiplies the condemnation of the Jews. Suppose that today God calls the Turks to knowledge of Himself and wishes to take them to be His own. If they revolt against God, they will be condemned. Suppose there are other people, which have had the Word for a very long time. The small children say, "We have been instructed from our infancy in the knowledge of God." Their fathers say, "Our fathers were nourished in the Word of God." Now suppose all these people turn from God. Are they not twice as condemnable as the Turks? Yes, certainly they are. That is what the prophet is trying to say.

Let us not imagine that the prophet takes the "Ancient Way" to be a way men had long been accustomed to. He wishes to say that God revealed Himself to Abraham and continued to do so up to Moses, to whom He gave the Law. The ways of Pagans could also be called "ancient," since they had laws. It is very likely that God never permitted His Law to be absent from the world, as it is said that Melchizedek did not serve strange gods but the true God. There has always been a small throng of righteous men.

We could even call the way of idolaters the "Ancient Way" in reverse! But the prophet wishes to speak otherwise, of course. He is saying that God chose the Jews and that He taught them in His truth. When he speaks of the "Ancient Way," he is not referring to the ways of men. No, to do so would be only a sweet lie. We should call the ways of men the "Ancient Lie"! If we wish to have truth, we must go to God. If we cling to men, we will have only incertitude and consequently suffer a total reversal.

Here we see the error of the Papists, who allege their teachings come from antiquity. It would seem that they have some foundation in this passage. They say, "Would God have permitted the world to have been so long in darkness?" But in what were their ancient teaching founded? Were they founded in God? No, in men! We must not rely ancient prescriptions; we must begin with God. The prophet says that "they followed unfrequented paths." The Papists fail by following well-beaten paths! These paths are not the best, as it is said that "the road to perdition is broad." When the prophet says that "they failed by not following the well-beaten path," we must suppose that he meant a path frequented by righteous men. The Jews, among other examples, had predecessors who were righteous men. They had the open road and yet they detoured into heavily trafficked lanes. Although they said, "We serve God," they served idols. They could well say, "We follow the Ways of the Egyptians and Babylonians." But why? Had their fathers followed these paths? No. The Papists will say, "We follow a well-travelled route!" How? They will point to the fathers and they will say, "Our Holy Father, the Pope, ordained such-and-such." Where are the prophets, apostles, and true martyrs? Alas! They mean nothing to the Papists. The Papists have good reason to claim that they follow a well-beaten path, for they do not follow the fathers that they should. They have good reason to claim that God has made them a great multitude, if by multitude we understand all those people damned to Hell! As we find our conductor in God, so it is He who must conduct our religion, just as Satan leads the band of liars and those who wish to be deceived. Whenever men walk according to their own inventions, there is only error. The prophet speaks of "ways" to denote the various paths men take.

However, if we examine them all very carefully, we will find that God has shown us only one way. If you detour from that path, you will go astray.

The prophet adds that "they have burnt incense in vain." By this word "incense," he signifies all idolatrous inventions, all that man has invented to serve God. He says this is all in vain. Why? Because "obedience matters more than a sacrifice." If we do not wish our efforts to be in vain, let us follow God's commandments and gain His approval. If, on the contrary, we do not follow His commandments, were we even to break our arms and legs in His service, it would all be in vain. We can well spend our money on sacrifices and the like; but it would be ill spent, for we would be unable to afford bread and meat. When men turn from the path to God, they lose their footing, as we see of bigots, who are quicksand for men. Right after they get up they have to go to confession. They have to fast. They have to go on pilgrimages here and there. They will say, "What? Since I did such-and-such with good intentions, must it all be in vain?" My friend, you have well your answer when the prophet says, "All is vanity!" When we see how God delivered us from all this, we are certainly admonished to hold fast to the Word of God, invent nothing of our own imaginations, rest contend with what He told us, and acquiesce to the sentence He pronounced upon us. So much the more are we encouraged to serve God, seeing that what we do is pleasing to Him. When we see that those who stray from the ways of God are worthless and that those who follow His will are sustained, we are encouraged to serve Him, seeing how kind He is and how approving of what we do, although it is of no value.

The prophet says that not only are idolaters condemned but that if we mix in idols with the service of God, all is lost. If we mix poison with wine, the wine becomes tainted. So it is when we mix superstitions in with the service of God. Ezekiel says, "Go and serve your idols. Do not associate with me." It is certain that the Jews, aside from their other altars, had the Temple. So it is with the Papists. When speaking of their best idols, they say, "Oh, we know well that the Virgin Mary is not God. We know well that baptism is good, but what harm is there in adding a little something to enrich it? When we have fire to signify the Holy Spirit, oil to signify the grace of God, and the vestment to signify innocence. Is not this a much richer experience than if we had only a little water? What? Communion depreciated by us? That would not please God! When the priest is adorned so ornamentally, each and every thread having significance, is communion not better served than it would be without such ceremony or by just handling out pieces of bread?" That is how the Papists wish to excuse their idolatries for appearance sake. "Serve your idols, for I do not wish to be with you," says God. Whenever we mix our ideas into God's service, He does not wish to share with us. If we wish God to approve our service, we must hold fast to His Word without any backsliding here or there.

The prophet says that God wishes "to make the land desolate." Here the prophet is saying that idolatry is such a displeasing vice to God that His vengeance will follow it always. In particular, when God gives a people grace to know His will and they turn from Him, punishment must follow. Men are never deceived by their ignorance. This is no excuse in the eyes of God. Men are deceived because of their unrighteous passions. That is why God permits Satan to ensnarl them in lies. God is sufficient to protect us, if only we would go to Him. Jesus Christ said, "If the truth delivers you, you will be truly free." All the machinations and deceit of Hell cannot harm our faith. If the Jews were deceived by false prophets, that happened solely because they were so deserving. God has ordained His service in such a manner that if we turn from it, He will send His vengeance upon us. On the contrary, if He is honored by us, He will multiply His grace in us. When the prophet speaks of desolate land, he is referring back to Moses, who is the well-spring at which all the prophets drink. Moses said: "If you abandon God, He will permit you to live in desolation and one will say 'Why has God done this? The land is destitute of God's aid and from this comes its desolation.'" When a man falls into poverty because of his sins, people mock and his at him. The prophet does not speak without reason, for he wishes to show how God detests those who abandon His service. Whenever we make what appears to us to be a small mistake, we are inclined to say, "Well, compared to those totally given to superstition, it seems like no big deal." On the contrary, God will say that it a horrible crime and He will take such terrible vengeance upon us that we will tremble. Each must take care not to mix anything in with His Word. Each must pay heed that God has called us. It must follow Him until I have joined with the faithful in this union of faith which we have in Jesus Christ.

Following this holy teaching, let us prostrate ourselves before the face of our good God, in full recognition of our faults. We pray that He touch us by true repentance, that we humble ourselves before Him. We pray that His Spirit strengthen us such that we will never stray, no matter what temptation befalls us. May He shed His grace not only on us, but on all the peoples and nations of the world, etc.

* * *

## (24) Saturday, August 10, 1549

I will disperse them with an east wind before the enemy. I will show them my back and not my face in the day of their calamity.

And they said, "Come, let us think up some devices again Jeremiah." Jeremiah 18.

Yesterday we saw that if one strays from the right path, one will stumble and fall; for a man cannot arrive at his own salvation unless he has knowledge of God. We saw that the fault of the Jews came from the fact they were deceived by seducers and false prophets, but that they were without excuse before God, who did not fail to punish them. Finally, we saw that when we turn from God, we ruin all the earth. I was said that the land was desolate and that each who saw it shook his head in amazement.

Now our Lord multiplies their punishment when he says that He "will chase them away by the noontide wind," which means that He will chase them away in a tempest. We know that the noon wind causes storms. This was especially true in Judah. It is therefore to multiply His punishment on these idolaters that He says He will chase them away by the noon wind. But the height of their misfortune is that He says, "I will show them my back and not my face", that is, He will not condescend to look upon them in their day of calamity. As I have said, that is the height of their misfortune; for when we are afflicted, the only recourse left us is to pray to God. As it is said in the Psalm, "Lord, will you abandon us and forget us when we are so afflicted? Lord, will you turn your face from us?" The last refuge that the faithful have in their affliction is to pray that God be merciful to them; for God has revealed such gratuity that He aids us as soon as we ask this of Him. God is not ignorant that we are in need. But Scripture had to have some way of speaking about God to accommodate Him to our crudeness; otherwise, we would not be able to understand what God says about Himself and His nature. When it is said, "Lord, turn you eyes upon me," this signifies that God is merciful, so that He is always ready to serve us as soon as we declare our needs. On the contrary, it is said that He will turn His back on the Jews, to signify that they will have to search elsewhere for their aid; "for I will not condescend to look upon them." When God speaks in this manner, it is to show us that we are totally unworthy of any reconciliation, that He does not chastise us out of paternal love, and that He will persecute us forever more, as we saw in the tenth chapter. Let us take care we wane neither to the left nor to the right of His will for fear that we will stumble and fall; for then we must expect the kind of punishment He now declares by turning His back on the people. It is impossible we return to God, save that the Holy Spirit converts us; and, insofar as we are unworthy, we cannot trust that it will do so.

The prophet adds that those who had been deceived by the false prophets conspired against him, saying, "Come and let us think up some devices against Jeremiah." Why? "For we have the

Temple in our possession, we have charge of the priests, we have the council of sages and others who govern all. Since we hold superior rank, we control the prelates, presbyters, sages, and prophets. We cannot fail to have Jeremiah under our thumb. Let us mock him and hear no more of him." Here we see what corruption there was in all of Judah, principally in Jerusalem, where the throne of God was supposed to be and where men were supposed to be able to hear the voice of God, as in Paradise. Nevertheless, it is said that not just one man but all were given to evil, not only the common people but the government as well, even prophets. We must conclude that there has been only evil in us.

Nevertheless, the priesthood was ordained by God; for it is said that "if there is a quarrel between you, go and ask the priest and hold to his ruling. If any refuse, they must be punished." Whatever the priest determines will be of God and not of men, for He has said, "Ask of my will from the prophets, and he will tell you." All this had been ordained by God, and yet we hear that all conspired against Jeremiah. The Devil brought disorder everywhere, for all was perverted at the time of Jeremiah. We see, then, that there is nothing so good or so holy that it cannot be changed over time. One could not so destroy a vineyard by turning pigs loose on it as man will turn things topsy turvy by his perversity. The man who is perverse is a terrible beast who instantly turns everything upside down. Seeing that we are all sinners and totally perverse in our nature, let us pray that God does not permit us to destroy all the things He ordained for our salvation. That is the first point.

Furthermore, we are advised not to be surprised when we see things happening today as they did at the time of the prophet, as there are many idiots who cause scandals wherever they go. Want some examples? Are not the Pope, the cardinals, the bishops, the prelates, and all the priests ordained by God? Yet it seems to these imbeciles that our doctrine is no good. Here is a beautiful example to show us that we must not be surprised by what happens. Let us compare the Pope with the High Priest. It is certain that the High Priest was in higher authority than the Pope. True, the Pope is called the "Universal Bishop of the Church." But what title has he from God? He is far from having the authority of his predecessors. There have been Bishops of Rome, righteous men, who knew well to say that the Popes are the precursors of the Anti-Christ. But on the authority of the High Priest, such rebels were condemned to death, as God had so spoken. God ordained the priesthood of Levi. But what ordination have the priests to their calling and position? True they will say that the bishops ordained them. But when they are ordained, are they told, "Go preach the Gospel"? They hold the office of priest, yet they have authority neither from God nor from man. It is necessary to conclude, then, that their sacrifices are worthless and are only an abomination before God. When we compare the ministers of the Ancient Church with those of the Papal Church, we find that the priest of the Ancient Law was ordained by God. On the contrary, the priesthood of Papism can find no passage in Scripture to demonstrate that they should be given any preeminence. They have usurped this office without any authority. The office of the ancient priesthood was ordained by God, and yet we see that the priests conspired with others against Jeremiah. If there was such a conspiracy against the servants of God at the time of Jeremiah, should we not expect as much today? Whatever grand title is claimed for the Pope or prelate, we should not be surprised. Let us subjugate ourselves to the Word, however all the world may oppose us.

Now the question arises: "How is it possible that God commands obedience to the High Priest and yet now commands that we do not obey the Pope?" We find the answer in the second chapter of the Prophet Malachi: "Behold," says the Lord, "I have broken the alliance I made with Levi, for I have made my alliance with Aaron, saying: 'The mouth of the priest should announce my Law, for his lips should keep knowledge and one should seek the Law from his mouth. You have not held to the alliance I have made. Therefore, I will throw shit in your face and render you contemptible to all the world, for you have not kept my ways according to my commandment." In brief, this is Malachi's message. He reproaches the priests for not having followed God's commandment. Why? "The priests must announce my Word and converse with me in peace and equity, and they must turn away people from their iniquities, and their lips should keep knowledge and one should seek the Law from their mouths. But they have done none of this. Therefore, I declare that they are nothing to me and that I will not constitute them in this office which they usurp. I disavow them." It was God's intention that the priest would proclaim His Law and that people would hold to his ruling. They had no authority to judge as they saw fit. Let us not misunderstand this point. He was obligated to answer whatever he was asked and to do so not in terms of his own inventions but in terms of the Law and teaching he had obtained from God and His prophets. So we see that the priests were the first to go astray and that they then corrupted the others into conspiring against Jeremiah. There is no reason why this sort of thing should happen, for we have a solution right here in this passage: Let us not break God's commandment by putting our faith in the teachings of false priests. We can well reject them as those who have abused their office and therefore are no longer worthy of our obedience. They are not servants of the living God, but are murderers, larcenists and seducers.

Here we see the ignorance of the Papists, who point to this passage in Deuteronomy that the High Priest my be obeyed. Yes, but they should pay heed to what Malachi says: "If the priest proclaims the teaching of God, he must be obeyed or God will be displeased. But if he proclaims the teaching of Satan, is he to be heard and obeyed? No, for he is so far from being a servant of God that God will throw shit in his face!" That is the authority God gives priests, according to Malachi. Therefore, if the Papists wish to defend themselves by saying that "the Church cannot error," they will suffer a quick set-back when we dispute them by the Word of God. All we have to do is point to this passage in Malachi to convince them. But if we do not work fast, they will point to passages such as: "You are my rock and upon this rock I build my Church." To support their confession, they will allege that it is said, "Show yourself to the priest." When they wish to support their invocation of the saints, they have their "Pro hac orabit ad te omnis sanctus." But if we really push on them, all they have to fall back on is, "We are the Church, and the Church cannot error." This amounts to the same thing as what the conspirators claimed: "The law will not perish from the priest, nor counsel from the sage, nor words from the prophet." This is to say, "Because we are priests, we have the authority of priests. Because we are sage and prophets, we possess all prudence." Jeremiah is finished. The Papists do the exact same thing today. If Scripture is mentioned to them, they claim that they are the Church and cannot error. Behold this marvel! Now, because Jeremiah was a servant of God, the Pope can claim nothing except that he has joined the band that erred at the time of Jeremiah.

To show that it is not merely one individual who conspires against Jeremiah, they say, "Come, let us assemble ourselves and think up some devices against Jeremiah; for the law will not perish from the priest, nor counsel from the sage, nor words from the prophet." Likewise the Pope will say, "Have we not councils?

Am I not the High Priest? Did not Christ say, 'Peter, I pray for you, that your faith not fail'? Since God has prayed for the Pope, it is impossible for us to error. Come, let us assemble ourselves and think up some devices in our hearts." Against whom? Against Jeremiah. Oh, then it is also against God! We can readily see that the Pope has good reason to claim that he is head of the Church, for he invented it himself. The High Priest in the Law was ordained by God, and every order of priests had its ordination in the Law of God to proclaim His Word; but the ordination of the priests in Papism is completely contrary to this. When the Pope or his bishops ordain priests they do not say, "I give you the authority to proclaim doctrine," but, "Go, sacrifice for the remission of sins of the people." That is how all the priests and all those members of Papal councils assemble against God. Their vocation is damnable, for they usurp what belongs to Jesus Christ alone, namely, the authority to reconcile God and man. Let us not be surprised when we see such masquerades and such a great number of mitered asses. Although we have not yet obtained such perfection as is fitting, God will not fail to sustain His own until the end.

Let us examine what defense the Pope has on his side when it is a question of how he sanctions his conduct and that of his people. There is no other way except, "General Councils, General Councils!" It is a good thing to assemble to settle differences in the Church. But how is it necessary to assemble? It must be done in the name of Jesus Christ. How is that to be accomplished? When the Word is in the midst of us and when we wish to resolve matters according to it. But if we see it is merely a meeting of men who are obsessed with their chaotic appetites and who do not care about God or His Scripture, are they assembled in the name of Jesus Christ? A child could answer that question. Let us not be surprised, then, by such masquerades where the Pope will say, "I am the High Priest and Head of the Church. I have the power to bind and unbind. I can open or close the gates to Paradise." There is no need to be astonished by all this, especially when we see how things are today. We see well how authoritative such a council can be, for it is merely a pack of fools. There will be a dozen mitered asses on one side and a dozen and a half on the other. What do they ordain? Here is their decree: All that they say must be obeyed, for the Holy Spirit presides among them. If we look at their deportment, it is enough to say that they are blockheads, drunkards, and whore mongers. In brief, they are given to all vices, as if they had deliberately conspired to anger God. Yet they are the one to be depended upon to settle differences in the Church. What purpose is served there? If we see that evil doings were cooked up against Jeremiah, let us now know that the Pope does as much against those who proclaim the Word of God faithfully.

True, they put on a serious facade when they say that "the Law will not perish from the priests." Yes, but that holds only if they proclaim the message God commissioned and according to

His measure, adding nothing of their own. When it says that "counsel will not perish from the sage, nor words from the prophet," that holds only if they undertake nothing on their own initiative. If these admonitions are heeded, God will be among them. But everything they proclaim witnesses against themselves; for the office of priest is to hold to the Law of God, and everything they do is contrary to that Law. That is how all will be confused. The offices of the sages and prophets is to resolve differences brought to their attention and to proclaim the Law of God. They are answerable to God when they pervert everything in His Church. The Pope says that he is the High Priest. It is necessary, then, that he hold to Scripture. Yet he mocks and shames Scripture. That is a witness against him, for he is evil and wicked because he does things contrary to the commission he pretends to have from God. The same is true of the bishops and doctors of the Church. True, these doctors are licensed, that is, given the authority to vomit up all their blasphemies. This title will cost them dearly when they so abuse it, for Saint Paul says, "The doctor must teach sound doctrine." When they act contrarily, they will be held accountable. When they say that "the Law will not perish from the priest," they show well what is the office of the priesthood. If God were to have spoken through the mouth of Jeremiah, He would not have said otherwise. But the priests, wishing to gain tyrannical power, say that the "Law will not perish from the priest" and then turn their backs on it. That is how God gets truth out of the mouths of false prophets, as He did with Balaam, who was wicked. Although he had gone expressly to curse the people of God, nevertheless God took him there unto Hell and he confessed the truth in spite of himself.

In conclusion, let us return to this passage in Malachi, namely, that when the priests do not hold with the Law of God, they are to be stripped of all authority and must not be obeyed. Why? God wishes to rule only by His Word and wishes each to accommodate himself to it. Those who God has ordained to teach others must first by schooled in the Law. God says through Malachi that the lips of the priest must keep truth and from his mouth one should seek the Law, for he is the messenger of the Lord. But God also says of the priests that "you have turned from my way and have caused many to stumble in the Law. Therefore, I will make you contemptible and belittle you before all men. You have not obeyed my commandment and you have been partial to people." Here, then, is what the priests did when Jeremiah prophesied in Jerusalem and they prose up against him, saying, "The Law will not perish from the priest, nor counsel from the sage." Here is why Ezekiel cried out in Babylon, "You say that the Law will not perish from the priests. I say that God reveals that you are destitute in the Law of God!" That is how they were condemned by Ezekiel, although they enjoyed popular acceptance in their opposition to Jeremiah.

Consequently the prophet shows us their great malice and cruelty, for they say, "Come, and let us mock him." They deliberated over some resolution against Jeremiah, thinking that this would be sufficient to cut the throat of him who wished only the destruction of the people. They thought that a verbal brow-beating would be sufficient to silence him, for they said, "Let us not listen to his words." However that Jeremiah might vanquish them, they held strong, knowing well that by opposing Him they oppose God. Although all this happened at the time of Jeremiah, it still goes on today. What is it that the Papists claim for their councils? Whenever they make some resolution, all the world must shut up and obey, even though they know well it is against God and His prophets. Regarding the faithful, they ask, "What are we to do with these heretics?" They answer, "Let us shut them up!" In these General Councils, with all these asses in the Pope's hire, they have resolved that there is a Purgatory, that the Pope is the foundation of the Church, that mass replaces the Supper of Jesus Christ, that all this tomfoolery in baptism is good, that we must not put all our hope in Jesus Christ but must devote a portion of it to the Virgin Mary and to the saints, that we can invoke them to aid us, that each can well have an advocate and fashion a patron out of his own imagination. Having so resolved, they say of God's people, "Can we tolerate such heretics? To the stake with them, to the stake! As they would baptize us with their tongues, it is only fitting we cut out theirs."

That is how they conspire against the faithful today, as they did at the time of Jeremiah. Satan may take on various guises, but he is always the same. Wherever he works, there is this obstinate refusal to hear the prophet's words. Today the Pope assembles his Councils. He is not content with just one but wishes to have two, or at the very least, two and a half, one at Trente and the other at Bologna. Now will they resolve that the prophets be heard and that Scripture be made public? No, certainly not! They will pursue their same ambition. They will say, "Let us take care that our estate is not diminished and that we suffer no breaches!" Here we see their impudence, for there is always some degree of error. But that does not matter to them. "If we enter into a dispute," they say, "that amounts to saying that you have failed in such-and-such, you are lacking in such-and-such." No, no, they wish to stand fast and hold to the greatest and most oppressive superstitions there have ever been. "Let us hold our ground," they say. "Although Scripture soars throughout the world and although each knows our own impudence, let us pay no attention to all that!" We see clearly their impudence.

If some of the weaker among us are shocked by seeing this display of Papism, let them be consoled by this passage in Jeremiah and let them not doubt that Scripture today does not have the authority it had then. We see that these wicked ones are so impudent that they care about nothing as long as they can maintain their tyranny. It is our task, then, that ministers of the Word of God take care not to abandon their office, knowing that it is God who ordained them. Although the wicked hold secret meetings to ruin us, be certain that God will sustain His Church against all their evil schemes.

Following this holy teaching, we prostrate ourselves before the face of our God, in full recognition of our faults. We pray that God not permit us to remain hardened, but that He soften our hearts, that we desire only to do as He says and to persevere in His Law. We pray that God confirm us in His Law, that we employ it to His service and can truly say we are His people. May we receive His teaching, that we never be diverted from it. May we hold fast to it, that He give us the grace to sustain us to the end. May He shed this grace not only on us but on all the peoples and nations of the world, etc.

* * *

All-powerful God, may it please you to give us the grace that early on we may turn aside your wrath and not so inflame it by our stubbornness that there is no remedy. Although it pleases you to chastise us for a time, do not completely reject us, that we may turn to you on our day of misfortune and calamity. May you always be ready to be reconciled with us. May you be appeased by us, that we know your mercy even when you are angry, until we experience in full and complete joy your grace and your paternal bounty in your heavenly kingdom, which was acquired for us through the blood of your only Son, our Lord, Amen.

(25) Friday, August 16, 1549

Hear me, Lord! Hear the voice of those who dispute with me! Will evil be rendered for good? For they have dug a pit for my soul. Jeremiah 18.

We saw that we should not be surprised by the great assemblies made against God and His Word, where the leaders claim such authority as if they were the Church of God. We have seen how there was such a masquerade against Jeremiah. We have seen that he was not deterred by that but persisted in his calling to the end. However that those who opposed Jeremiah pretended to be sages, he remained loyal to God, knowing He is his guarantor. This gave him the confidence to repel all assaults made against him. When we have God on our side, we need not fear anything, so let us take care that we are not among His enemies. As we have told the Papists that we are adorned by the Word of God, let us take care that we do not become enemies of those who administer it and do not say, "Let us mock them"; for this has been done by those of superior rank in the Church.

These individuals mocked Jeremiah because they could not stand the fact that he reprimanded them, that he made manifest their iniquities, that he spared them nothing, that he reprimanded all the orders of priests. Although these priests were very much esteemed by the people, the prophet publicly throws himself against them and declares their errors. That is why they were enemies of Jeremiah, for they could not stand to be reprimanded. That is why they rose up against him. That is why they said, "Come, let us mock him and hear no more of him." All we have to do is give him a good tongue lashing and he will fall; for we are possessed of authority, we have counsel, we have the Law." In brief, if we inquire into what precipitated the greatest battle the prophets had, we find it was their zeal for God along with the fact they, by virtue of the Holy Spirit, revealed the turpitude of evildoers. That is why the prophets were so hated. We see in Amos and Micah how the evil one waited in ambush to contradict those who reprimanded them. Men do not wish to be reprimanded; men wish to be flattered. When they have neither a sword no the authority to strike back at those who reprimand them, they resort to all sorts of underground subterfuges. They devise one cunning plan, then another. They think they can well forestall those who reprimand them by the Word of God. How? By snaring them with underground traps. That is why we must take care not to associate with them. The prophet is not speaking here of infidels or those who make a profession out of being enemies of God; he is speaking of those who put on a facade of being among the leading pillars of the Church of God.

He explains this more clearly when he says that "they have dug a pit for my soul." He complains not only that they conduct open warfare against him but that they hatch all sorts of treacherous plans to put a stopper in his mouth. These plans are aimed against us. If that happened at the time of Jeremiah, it is perhaps more so the case today. Men do not like to be reprimanded. How many today owe up to their vices as they should? On the contrary, there is not one who does not become incensed when reprimanded for his vices. Just as our Lord wishes each and every word of Scripture to be applied to the needs of the times and to combat the reigning vices, so the evil one today turn each and every word of Scripture into ridicule. Why? Because they are reprimanded for their vices. They say, "Hah! We do not have to put up with those who reprimand us. They think that they are a cut above us." We reply, "Do you scum think that you give God His authority?" Today we must fight against those who feign serving God. They dig pits for the faithful today, just as they did for Jeremiah.

Let us turn now to the outcome of Jeremiah's situation. For a time the evil ones were in vogue and held the prophets in no esteem whatsoever. They said, "Ah, well, so we lose Jeremiah. He is only one man! For everyone lost, two are recovered. The seed of preachers will not fail. We will recover enough of them! Yes, yes, it is such great foolishness to prize one man!" That is how it seemed they must triumph. Listen to the words of the prophet, "Hear me, Lord! Hear the vice of those who dispute with me! Will evil be rendered for good? Must I not be recompensed? Lord, you are my witness that I interceded for them when I saw their downfall was imminent. I came forth, seeing that they were destroying themselves by such great evil. You know that I spoke well of them to you and that I tried to rescue as many as I could. Now my payment is that they plot against me! Their malice may not be perceived at first glance. If men do not know their evil machinations against me, you, Lord will be my witness!" Here he shows that men are such hypocrites that they will feign being the finest Christians in the world, although they are more wicked than can ever be said. We need not go into a detailed exposition of this passage; for we can readily see how it is a mirror of our situation today, in which the evil ones turn into ridicule the words of those who proclaim the truth. They will ask among themselves, "Who has asked for their opinion? Who has said a single word to them?" And those who mock even more viciously will ask among themselves, "Who gives them these words?" They are more venomous yet when they are in their evil synagogues, the taverns; for there they vomit up all their blasphemies and cut up the faithful as they so desire. Jeremiah, then, turns to his Judge and says, "Lord, however the iniquity of my enemies be not apparent to men, you know my innocence and how I have struggled to lead them to salvation. You will not judge them in the manner of men, for you will judge them in truth."

At the end, he adds that "their wives will be widows on the day of His wrath." This shows us the outcome for those who battle against God. Although they seem so cunning that they are indestructible, in the end they will meet their Judge. Here Jeremiah is not carried away by wrath or anger. His prayer that his enemies be crushed on the Day of Wrath is the sentence that God pronounced on these people. "I am resolute," says Jeremiah, "that you will punish the iniquities of the wicked and approve of me as your servant. That is what I wait upon and I will persevere in my office despite my enemies." His "amen" signifies his total acquiescence to the will of God.

Now, to better understand matters, let us note in first place that even before the time of Jeremiah, prophets had prayed against their enemies. They did not seek to influence God's judgment; they waited upon God to reveal His will. That is what we must do. We are inclined to great rage against our enemies, but we must pray to God that it please Him to return them to Himself. Instead, we are often carried away by our wrath against them. We must strive to correct this vice. Let us not strive to get a head start on God's judgment; let us wait upon Him to judge. When we read in Psalms and in other passages in Scripture that David, Jeremiah, and others demanded vengeance upon their enemies, let us note carefully that their wrath had not made them reckless; for they prayed for vengeance only after God had revealed to them it was His will to punish these people. David and the others, then, had no difficulty saying, "May your wrath fall upon them!" They did not try to get the jump on God, for they waited for sure and certain revelation.

Now it is necessary to note one other thing here. They were not moved by carnal passion, as we are so often, but by their devotion to God. If the name of God is blasphemed, that is of no importance to us. But if injury befalls us, we will return evil for evil. If we have offended God five hundred times, we will say that this is no big deal. We pay more attention to ourselves than to the honor of God. That is not as it should be, for we should not put our honor before God's. We should forget ourselves and strive only to serve God in all righteousness. If we do otherwise, we will exceed our limitations. If a man is offended and demands God revenge him, he does evil. Those who disdain the sword to revenge themselves think that they are just and patient before God. Nevertheless, they will not fail to ask God to avenge them, as if God were their servant and executioner. You wish to be brigands and you wish God to give you the sword to commit your acts of brigandry and murder! Whenever any one offends you, you cannot demand God revenge you without offending God. We cannot say that the prophets, David, and other righteous men in Scripture demanded vengeance; for we have absolutely nothing in common with them. We cannot say that David demanded God to revenge him, for he symbolizes the person of our Lord, Jesus Christ. We can transgress in our zeal for God, as did the apostles when they demanded that fire descend from the sky to devour their enemies, as did Elijah, who made a similar request, which was granted. Jesus Christ says of them that "they do not know by which spirit they are led." When we wish to do likewise, Christ will always say to us, "You do not know by what spirit you are led." Let us not assume that God avenges us as we so desire. Let us guard against such intemperate zeal. Let us wait upon the counsel of God and hold to it. We have a long way to go before we will have such zeal as had the prophets.

Let us return to our main point, namely, that the prophet is not an angry man who demands of God whatsoever comes into his head. No, certainly not! When he knows the will of God, he acquiesces to it by saying, "Amen," just as we say, "Your kingdom come." We certainly wish that the enemies of God are destroyed, but let us not be hasty. Let us wait upon God's judgment, for it is up to Him alone to determine the time when His enemies will be punished. That is what Jeremiah did; he prayed that God's sentence be executed. Was he carried away by his zeal to punish? No, certainly not. He proceeded according to God's revelation. We see that in the end those who rise up against God will be destroyed. God is their Judge, not merely for a time, but until the end of the world. It was not just in Jeremiah's day that people thought that for every prophet lost, a hundred more crop up. Today, these mockers say of preachers, "Their seed will not fail," as they said in Jeremiah's day. If they were aware such a statement amounts to a declaration of war against God, they would not be so bold. But they think that they are waging war against only man. Whatever is addressed to those who bear the Word of God is addressed to God Himself. All those who cannot tolerate the Word of God having free range and all those who cannot accept being reprimanded are rebels against God. Am I to blame if my tongue pronounces the sentence of God? Because God will have me bear His Word, you must not look to my person. When the wicked aim against me, let them know that the credit goes to God. The prophet Jeremiah summoned God to sustain his cause, saying, "You must take matter in hand. If I have deceived, it is you who are the deceiver. If I have lied, you are the first liar," as if he were saying, "Just as it is impossible that God is a liar, so it is impossible that my words are lies." Those who rebel against God will have to flee far, for God can well drag them in despite themselves. It would be better for them to answer Gods's summons and to ask for His pardon than for them to be dragged into hear their sentence, which will be executed without any hope of salvation.

There is good reason why God's vengeance is so cruel against those who rebel against Him. We all condemn ingratitude. There is not one of us who does not condemn this vice. In times past, there was no law passed against ingratitude. Why? Because it is so against the nature of man that one cannot bear it. We have this innate impression in our hearts and this natural light which say that there is no greater vice than ingratitude. Now, when men are so ungrateful that they do not wish to hear the Word of God, they are ungrateful not only towards the preacher but also towards God. Those who faithfully preach the Gospel did not come to this calling by themselves. There would never have been such preacher if God has not sent them, as Saint Paul says. We express great ingratitude wise up against good preachers. Our ingratitude is more abhorrent yet, insofar as God sent them to proclaim His Word. What, then, will happen to us if we rise up against them? The prophet says that God will not only condemn the infidels but also the hypocrites who put on the facade of being the Church when in fact they plot in secret against the faithful. God's vengeance against them is never cruel. Why? Their ingratitude is so great. That is what the prophet means when he asks, "Will evil be rendered for good?" This is not only to show that ingratitude reigns today but that each of us knows well that it is an evil vice to be condemned. That is why the prophet speaks as if it were a foregone conclusion that ingratitude is a great sin.

"You know, Lord," says the prophet, "that I interceded many times for their salvation." Here, I say, the prophet teaches us that we have the same responsibility. We must not only preach; we must pray to God that He deliver unto salvation those in our charge. When we see that they have gone astray, let us pray that God see our pain. Although the wicked think that they have no greater enemy than ourselves, God witnesses to the contrary. Here is the kind of zeal those who preach the Word must have: No only must they be God's messengers to men, but they must also be intercessors, that God return the errant ones to Himself. After we have preached, let us go off in private and pray that our teaching be not rejected by the evil ones, that it please God to bring them to their senses, for Satan has turned their heads around.

Why is it that the prophets are so harsh? It seems that Jeremiah desires only the destruction of his people. He speaks of cities being destroyed, women being widowed, children being orphaned, and the Temple itself being knocked down. How can he say such things? He seems to contradict his own prayer. Let us note, then, that when he speaks of God's judgments, it is in order that they might be diverted, that they might not befall the people. He does not proclaim God's judgments because he wishes the destruction of the people, but in order that he might forestall them, if at all possible. Another reason is that when the prophets saw that the wicked did not receive their teaching, they wished God's vengeance to fall upon them in order that they might return to Him. Saint Paul says that God put the rebels of his time in the hands of Satan, that they be saved on the Day of the Lord. We so ardently cry out after the evil ones, not because we wish them ill, but because we desire they return to God. When we preach, let us take care that we do not put off the listeners by verbally molesting them. It is bad enough that they have already stopped up their ears and do not wish to hear a single word of what we have to say whether we preach in the taverns or in the Churches. When we see sinners with their ear muffs on, we may desire to punish them severely. But that is wrong on our part. They already have their own executioners, the devils which suck them down into Hell. Let us, then, look only to their own salvation. If they do not wish to follow us, let us pray God punish them, that them might be saved. That is what the prophets did and that is what we must do. If we see we cannot lead the wicked ones to God, let us be content to leave matters in the hands of God. That is what the prophets did and that is what we must do, for we are in the same charge.

The prophet says that "they have dug a pit for my soul." This signifies that, as I have said, the hypocrites put on such a facade of innocence that it does not seem they would wish to molest anyone. They wish to be esteemed as the pillars of the Church of God while all along they have been laying secret ambushes for the faithful. If we wish to follow the prophet's example, we must battle not only against infidels but also against those who feign serving God and being among the first to maintain His Word and serve His cause. When we see they wish to destroy everything, we must not lose courage; for the prophet was victorious in the end. He speaks of the Day of Wrath to show that he perseveres in his calling, patiently waiting for the wrath of God to ripen. We must do likewise, although we are bitten by dogs who incessantly bare their fangs at us. Let us be patient, knowing that God can destroy them. Whatever the case may be, let us pray for those in our charge that it please God to return them to Him; for God is the same today as He was at the time of Jeremiah and He has not changed His mind. Let us persevere in our calling. Let us be certain that those who turn from us will go visit the Devil.

Following this holy teaching, we prostrate ourselves before the face of our good God, in full recognition of our faults. We pray that because He has given us His yoke, to which we must submit, that He permit us not to reject it. We pray that we so submit to it by virtue of the Holy Spirit that we wish no other thing than to bear it to the end of our days. We pray that He permit not Satan to dazzle and deceive us. We pray that we may give rise to good ministers who, etc.

* * *

All-powerful God, you call us to repentance daily and continually through your teaching and your Spirit. You reveal that you are always ready to be reconciled with us. Give us the grace that we do not reject such an invaluable good and that we give ourselves totally to you ion a peaceful and gentle spirit. Give us the grace that we do not provoke your wrath such that you reject us and show us no mercy. May we forestall your Last Judgment and remain in your favor. May we receive the good you do us by reconciling yourself with us. May we be acceptable to you and agreeable to the name of your only Son. May we persevere in our vocation, until we come to share in the joy of our eternal heritage, which has been acquired for us by the blood of your only Son, our Lord. Amen.

TEXTS AND STUDIES IN RELIGION

1. Elizabeth A. Clark, **Clement's Use of Aristotle: The Aristotelian Contribution to Clement of Alexandria's Refutation of Gnosticism**
2. Richard DeMaria, **Communal Love at Oneida: A Perfectionist Vision of Authority, Property and Sexual Order**
3. David F. Kelly, **The Emergence of Roman Catholic Medical Ethics in North America: An Historical-Methodological-Bibliographical Study**
4. David Rausch, **Zionism Within Early American Fundamentalism, 1878-1918: A Convergence of Two Traditions**
5. Janine Marie Idziak, **Divine Command Morality: Historical and Contemporary Readings**
6. Marcus Braybrooke, **Inter-Faith Organizations, 1893-1979: An Historical Directory**
7. Louis William Countryman, **The Rich Christian in the Church of the Early Empire: Contradictions and Accommodations**
8. Irving Hexham, **The Irony of Apartheid: The Struggle for National Independence of Afrikaner Calvinism Against British Imperialism**
9. Michael Ryan (ed.), **Human Responses to the Holocaust: Perpetrators and Victims, Bystanders and Resisters**
10. G. Stanley Kane, **Anselm's Doctrine of Freedom and Will**
11. Bruce Bubacz, **St. Augustine's Theory of Knowledge: A Contemporary Analysis**
12. Anne Barstow, **Married Priests and the Reforming Papacy: The Eleventh-Century Debates**
13. Denis Janz (ed.), **Three Reformation Catechisms: Catholic, Anabaptist, Lutheran**
14. David Rausch, **Messianic Judaism: Its History, Theology, and Polity**
15. Ernest E. Best, **Religion and Society in Transition: The Church and Social Change in England, 1560-1850**
16. Donald V. Stump *et al.*, ***Hamartia:*** **The Concept of Error in the Western Tradition**

17. Louis Meyer, **Eminent Hebrew Christians of the Nineteenth Century: Brief Biographical Sketches,** David Rausch (ed.)

18. James Jenkins, **The Records and Recollections of James Jenkins**, J. William Frost (ed.)

19. Joseph R. Washington, Jr., **Anti-Blackness in English Religion 1500-1800**

20. Joyce E. Salisbury, **Iberian Popular Religion, 600 B.C. to 700 A.D.: Celts, Visigoths, Romans**

21. Longinus, ***On the Sublime***, James A. Arieti and John M. Crossett (trans.)

22. James Gollnick, ***Flesh* as Transformation Symbol in the Theology of Anselm of Canterbury**

23. William Lane Craig, **The Historical Argument for the Resurrection of Jesus During the Deist Controversy**

24. Steven H. Simpler, **Roland H. Bainton: An Examination of His Reformation Historiography**

25. Charles W. Brockwell, Jr., **Bishop Reginald Pecock and the Lancastrian Church: Securing the Foundations of Cultural Authority**

26. Sebastian Franck, **Sebastian Franck, 280 Paradoxes or Wondrous** Sayings, E. J. Furcha (trans.)

27. James Heft, **John XXII and Papal Teaching Authority**

28. Shelley Baranowski, **The Confessing Church, Conservative Elites, and the Nazi State**

29. Jan Lindhardt, **Martin Luther: Knowledge and Mediation in the Renaissance**

30. Kenneth L. Campbell, **The Intellectual Struggle of the English Papists in the Seventeenth Century: The Catholic Dilemma**

31. William R. Everdell, **Christian Apologetics in France, 1750-1800: The Roots of Romantic Religion**

32. Paul J. Morman, **Noel Aubert De Verse (1642-1714): A Study in the Concept of Toleration**

33. Nigel M. de S. Cameron, **Biblical Higher Criticism and the Defense of Infallibilism in 19th-Century Britain**

34. Samuel J. Rogal, **John Wesley's London: A Guidebook 1738-1791**

35. André Séguenny, **The Christology of Caspar Schwenckfeld: Spirit and Flesh in the Process of Life Transformation,** Peter C. Erb and Simone S. Nieuwolt (trans.)

36. Donald E. Demaray, **The Innovation of John Newton (1725-1807): Synergism of Word and Music in Eighteenth Century Evangelism**

37. Thomas Chase, **The English Religious Lexis**

38. R.G. Moyles, **A Bibliography of Salvation Army Literature in English 1865-1987**

39. Vincent A. Lapomarda, **The Jesuits and the Third Reich**

40. Susan Drain, **The Anglican Church in the 19th Century Britain: Hymns Ancient and Modern (1860-1875)**

41. Aegidius of Rome, **On Ecclesiastical Power: De Ecclesiastica Potestate,** Arthur P. Monahan (trans.)

42. John R. Eastman, **Papal Abdication in Later Medieval Thought**

43. Paul Badham (ed.), **Religion, State, and Society in Modern Britain**

44. Hans Denck, **Selected Writings of Hans Denck, 1500-1527,** E. J. Furcha (trans.)

45. Dietmar Lage, **Martin Luther on the *Imitatio Christi* and *Conformitas Christi* and Their Relationship To Good Works**

46. Jean Calvin, ***Sermons on Jeremiah,*** Blair Reynolds (trans.)

47. Jean Calvin, ***Sermons on Micah*,** Blair Reynolds (trans.)

48. Alexander Sándor Unghváry, **The Hungarian Protestant Reformation in the Sixteenth Century Under the Ottoman Impact: Essays and Profiles**

49. Daniel B. Clendenin & W. David Buschart (ed.), **Scholarship, Sacraments and Service: Historical Studies in Protestant Tradition *Essays in Honor of Bard Thompson***